CLEARING IN THE WEST

WEST

My Own Story

BY

NELLIE L. McCLUNG

TORONTO
THOMAS ALLEN LIMITED

PRINTED AND BOUND IN ENGLAND BY
HAZELL WATSON AND VINEY LTD
AYLESBURY, BUCKS

To

MY ELDEST BROTHER,

WILLIAM SCOTT MOONEY,

IN LOVING MEMORY.

CONTENTS

CONTENTS

CLEARING IN THE WEST

CHAPTER I

THE YOUNGEST OF SIX

SNOW comes early and often in Grey County, Ontario. In 1873 it fell heavily on October the twentieth, in thick wet blobs that sent the cattle into the straw-stacks to escape the driving storm. The horse-power threshing-machine at Robert Lowery's farm, near Chatsworth, was forced to give in to the storm at four o'clock in the afternoon, and let the hands go home, because the sheaves were too wet to go through the separator.

When young Will Mooney, who, though only fifteen, was as good as a man, and had been cutting bands all day, reached his home, on the Garafraxa road, he was wet and cold and hungry, but the sight of the doctor's cutter at the front door drove out every sensation but one of extreme anxiety and quickened his steps into a run. He opened the back door softly, to be met by a rush of hot air, in which there was a trace of carbolic acid and warming flannels and fresh bread.

Two of the neighbor women, Mrs. Edward Lowery and Mrs. Charlton were in the kitchen, talking excitedly though in subdued tones; the matter of the doctor was under discussion. "We did not need him," said Mrs. Lowery, "and Mrs. Mooney did not want him. What is there for a doctor to do in a perfectly natural birth? We brought her through before, and could have done it again. A doctor is all right in case of a broken arm or maybe scarlet fever, but an increase in the population is a natural thing surely."

Her companion spoke up. "I gave him a look when he asked me if I had scrubbed my hands in carbolic, I said, 'Young man, we use soft soap here, and we've found it very good and I may say, women have helped each other here for a long time, and we have not lost a case yet. I hope your record will be as good when you've been here as long.'" Then they noticed that Will had come in, and motioned to him to be quiet.

"Is mother sick?" he asked anxiously.

"She'll be worse before she is better," Mrs. Lowery replied mysteriously. "Dr. Dumball is here now, your father brought him and it will soon be over. Everything is all right. You are going to have a little brother or sister, Willie. . . . Come over here to the stove, and get off your wet shoe-packs. Tish will get you dry clothes, you're soaked to the skin, I know."

Tish, a fine young woman of twenty-one, who had been helping in the kitchen for the last two months, produced a pair of dry socks from a basket of clean clothes under the long table, and taking his overcoat shook the snow off it, at the back door, and hung it in the passage.

Then she went back to her bread, which was just ready for the oven. In birth or death, or any other human upheaval, a batch of good light bread never comes amiss.

"Is mother very sick, Tish?" Will asked again.

"Bad enough, I guess," Tish said, shoving a pan of bread into the high oven, "but you know she never lets on. I was talking to her half an hour ago; she said she thought you'd be home soon and to be sure and get you to change your shirt too."

She felt his grey flannel shoulders.

"It's just a little damp—but slip upstairs and put on a dry one, she'll be asking."

"I hope it is a boy," Will said thoughtfully, when he came downstairs. "We've girls enough."

Hannah, three years old, was sitting quietly in her high chair, playing with a counter of colored beads, and took no notice of this bit of brotherly candor.

"If it is as nice a little girl as Hannah, she'll be welcome," Tish remarked. "She's the best child I ever saw. She has been sitting there for an hour; you'd think she knew.

When the news broke with the shrill cry of the infant, uttering the age-old protest, Will was somewhat taken back, and disappointed. It was a girl!

He ran out to tell his father who was in the big barn flailing peas.

An hour later, Will was let in to see his mother, who lay in a high four-poster bed, in the bedroom off the parlor.

He kissed her affectionately and asked her how she was feeling. She told him to look behind her, and there in a new white shawl he saw a wrinkled little face framed in jet black hair, with two small pink fists doubled up beside its cheeks.

He was sorry for his mother; she must be disappointed too, and it wasn't her fault, so he kissed her again, and told her it was all right. The Irelands had three girls too, and the Charltons had four, and maybe the next one would be a boy.

My first memory is of a snowy afternoon too, one that seemed likely to last forever. I had stationed myself on a stool in front of a window and inside the lace curtain to watch for Lizzie, and Hannah and George and Jack coming home from school. At first it was pleasant to watch the snow making a pattern against the dark bulk of the barn, and putting big white knobs on the fence posts, but my heart was too burdened to see much beauty in anything.

I had heard a bit of bad news! One of the neighbor girls, named Hattie—I forget her last name—came over to borrow something, and I hid behind the curtain when the dog barked a warning and I saw her coming. I did not like Hattie, or any one of her unpalatable family, and for the same reason. They kissed me every time they came in. Not only kissed me but tried to make me bite my tongue by chucking me under the chin. So I went into hiding when any of the tribe drew near.

Hattie and mother talked without knowing I was in the room, and Hattie said they were not going to have a Christmas tree this year, for Zebbie had found out there was no Santa Claus and it was no fun now, when there was no one who believed. These were her very words.

I thought mother would surely contradict her, but she didn't. Then I made up my mind that I would wait right there to see what Lizzie, and George and Jack and Hannah would say. I was afraid to ask mother—afraid it was true—I knew she would not withhold the truth, if I asked her. . . .

I must have begun my vigil in the forenoon, for it seemed fully two weeks before I saw the four welcome figures turning in at the gate, and snow balling each other as they came down the lane. Little they knew of what awaited them!

I got a hearing with my brother George first, and he cautioned me about speaking to anyone else, for he said he knew exactly what to do. He could show me that Hattie was wrong. And he did.

The night before Christmas he took me out, and showed me the hay and oats he had placed in an old water-trough for Santa Claus' reindeers, charging me to look well at it, and to observe that the roof leading to the chimney had no tracks. I observed these things. On Christmas morning, I was taken out again for observation, and found the hay and oats gone, and tracks plainly visible on the snowy roof. There were other proofs too, that thrilled me to my heart's core. In my stocking, hung beside the fire, were, carefully wrapped in red tissue paper, a dappled gray tin horse, and a blue glass mug, with "Love the Giver," on it in white letters.

I wondered what Hattie would say to this!

That was a glorious Christmas. The whole house was full of surprises. There were paper balls hung at the windows, and spruce boughs glittering with diamonds over the doors, and a new scarf for me, dark brown, "to match your eyes," Elizabeth said. It looked very much like the pale blue one Hannah used to have, and the color made me think of the butternut dye that mother used for carpet rags, but I am glad to record I was too much of a lady to say so. The tin horse, all so nicely dappled, with a red saddle painted on his back, was the high spot of that Christmas and though he divided in two before the day was over, I set one before the other, and had a team. The smell of the paint on the horse was delicious to me, and still is the real aroma of Christmas—that tin toy smell.

I remember that Christmas, because it was the last year that I was a true believer.

We lived a mile from Chatsworth, on the Garafraxa road, in a stony part of the county of Grey. The stones lay over our farm like flocks of sheep. But one can grow accustomed to stones. They were merely a part of the landscape to me. Our barn was a fine big one painted red, with great doors in the loft that swung outward to receive the winter's hay. The hay-loft could be reached from the inside by a ladder on the wall. Once we found a tramp had slept in the hay-loft and "it was a mercy he had not set fire to it." Instead he called at the door the next morning and thanked us for letting him stay, and was asked in for breakfast.

The house was of dressed timbers, cut from our own logs, and the outside was white-washed, and looked very well under the hard maples.

There was a spring of cold water coming out of a bank behind the house, and over this little stream the milk house was built, a small white-washed building with a flagged floor, the centre of which was a tiny pond edged with stones, where the milk-pans stood cool and sweet. That perpetual stream of crystal water that ran in and ran out, losing itself in a green meadow below the house was a fragrant memory to all of us and even after we moved to Manitoba and were comfortably established there, my mother still mourned for that living well of water that bubbled out of the hill and failed not in winter or in summer. It was a "drink from the spring," that she craved more than anything else, when the tides of life ran low.

Being the youngest of the six children, I received much of my early education from my brothers and sisters. Will, my eldest brother, who was fifteen when I was born, was my devoted friend and champion, always. He was a tall boy for his age; had curly brown hair, fine brown eyes, creamy skin and red cheeks, and I think he was my mother's favorite child. In the winter of the deep snow, seven years before I was born, my father had bronchitis and it was Willie who helped mother to care for the cattle and horses. He was only eight years old, hardly able to swing an axe, but he chopped wood until his nose bled. The snow was so deep that for three weeks no sleigh could get through, and she was there alone, with a sick man, and three small children, one a baby a month old, and ten head of stock to feed and water. My mother was not given to tears, but her eyes were always wet, when she talked of that hard time, and how Will's brave young spirit had never faltered.

My second brother, George, two years younger than Will, was a natural trader and a successful one. George always had interesting things in his pockets—alleys, and knives and pretty stones, and once a knife that in addition to two blades, had a pair of scissors which shut up like a blade. I remember hearing George closely questioned on the subject of "steel knuckles," which, in some mysterious manner were being put in circulation in our neighborhood, and every possible avenue of distribution was being canvassed. But George was not guilty of any connection with this form of armaments though he did say that he thought "steel knuckles," plenty of "steel knuckles," enough for everyone, would prevent all fights, for everyone would be afraid to start an argument. George's best line was jewelry, the costume jewelry of the late seventies, and in return for a used horse-collar, honorably earned by pulling weeds in a turnip patch, he received a gorgeous stock of rings and tie-pins from a band of gypsies camped on the commons. The rings and pins were kept under a stone in the potato patch, and George might have carried on his business free from discovery but that his kind heart betrayed him, as it has many another good man.

I burned my arm one evening by falling on the stove from my high chair, and to stay my screams George brought me from his treasure chest, a solitaire ruby ring, the ruby being, as I remember it, quite large enough for the parking light on a car. When the uproar had been calmed and my arm was resting in a cold starch pack, Mother had time to go into the matter of the ring, now tightly clutched in my good hand. George told the truth—he was never known to depart from it—and that enterprise came to an end. But the ring, which I with an invalid's privilege was allowed to keep, helped more than the starch to heal my arm.

My eldest sister, Elizabeth, deserves a whole book. She was everybody's friend. She could comb hair and make curls without hurting. She could find things that had been lost for days. She knew where everything was. She could think of games to play and even make up games. She could take thorns from fingers, and understand how dresses got dirty. Her hair was bright brown and her skin clear and white; so clear and soft, that one of the neighbor girls, (Hattie's sister) circulated the report that Lizzie Mooney washed her face every night in buttermilk, which my mother indignantly denied. But Elizabeth, with that fine philosophy which has helped her over many rough places in life, said nothing, but began to do this very thing to see if it had any virtue, and to-day, though she has faced hot winds in summer and cold winds in winter, she has never lost her apple-blossom complexion.

Hannah, who had the reputation of being the best child Tish ever saw, was a round-faced little girl with large, dark blue eyes and auburn hair, like mother's mother, Margaret Fullerton McCurdy. Hannah spoke only when she had something to say and was always listened to with respect. She could read when she was seven, and read stories to me—on conditions. I did not go to school until I was ten, so Hannah had several good productive years when she measured out to me a dole of fiction in return for sundry little chores. When she was reading, and I was sweeping the floor, and listening in a trance of delight to "Davy and the Goblin," or "Children of the New Forest," sometimes in my rapture I would forget to sweep and leaning on the broom-handle gaze open-mouthed through the golden door she had opened for me . . . . until the silence of the room made me remember my bargain.

Hannah had rather a hard deal in the matter of her name. Mother had intended to call her "Margaret Alice," but a friend of hers came back to Chatsworth to visit, and everyone was doing things for the visitor and mother named the baby for her, "Hannah Maria Conger." I thought it a very beautiful name, but the owner of it has not thought so, although she carries it gracefully and without complaint.

My youngest brother, Jack, five years my senior was a sturdy, square little chap, given to fighting, and walking the ridgepole of the barn. He was only five years older than I, but I never seemed to catch up to him. There was a selection in the readers of that day beginning:

> "The rocky John Thomas,
> The hedger and ditcher,
> Although he was poor
> Never cared to be richer,"

which never failed to draw fire from my youngest

brother, who hated it violently. Perhaps he was repelled by the lowly occupation of his namesake, or his lack of ambition, but anyway it registered. I used it myself against him, but only when I was at a safe distance. Jack had a great distaste for anything sentimental and always went out, when a story was being read to us, which had anything in it of love or courtship. He said he "would never get married: he would live with a man and keep dogs."

CHAPTER II

THE FAMILY

MY father, John Mooney, came to Bytown in Upper Canada from Ireland in the year 1830, crossing the ocean in a sailing vessel which took ten weeks to make the voyage. He was then a lad of eighteen, who had never done anything but go to school, but the famines in Ireland were driving the young men to seek their fortunes elsewhere; and already some of his kinsmen had made the venture of coming to the New World. His two older brothers, William and Thomas came with him, and a cousin, Robert Clarke.

My grandfather, William Mooney of Nenagh, Tipperary, near the rock of Cashel was a steward for a nobleman, and lived in a fine stone house, "rent free, with kail yard and byre," and had what was considered a good position, but the family was large and growing, so he was quite willing to let the three eldest boys go, and outfitted them generously with hand-woven blankets and frieze coats.

My father's mother, Elizabeth Scott, had died when he was eight years old, and my grandfather had married again, and the second family, numbering five, would be enough for him to look after. Maria, my father's sister came out the next year, and on her arrival in Bytown, married Robert Clarke, the cousin, who had come out with my father.

My Uncle Tom, who was a school-teacher, soon found a position in a settlement school near Bytown. William who could make a fiddle "do everything but talk," was a welcome guest at George Clark's tavern, on the Main street of the four-year-old village. My father went with the shanty men, who were bringing down rafts of logs on the "Grand River," as the Ottawa was called then. It was a rough life for a boy of eighteen, but wages were good and there was plenty of companionship, and adventure. Bytown, named for Colonel By, came into being by the building of the Rideau Canal, begun in 1826 by the Imperial Government, and a great project it was, to open a waterway between Bytown and Kingston, a distance of one hundred and twenty-six miles, at a cost of one million pounds. The money came from the Old Country in half-crowns, packed in kegs which helped to put silver in circulation in Canada.

He remembered seeing Colonel By many times riding on his black horse, as he watched the progress of his men, and when many years later the name of Bytown was changed to Ottawa, my father thought it a great pity to lose the name of this fine soldier whom every one admired.

The shanty men, mostly French and Irish were a wild crew, he said, with whiskey running free in every shebeen, and many a time the streets of Bytown were filled with drunken, cursing fighters. He remembered seeing an Irish Roman Catholic priest, with a horsewhip flogging the members of his flock into a better frame of mind, and demanding that they appear at the confessional the next day. And they did.

After several years of logging, and many narrow escapes from drowning, he began to think of farming as a better and pleasanter way of living. He had earned good wages on the river but he had saved very little. He knew of the new gravel road that was being built from the Georgian Bay to Toronto, in the western part of the Province, and that free grants of land could be taken on each side of the road. He had heard about it first from a Methodist missionary, who worked among the Ojibways, still farther west, and who had come to Bytown to visit his relatives there.

The Shouldice family, cousins of the Mooneys, living in Neapean, had made the move, making the trip safely across Georgian Bay in a bateau, by keeping close to the shore. While this matter was being turned over in his mind, Bytown suffered an outbreak of typhoid fever, and his brother Tom took it and died. Later in the same year William also died, and my father, alone now, except for his sister, Mrs. Robert Clarke, who lived in Neapean decided to make the move.

He made the trip across the Georgian Bay in 1841, took up the free grant of fifty acres, and by helping to chop out the road earned another fifty acres, and then settled down to the tremendous task of clearing his land, which was all heavily timbered with hard maple, hemlock and elm. Each fifty-acre lot had a frontage of forty rods and a depth of two hundred rods. The first ten years seem to have been a sort of endurance test, and I remember of hearing the sad but heroic tale of one settler called Barnes, thirteen miles down the road who actually died of starvation and no one knew of it until he was dead. He had tried to live on cow-cabbage, refusing to take any of the potatoes or cow's milk from the children.

In 1850, the township of Sullivan, on the west side of the gravel road, was organized in proper form, with a reeve and a council. The records show that John Mooney was the first treasurer, and received for his labors the sum of one pound, ten shillings. There were one hundred and thirty-three ratepayers and the amount collected was one hundred and twenty-three dollars and eighty-one cents, and after all expenses were paid there was a balance on hand of eight dollars and twenty-six cents to start the new year. So the balance was on the right side of the ledger. They built a school that year, and there was a stipulation that any religious denomination might use the building. Each child who attended the school must pay at the rate of one shilling and sixpence per month, and each third child was to be taught free of charge. The teacher boarded around. William Buchanan who was the first teacher received a salary of twelve pounds per annum.

The gravel road was called the Garafraxa, which is

surely as fitting a name as any gravel road ever received, and was completed to Toronto in 1842.

My Uncle Tom, the school-teacher, has always been a shadowy figure to me, leaving no trace of his personality in my memory, though I do remember a box of old Irish school-books in calfskin bindings, yellow vellum and long s's with his name written in them in violet ink. But William, the boy who could "turn the heart in ye," when he played the "Irish Lament"—William with his brown eyes and auburn hair, slim and straight as a gun-barrel; with a laugh that you would hear in a room full of people, for the lilt of it; William who was talked of in all the lumber camps and on the rafts, as the men were coming down the rivers; who died in his twenty-fifth year in a noisy room above the bar in a Bytown tavern, where he had so often played for dances, was one of my infant heroes, and I was disposed to boast about him, when I played with other children, though he was dead forty years before I was born. When I heard music that swept my young heart with longing, I knew it was something like the performance of my Uncle William. My father had been up the river when William died, and he never ceased to regret his absence.

After taking up his land on the Garafraxa, my father married Jane Shouldice, his cousin, but Jane lived only a little over a year.

When the news went back to Nenagh, Ireland, that Johnny's wife had died, and that Johnny was the only one left of the three fine lads who had sailed from Limerick, and that he was alone on a bush farm, old Judy Connor, one of the servants in my grandfather's house in Nenagh—and she was then fifty years of age— braved the terrors of the Atlantic, and came all the way to Sydenham to keep house for him.

In 1858 he married my mother, Letitia McCurdy, who had come with her mother, Margaret Fullerton McCurdy, and a younger sister Ellen from Dundee, Scotland, the year before.

Judy Connor lived with them all her days, and it has always been a regret to me that I was not born early enough to have met Judy, in the flesh, with her belief in fairies, and banshees.

Judy at certain times and seasons, that had to do with the moon, took the precautionary measure of leaving a pan of milk on the grass for the fairies to wash in. It seems it was always done in Ireland to keep the little people in good-humor. But one night my mother, who did not believe in fairies, gave the milk to the pigs, and used the pan for something else, and the next day she slipped on a stone in the milkhouse, and turned her ankle, and Judy told her it was "well for her, it wasn't worse," so the pan was left thereafter. When Judy lay dying, she had everyone listening for the banshee, who should, by all the laws of compensation and tradition, have cried below the window, but no sound troubled the stillness of the maple trees around the house, until Watch, the dog, sensing that something was happening, lifted his head to the stars, and howled drearily. Judy heard him through the shadows that were closing around her, and opening her eyes, she looked at my mother in triumph. "Now, thank God, I can die," she said, and she did!

Mother's father, Duncan McCurdy, who was of the McCurdy's from the Isle of Bute, had died of cholera in the outbreak of 1856, in Dundee and it was then, with their breadwinner gone, and under necessity to make their own living, that the women of the family came to Canada. An older sister, Elizabeth, was married to a man named John Taylor in Dundee, and stayed behind, afterwards emigrating to Australia.

My grandmother's two sisters had emigrated two years before with their families, and settled in the township of Holland, east of the Garafraxa where the land was more fertile than in Sullivan, where my father settled. As a result of this, the Holland relatives, as the years went by, prospered more than we did and grew comparatively rich. The two aunts were rather patronizing to my grandmother, whom I remember as a slight little woman, in a gray dress, with' reddish hair, who was always ready to tell a story to me. Her two sisters, older than she, did not even talk like anyone else, accounted for by the fact, that in Scotland they had lived in "Enbro," and so rather despised the more commercial city of Dundee. As a final proof of their magnificence, in each of their homes in Holland, there was an organ, but they did not call it that. It was the "instrument," and could not be played on Sunday. I was taken to one of their homes once and there was no music from the "instrument;" it stood in the corner, a complicated bulk of carved wood, and red velvet, locked tight and ornamented with two high and fluted gray vases of dead grass. The red velvet, showing so enticingly through the wood-carving called to me to poke one small finger through and see for myself if it could be pushed back, but some good angel stayed my hand.

CHAPTER III

THE HOUSE AND THE PEOPLE

MY memory of our old house is somewhat shadowy, but I know that smoked hams hung from the rafters in the kitchen, and from one corner were suspended brown festoons of dried apples, done by a paring-machine which went around the neighborhood. The walls of all the rooms were white-washed, and only the big log beams that held up the ceiling were left in their natural state. The floors were pine boards and were scrubbed every week, using very little soap, for soap yellowed the wood. Elbow grease was the thing! The heating was done by a huge cook-stove, with a high oven, in the kitchen and a round heater in the front room which had a drum upstairs to collect and radiate heat to the bedrooms. Seats near either stove was much prized for the outer area was very cold when the north wind swept down from the Georgian Bay.

The floor had lengths of rag carpet in pale stripes and there were red and brown mats, hooked in circles and triangles. The inside doors were home-made ones and had buttons of wood instead of latches. The two front windows had hand-knitted curtains, done by mother, in a fern pattern and paper lace valentines were hung on them.

Two pictures, I remember very well, "Winter," and "Autumn." Two beautiful women—"Autumn," wreathed with red leaves and purple fruit, and "Winter," dressed in white fur with holly berries on her cap. "Winter," with her soft eyes was my ideal of beauty and I determined to be just like her when I grew up, if it could be arranged. These prints were given as premiums with the *Montreal Family Herald* and *Weekly Star*, and there were

18

really four in the series, for I had seen "Spring," and "Summer," at my aunt Ellen's house. There was a steel engraving of the Battle of Waterloo, which I did not like. In it, Wellington and Blucher on their horses, were shaking hands across the bodies of the slain. Dead men and horses carpeted the field, and one young fellow was trying to raise his head, and his face was full of pain. Jack said, I was crazy to cry about it, for the dead men and this wounded one were all Frenchmen and our enemies and it served them right; but even so, he could not explain away the dead horses.

There was another horrible black and white print, "The Stag at Bay," of a poor tired stag with his back to a rock, facing a pack of fierce and snarling hounds. He was trapped, and beaten with no hope of escape, but he was still fighting.

There was one pretty chromo called "The Old Mill Stream," which showed a rapid stream, the mill-race, bright blue in color, from which a beautiful dog, a big tawny fellow, had just saved a little girl, with golden curls and pantalettes, from drowning. She lay on the grass very wet and pale, but her mother was running across the green with outstretched arms.

There was another colored picture of a girl in a long white nightie, and golden hair holding herself out of the water by hanging tightly to a wooden cross set in a rock. White gulls flew overhead, and I knew she was cold and wet.

I was taken to Sunday-school in Chatsworth, by Elizabeth and Annie Stevenson, who made a chair and carried me when I got tired. Annie was a lovely girl, who wore a hat with plumes and seemed to belong to us.

The Sunday-school was held in the church, with green baize curtains to divide the classes. But there was no room for the "Busy Bees," one Sunday so we were taken across the road to the parsonage parlor, and the minister's wife told us about "Moses," who had a little bed of switches smeared with tar, to keep out the water, and was put in the river for safe keeping; and then she took our collection, one copper each, tied in a knot in our handkerchiefs. It took quite a while to extract the coins, because we had chewed the knots. Six cents was the day's receipts. We stood around her when she played her little organ, which had white teeth all right, but no high top like the "instruments" in Holland. And she asked us all to come back, and told us the school had grown, so we would come there every Sunday now, and we were glad. When I went home, and released the big story about "Moses," being put in the river, I was disappointed to find they all knew it!

I received a small card each Sunday with a verse set in a little frame of flowers, and there was a hope held out that four small cards would be rewarded with a big one, but I never was able to put it to the test for I could not keep the little cards. They got lost.

My first time to be in church was at a revival meeting held at the Sauble, where Rev. Mr. Read, the Methodist minister of Chatsworth, was holding special services and when father and mother went one night, they had to take me for it seemed there was no way of leaving me. My mother, being a Scotch Presbyterian, did not hold with revival services and testimony meetings and confessions, but father was an out-and-out Methodist, and had experienced the strange, "warming of the heart," that John Wesley wrote about in his Journal.

We were late for the meeting and the altar call was sounding when we entered, and crowds of people were pressing forward; and as many more came in when we did, we found ourselves among the seekers, and we knelt there with the others. Mr. Read put his hand on my head and said no child was too young to be reconciled to God, and he was glad to receive the lambs of the flock. I was the only child at the altar and I liked him very much for being so friendly.

He was a tall man with brown whiskers and a cheerful face. He moved his ears when he talked which I thought very clever of him. I had a trick too, just learned that day from my brother Will. I could shut one eye and keep the other one wide open, and I thought he might like to see me do it. So when an old man who stuttered, was giving his testimony and holding back the meeting with everyone getting impatient, I kept my one eye on the minister and the other one shut.

Mother said after we went home, that Mr. Read was too light a man to be preaching the gospel, for when poor old Samuel Norton was speaking he actually began to laugh, though he had tried to turn it into a cough. My father was loyal to the minister and said there was no harm in a laugh at any time, and it would be better if there were more laughter in the churches.

But mother refused to accept this, and said, there was a time to laugh and it was not in the church. I didn't like to hear Mr. Read criticized, so I said I wanted to go again for I wanted to make my peace with God, and that stopped the argument. Mother was ready to talk to me then, and tried to explain what it meant to be a Christian. She said, I would have to stop mocking people; for that was my besetting sin; though it was not so much my fault, she said, as it was the fault of older people who encouraged me and laughed at me. I knew who the older people were and I was sorry that I had drawn my father into another argument.

The only people I had ever mocked were mother's two aunts, who lived in Holland—two thin old ladies who owned the "instruments," who dressed in black silk made with tight bodies and full skirts, and wore mutches, and knit with flashing steel needles. They came to visit us once a year anyway and when that happened, father took to the barn. He always had peas to flail when the aunts came.

I loved to listen to them and get their stories, just as they told them, which was not always easy, for the aunts to save time talked both at once. On account of the bad roads in Holland, they did not get out much, and when they did they talked without a pause. I sat near them, drinking in every word and they often said I was a nice quiet child. When I had gathered a good earful I made my way to the barn to tell my father, and with two bright straws for knitting-needles, I relayed what I could remember, and so well received was my recital, I often stayed out until I was nearly frozen. It was not only their words, but their peculiar accent that gave my recital merit. They had a queer droning way of speaking.

But now, having renounced the world, I knew I would have to give this up. I must not mock my mother's aunts! I hoped they would not come soon, not until I was stronger in the faith, for the pleasure of seeing my father lean on his flail and laugh until his eyes ran with tears, was hard to forego, and I knew so many of their stories now, it seemed too bad to waste them. There were times when I looked back, like the children of Israel, and longed for my degenerate days.

The catechism helped to keep my spirits aflame. In it I seemed to have had special mention. "What is your name?" was one question, early in the book. "M or N," was the answer, so I hoped from that, that I was numbered with the blest and for the time, at least, continued in the way.

It was a mellow evening in early autumn, for the apples were ripe on the trees behind the milkhouse, their bright red globes gleaming in the gray-green leaves, and there was a smell of ripening grain in the air, and a blue haze dulled the horizon, and blotted out the hills.

I was being taken down to the lower meadow by Lizzie, the good angel of my childhood, for this was the evening when the pigs were being killed, and my heart was ready to break. Not that I had a pet pig or cared about the pigs as individuals. I was a little afraid of pigs, and thought they were greedy, ill-mannered brutes, but even so, I felt they had a right to live, or at least to die without pain.

All day I knew what was coming! The pigs were being starved for the killing, and they squealed in their pens and quarrelled among themselves. The hole was dug for the barrel, which would be filled with boiling water from the boiler set on stones with wood laid under. The gruesome scaffold had been erected, and the whole farmyard had been changed from a friendly playground, to a place of evil.

We walked over the hill behind the house just as the sun was dipping into the mist of evening, and a queer green light came into the upper and eastern sky. Lizzie's hand was very comforting in mine now that my world had gone wrong, and the sorrows of life were overflowing. She told me she had a new pattern for a dress for me, with a little scalloped collar, which would be edged with turkey-red, and the tie-backs would have scalloped ends, and the dress would have red pearl buttons, with one on each pocket.

We sat beside the little stream just before it lost itself in the meadow, and she found stovepipe grass for me to piece together into a chain.

She thought that by taking me over the hill the sounds would not come through, but just as I had almost forgotten why we had come, in my delight and surprise at the honey sandwiches which she had produced from under her coat—the terrible cry came drilling through the hill, and tore through us like a thousand poisoned arrows. I knew then, that life was a place of horror, in spite of flowers and trees, and streams, and I flung myself down on the grass and cried my heart out in an agony of helplessness. I remember how she put her two kind hands over my ears, but that piercing cry came in at every pore of my body.

Lizzie told me God made pigs for meat for people. They were of no other use and if they were all let live there would be pigs everywhere, and how would I like that? But I asked her why they had to suffer like this; why didn't God make them like trees or grain? *They* didn't squeal when they were cut down. God could have done that, if He wanted to. He made everything. Lizzie admitted she did not know why there had to be such pain in the world; she said she often wondered, but it wasn't right to criticize God, His ways were always right. But I was rebellious. I didn't think much of the world, and I was through with being a Christian. I didn't love God, and I was going to be like uncle Abner and not care for anything, but just having a good time. I'd go to the dances when I grew up, and put hairoil on my hair and stay out late. And I would mock the aunts, I would mock them worse than ever, and I didn't care how soon they came, and I was through with Sunday-school and would burn my tickets.

Lizzie did not try to stem my outburst. She let me rave on and in the raving I found relief. I knew my words were wild and wicked, but in some way they restored me. Wild words were safe with Lizzie; she would never remember them against anybody; they fell around her like dust that is blown away. Every family needs one member who has the gift of listening, and forgetting.

It was quite dark when we got home, and Lizzie led me around to the front door and we went upstairs. The house was heavy with the smell of rendering lard, which reminded me there would be doughnuts to-morrow and I resolved I wouldn't eat one—or at least very few of them. Mother came up to see me after I had gone to bed and told me the pigs' suffering was all over in a minute, and I must put it all out of my mind. Father knew exactly how to kill a pig with the least possible amount of suffering, and he just hated to do it too; when he was a little boy in Ireland he always ran away to the bog when the pigs were killed, but now he knew it had to be done and he always did it himself, just to be sure it was done quickly. I was glad to know that he hated to do it, for I adored my father and couldn't bear to think him cruel. I ate the remainder of the honey sandwiches and went to sleep.

People who write about their own family usually tell much of family tyranny and msunderstanding, and in the minds of many, parents and children are natural enemies, but I have not much to say about parental oppression. My people were hard-working folk, greatly concerned with the problems of making a living, tired many a time with the day's work and perplexed with life's cares, but they were never too tired or busy to comfort a sad little heart, or do their best to direct a lost young pilgrim back to the highway of happiness.

CHAPTER IV

ECHOES FROM THE WEST

I HAVE a wistful memory of the sunlit populous farm-yard, over which fresh yellow straw drifted as the wind blew, and where I could rove at will, without a care or a fear. The white house under the red maples, with bright sumach trees in front, threw back the sunshine in a dazzle that made me wink my eyes, but I loved to look at it. There was something about it that satisfied me. It was so sure and safe.

As I drifted around the farmyard, I liked to sing, swaying and dancing to my own music. Mother had heard Jenny Lind, the Swedish nightingale, before she came to Canada, and although my mother was not a singer, she made us understand the moving power of a great voice.

> "Come, arouse you, arouse you,
> My brave shepherd boy
> To the fields, now and labor away,
> The dew is sparkling in the beam,
> The kine are thronging to the stream!"

That was all I knew but as I sang it, I could hear that golden voice rising and falling in a rushing, sweeping melody that sang in my veins, and wrung my heart with emotion. I never sang this when anyone could hear me for always it made me cry. . . .

I have heard some of the world's great singers since then, and felt the magic of good music, but never have 1 been more transfigured or intoxicated with sweet sounds than when, in my fancy, I heard the voice of

Jenny Lind, coming to me out of the long past, and from far across the sea,

> "The dew is sparkling in the beam,
> The kine are thronging to the stream!"

An Ontario farm, in the early eighties, was a busy place, and every one on our farm, moved briskly. My father often said of my mother that she could keep forty people busy. She certainly could think of things for people to do. Maybe that was one reason for my enjoying the farmyard so much. I loved to sit on the top rail of the fence, and luxuriantly do nothing, when I was well out of the range of her vision. Mother herself worked harder than anyone. She was the first up in the morning and the last one to go to bed at night. Our teams were on the land, and the Monday morning washing on the line well ahead of the neighbors'. I know now these things compensated her for the busy life she led, for everyone has to be proud of something.

But I often wished we could all slow down a bit. I wanted to hear more talk. I wanted to do some of it myself too. It seemed too bad to be always rushing. Early to bed and early to rise! To-morrow always crashing in on the heels of to-day! I heard Will say he was tired of working on a treadmill. I knew he felt like the horses on the threshing-machine; drawing, and walking round and around in endless circles, always going but never arriving. Lizzie, too, who changed her dress the very minute she came in from school and never stopped until bedtime, had often told me to play all I could, and sleep all I could, for when I was big enough to work there would be plenty of it to do.

Even the twenty-fourth of May which is second only to Christmas, had to have its dole of work done in the morning, or there could be no picnic in the afternoon. I remember rising in the gray dawn with the others, and

B

helping in a feverish potato-planting drive, so we could all go to a picnic at the Sauble at two o'clock.

One morning, Hannah and Jack had to have pens, and were sent out to look for enough eggs to make the purchase. Three dozen were found, and after a casting up of figures—copybook ten cents, pens five cents, with eggs ten cents—it seemed a fair hope that the purchase could be made. Of course, there was always the danger that eggs might go down, in which case Hannah would have to wait the pleasure of the hens for her copybook.

Jack was elected to carry the egg-basket for he was ten, and Hannah was only eight. But at this juncture dissension arose. Jack would not carry an egg-basket. He would do anything but that. Carrying eggs and peddling eggs was not a man's job, Hannah would have to do it. He did not care if he never got a copybook.

Mother could hardly find words to express her indignation. He should be glad we had eggs to sell. Everyone sold eggs!

Jack set his jaw, and repeated his contention. Hannah, who never wasted words, took the basket and departed. She was half-way to the road before her absence was noted.

This was in the early morning of a rainy day, and both Will and George were in the house, and had heard the discussion. "That lad will never make an Ontario farmer," George said.

Will was eating his breakfast, and suddenly shoved back his plate. "I know how he feels, though I must say it has hit him early. I am tired of the butter-and-egg business too! It does seem that hard work, early and late, should bring in a little money—real money that would be a pleasure to spend. Now we have to sneak in with a basket of eggs, or a crock of butter, when we want a pair of boots or a new tie. . . . The soil is too gravelly and light to grow a decent crop—and the more stones we pick off, the more come up from below. By raking and harrowing, and coaxing them along, the fields will raise cattle-feed and chicken-feed, but no big crops that can be sold for cash. The County of Grey is on a narrow gauge and always will be."

Mother was standing beside the stove listening to them.

"What can we do, boys?" she said anxiously. "We're here and we've got to live. Your father cleared every bit of this farm, and we can't just pick up and leave it, and where would we go, anyway?"

Will got up, and began his preparations for going out; a rainy day had its own activities, the seed wheat had to go through the fanning-mill.

"Mr. Cameron has a book about a trip a man made with a dog, from Fort Garry away West, and it's a wonderful country, he says; the man's name is Butler, and he came from Tipperary, near Nenagh too."

Father suddenly became interested. "Look at that now!" he said.

"But can you believe what you read?" mother asked lapsing into her Dundee accent. "Pen and paper refuse nothing."

"Mr. Cameron believes it," Will said. "I was in there the other night with the boys, and he read us about a buffalo hunt that was great. Thousands of buffaloes on a plain a hundred miles wide, and not a tree or a stone."

Will knew he had quieted every doubt, in mother's mind, for Mr. Cameron was the Presbyterian minister in Chatsworth and had recently come from Scotland. "And there are letters in the Toronto *Globe*, written by a man called White, saying there's room for millions of people in the North-West. . . . and you know what George McDougall said."

"But the cold is terrible in the North-West," mother said. "I remember the geography we had in our school at home said, that the haymakers were often frozen in their tents, and the country should be left to the Indians."

"There's plenty room for the Indians, too," said Will. "We've no idea of the size of the North-West. . . . Mr.

Cameron says the Rebellion of 1870 did one good thing, it brought eastern men out there, and let them see the country with their own eyes. They saw it, and saw its good soil, and now there is a real movement to take up land. I'd like to be going, I certainly want better soil than we have here."

Thomas White's letters in the Montreal *Gazette* and Toronto *Globe* were handed about and read, and discussed at Breeze's store and in the tavern. The majority of the farmers were skeptical. No country could be as good as this! It was a scheme of the land agents to get honest men's money! Men who had the best farms in the community spoke this way, but men, particularly young men, who worked on stony farms listened eagerly. Chilblains and stone bruises made their minds receptive.

In the winter of 1878, our neighborhood had a visitor. Young Michael Lowery, who had been gone two years, came home. He had gone to Manitoulin Island first, and then drifted west to the Red River country, where he had fallen in with freighters, earned good money with them, and with it had outfitted for farming, and settled on a piece of land in south-western Manitoba, where the railway was already surveyed.

Young Michael had really come back to be married, but for family reasons that purpose was carefully concealed. There was still some doubt that he would be able to get his girl away from her aunt, who was a masterful woman, and knowing her niece's ability as a housekeeper, did not propose to lose her without a struggle.

He was a handsome young giant and wore a shaganappi coat, heavily beaded and fringed on the seams with doe skin, and a red scarf and toque; and he had with him a box of moccasins and gloves made by the Indians. He had many tales to tell of good hunting, big game, narrow escapes, friendly Indians, and above all in fascination for the dwellers along the Garafraxa, hundreds of acres of land, without a stone, or a bush, waiting to be taken. There were strawberries so plentiful and luscious, that his oxen's feet were red with them as he ploughed the willing sod, young Michael said; and there were wild plums and cranberries, spilling on the ground, with no one to pick them.

Young Michael must have told his story well, for the quiet waters of our neighborhood were stirred to their depths, and discussions raged in every farmhouse. As a rule the older people scoffed at the idea that any place could be as free from "drawbacks," as Michael claimed for the North-West. The Hemstock family shook its composite head and said, "Green fields are far away. What about orchards in the North-West? Can apple trees live in that frosty country?" The Hemstocks had a whole acre in fruit trees and a purple grapevine that covered a stone fence. The Charltons on the next farm had had a relative in Minnesota during the trouble with the Sioux and nothing would move them from the security of Grey County.

But the young people kindled to the picture young Michael painted—they could see the sea of grass and the friendly skies above it, and they could feel the intoxication of being the first to plant the seed in that mellow black loam, enriched by a million years of rain and sun.

My bother Will caught the fever and when his chores were done, cleared out every evening across the fields to Robert Lowery's where young Michael was staying, and did not come in till all hours, maybe ten o'clock.

Echoes of Michael's comparisons drifted in through Will's conversation. "Out West they do things in a big way," Will said. "Fifty acres is the size of a field not a farm. And there are no coppers, Michael said; he hardly knew what they were when he saw them."

"How do they get on without them?" George asked incredulously.

"They don't haggle about trifles," said Will, "a thing is either five cents or ten cents. If it is less than five cents they give it to you."

"That would save a lot of counting of collections," mother said, "but it might keep some people from church too. . . . It always makes me feel mean to see people put a cent on the collection plate; especially them that can afford more. To see a woman with a nice braided dolman put a penny on a plate is about as mean a sight as I know."

"This kind of pocket handkerchief-farming makes people mean—Michael says the people of Grey County would kill a flea for the hide and tallow," Will remarked.

Strangely enough, my mother was more impressed than my father with Red Michael's story. She questioned him closely, and unlike some other questioners, listened when he answered. I think Michael liked talking to her.

"We'll have to go some place, John," she said one night to my father. "There's nothing here for our three boys. What can we do with one-hundred-and-fifty stony acres? The boys will be hired-men all their lives, or clerks in a store. That's not good enough!"

Father was fearful! There were Indians to consider, not only Indians, but mosquitoes. He had seen on the Ottawa what mosquitoes could do to horses; and to people too. No! It was better to leave well enough alone. Had any of us ever gone hungry? And now when we were getting things fixed up pretty well, with the new root-house; and the cook-house shingled, and the lower eighty broken up, and a good school now, with a real teacher, and an inspector coming once a year anyway, and a fine Sunday-school too, and all sorts of advantages. . . .

We all knew mother was agitated as she went around the house, for she banged doors and set down stove-lids noisily. And she kept everyone going at top speed. Even I knew she was in some sort of tribulation of spirit. . . . When everything else was done, the leach had to be watered; and that was one little chore I could do.

The leach was a small barrel of ashes, set up on a trestle, high enough to cover a black iron pan. The barrel had small auger holes bored in the bottom, and the innumerable pails of water poured on the ashes would at last run through in reluctant black drops, and then the leach was said to be running.

The lye thus extracted was used for making soap, and the day the soap was made was a hay of high adventure. The operation took place outside in a big black kettle that was never used for anything else. No ordinary day would do; it had to be a clear bright day with no wind, and the moon had to be on the increase or the soap might not set. Over a blazing fire, made in a hole lined with stones, the grease and lye were fused in the old black pot and stirred all the time, from left to right, with a hickory stick. All persons of six or under were excluded from the ceremony, but there was nothing to prevent persons of six or under from climbing out of an upstairs window, reaching the sloping roof of the kitchen, lying flat on the edge and looking down.

There was a fascination in the fiery boiling of this billowy mass, threatening every minute to boil over. My mother, in a sprigged blue print dress, tucked tightly between her knees and her head rolled in a red handkerchief stood on the windward side, stirring with a quick motion. Wooden boxes stood ready to receive the soap when it was done. No one must speak to her or interrupt in any way when the boiling was going on, for there was a moment when the pot must be removed and if that moment were correctly guessed the soap would harden. My mother was the High Priestess of all domestic rites to me, so of course she knew the exact moment. I had no doubt she invented soap-making, and I was very proud of

her cleverness, and sorry for the little girls whose
mothers couldn't make soap and so had to use the
"boughten" kind.

And there was a real trick in making soap. Even my
Aunt Ellen had a failure once, and my Aunt Ellen was a
very clever woman, and one of the delights of my childhood. Aunt Ellen lived in the village and we often went
to see her. Uncle Abner was a blacksmith, but he only
worked in the afternoons. Uncle Abner had blue black
curly hair, and big blue eyes, and the longest moustache
ever seen. When I sat behind him I could see both ends.
People said Uncle Abner was lazy, and really good for
nothing, but playing the fiddle at dances. But they did
not say that to Aunt Ellen, who adored him. People said
she was too proud to admit that she had made a bad
bargain. Aunt Ellen said people did not understand
Abner. Naturally he liked company—why shouldn't he?
He was the life of the party wherever he went; and when
he was out late so many evenings, he just had to sleep
in in the mornings. But he could do as much in an afternoon as most men did all day. Uncle Abner made me a
little basket from a walnut shell, and a gold wire brooch
with my initials. My mother did not quite approve of my
Uncle Abner but she qualified her criticism by saying:
"For all that, he has a nice way with him." Uncle Abner
was frequently cited in matrimonial arguments along the
Garafraxa. Indignant husbands, hard-working and
steady, who felt they were being unduly criticized for
some slight misdemeanor, wished they were more "like
Abner Patton and then they might be appreciated, by
gum."

Young Michael certainly had troubled the waters, with
his stories of the far West. All day long, while the work
of the farm went on, at high speed, not much was said,
but at night the rafters in the kitchen rang with words.

Unfortunately I had to go to bed, but Hannah relayed

all to me, with shrewd editorial comment, and long before any decision was reached, told me she was sure we were going. She based this belief on the fiery way mother was working. There was another quilt on the way; and the leach was set up again. Arabella Cresine was coming to sew as soon as she was through with the Charltons.

We began to be sorry for the young people who had to stay forever in Grey County.

I wondered what we would do with the dogs. . . . Aunt Ellen might take them; they had two already, but a dog more or less did not matter. Uncle Abner would like the brown spaniel, but not old Watch, who had no beauty or grace, just a stern sense of duty. All day he watched for hawks and answered the call of the hens. He never left the yard, never played, never had any fun, never wagged his tail and nobody liked him but mother, who said if he were young she wouldn't take a hundred dollars for him. Nap, the spaniel was a joyous pup, with silky brown hair and creamy white trimmings. He could sit up and beg and bring back sticks, and play ball; would not go after the cows, or chase a hawk, or do anything useful, but he was light of heart and had a welcoming bark for everyone. My father called him "play-boy," and said it was too bad that the two dogs could not be combined.

He explained all to me one day when I was picking potatoes for him in the field between our house and the road. He said old Watch did not need to be so cross and grim and suspicious, and Nap might easily learn to be useful without losing one bit of his playful ways. People were the same. And then he went on and said that was one reason why Christ was sent to earth—to show people that a Christian might be, indeed must be polite and pleasant, and full of fun and fond of music, and pretty colors and yet serious too and earnest. And he told me to think about this and try to combine the virtues of Watch and the friendliness of Nap, in my own life.

I asked him then if it were wrong for me to mock the aunts.

He stopped his work and looked over toward the house, before he answered; his voice fell, as if he were afraid the wind might carry it.

"Your mother thinks it is," he said, "she thinks it shows disrespect. I do not think so. They are funny, queer stiff old ladies, set in their ways and right in their own eyes. It's no harm for you and me to have a laugh over them, a laugh is as good as a meal or an hour's sleep. But perhaps we had better not offend your mother. We know that would be wrong, we'll just keep it to ourselves and not be hurting anyone's feelings."

"What makes mother like that?" I asked after awhile.

"She's Scotch," he said, "they're very serious people, a little bit stern, but the greatest people in the world for courage and backbone. The Irish are different; not so steadfast or reliable, but very pleasant. Irish people have had so much trouble, they've had to sing and dance, and laugh and fight to keep their hearts from breaking."

"I am glad you are Irish," I said. I stopped picking and straightened up. It was a lovely autumn day, with a sky as blue as an enamel plate. From the yard came the contented sounds of hens cackling and turkeys gobbling. White clouds, with gray wrinklings idled over our heads. The wind lifting the potato stocks made a dry rustling that subtly spoke of winter, when there would be long dark days, with frozen window panes and stinging winds that made it impossible to play outside. But this day, full of the abundance of harvest was made for joy and singing, and we went on with the digging and sang as we worked:

> "Shule, shule, shule, agra
>   Its time can only aise me woe
> Since the lad o' me heart
>   From me did part
> Schedate, avoureen, schlana.

I'll dye me petticoat,
   I'll dye it red
And through the world
   I'll beg me bread,
   I wish in me heart
   That I was dead.
   Schedate, avoureen, schlana."

The words were sad, but not the singers.

CHAPTER V

The Decision

ONE day the whole question of emigration to the far away Red River was suddenly decided. The vapor of argument and opinion suddenly lifted and blew away, and before us stretched a straight hard road, from which there could be no turning back.

The spring plowing was going on this bright windy day in May; and because of the high wind and eddying dust I was playing in the kitchen; I had just come over to the long table to watch mother kneading her bread, which squeaked as the air-bubbles broke. All in a moment the door flew open and Will came in, with a gust of wind.

He must have made a dramatic entry, for I can remember that his face was white and his eyes had turned strangely black. Mother turned around from the table and stood without speaking. Will threw his hat on the floor and every sound in the house suddenly ceased.

"I am done!" he said, and his voice shook with rage. "I am quitting right here! I'll never put another plow into the soil of Grey County, I'll go west, if I have to walk!"

Mother went to him and helped him to the sofa.

"You are hurt Willie," she said anxiously. "Did the plow hit a stone?"

Will nodded. "It knocked my wind out," he said; a hidden stone—there's no end to them, but I'm done. I've quit!"

There was no argument. Will would go at once and if he liked it we would all go in a year.

The day Will left I cried bitter tears. I think every one cried but my mother. She said there wash no need of tears, we should be glad we had a brother brave enough

38

to go out West and find land for us, and we would all be together soon, and there would be plenty to do in the year getting ready for the big move, and there would be need of every one, even to the youngest. I knew that meant I would have to go on watering the leach.

We all walked out to the road with Will and waited for the stage, which would take him to Owen Sound, and he would get on the *Francis Smith*, the boat which sailed that night. He wore a pale grey shirt, with a blue tie caught in a gold ring, and had a new grey felt hat and carried the only valise we owned. I knew he would conquer the world.

The next night came the storm which beat the *Francis Smith* upon the rocks. The gale came suddenly in the night and wakened me with great flashes of lightning followed by peals of thunder that shook the world. First a flash and then a burst of thunder and pelting rain in one deafening confusion. I turned my face into the pillow, but could still see the flashes. Then the rumbles began to come from farther away and the rain slackened too. Suddenly I thought of the boat and sat up! Would the storm be on the Lakes? A flash of lightning showed me mother kneeling by her bedside in her nightgown, her long dark hair hanging down her back in two braids; and through the dark I heard her praying: "Thou, who didst walk the waters on the Sea of Galilee," she pleaded, "walk it again on Lake Superior and save the *Francis Smith*; O, still the waves and let the passengers be saved, even if the vessel is smashed to pieces on the rocks, stoop, O Saviour, stoop and save."

I prayed too, but my petition was a simple one. I made a little tent of my hands before my face and whispered in the dark: "Dear God, take care of Will—he's my biggest brother and he's going to find good land for us. He's a good fellow, and if he should get drowned we can't go West. Amen."

Having thus delivered myself I went to sleep again and slept till morning. I knew it would be all right. God

would not go back on mother. My father must have felt
the same way, for he slept the night through. At daylight mother wakened him and they drove into Owen
Sound and found that all the passengers had been taken
off the ship, and a few days later we got Will's letter,
telling us about the storm.

After that Will's letters became the great events of
our lives. He had joined a surveying party and was
lucky to get on it. Now he would see the country and be
able to choose the best land; he wouldn't forget to have a
running stream on the farm and there would be good
black loam. He was well and happy and letting his
whiskers grow. . . .

He found a place near the Souris River. . . . We would
write to Grand View now and he would get it some
time. We must not be anxious if we did not hear from
him, and would we give this letter to Annie Stephenson to
read? He had only one stamp. . . . He would draw a map
of the township for us. . . .

He was going to camp in the bush with a man called
Macdonald, and cut logs for the house when the cold
weather came. Maybe he would get a chance to send a
letter out, anyway he would be all right in the camp—
there was plenty of firewood and they had a tin stove and
lots of pork and beans, and rabbits were plentiful. He
hoped we could sell the farm. There was plenty of good
land there lying waste. He would come to Winnipeg to
meet us in May. . . .

In May, 1880, we all sailed on the *City of Owen Sound*.
I remember taking leave of the old home which had been
bought by a man named Crawford. I was dressed in my
best dress, the day we left, for I was going to have my
picture taken in Owen Sound. It was a black and white
farmer's satin, second mourning for my grandmother
who had died the year before. I had white cotton stockings, knit in a feather pattern, and high laced boots.

The neighbors helped us to draw our stuff into Owen

Sound. Hannah and I rode with Caleb Morgan, Mr. Conger's hired man. It was a bleak windy day, with light clouds rolling, but we were warmly wrapped in a blanket and sat on the high spring seat with Caleb. He confided to us as we rattled along that he fully intended to get out West himself sometime, but what could a man do with his mother and two sisters to support?

Mother and father rode in our own wagon ahead, driven by Mr. Crawford, who had bought the horses and wagon, and was helping us now to get our stuff on the boat.

We stopped in Chatsworth and went into the cemetery. On grandmother's grave mother put a wreath of paper flowers, in a little box with a glass lid, which Arabella Cresine had made for her. There was a new white stone with her name, "Margaret Fullerton McCurdy." There was a little grave beside grandmother's with a white lamb at the head and this was where the little brother, John Wesley, whom I had never seen, was laid. I had been there before and knew about this little fellow, who was the smartest, best child of us all, and one Sunday he had come home from Sunday-school with his Berean Leaf and said his verse, "Let not your heart be troubled," and he was dead at noon on Tuesday. I tried to feel sad when I looked at the little stone. . . . mother cried when she knelt beside the little mound and said, "We're not leaving you Johnny, for you're safe in heaven, and I carry your memory in my heart and always will . . . and when the other children all grow up and leave me, I'll still have my wee bairn. . . . And when my time comes you will be the angel sent out to meet me, and you will say your verse to me then. . . ."

Near Inglis Falls we stopped again to say good-bye to the McMickens, who kept the tavern there. Mrs. McMicken was my father's niece, and Robert her boy, eighteen years old was sick with consumption. He had grown too fast. There were great deers' heads of the hall, and a cabinet of stuffed birds on the landing of the stairs. We were all taken in to say good-bye to Robert, who lay as white as the pillows on his high bed.

In Owen Sound, Hannah, Lizzie and I stayed at Mary Little's. Mary had gone from our neighborhood some years ago and set herself up in dressmaking, and had done well. She was a thin darting little woman with a heart-shaped pincushion of red velvet hanging from her leather belt. Across from her house was a great yellow house, whose eaves and windows and verandah were all edged with wooden lace.

At Silver Inlet, we went ashore to see a cousin, who had the name of being a bad housekeeper. She read novels, paper-backed novels, day and night and would neither knit nor sew. Novels were a form of poison. I knew that, but mother spoke well of poor Lucy in spite of her weakness. She was as good-natured a soul as ever lived, and would be a good woman, if she could only leave the cursed novels alone. Maybe she had done better in her new home. Anyway, we would call and see her for the boat stayed two hours.

We trailed up a long hill, with a narrow sidewalk of two boards and houses standing one above another. We found Lucy's house quite easily. There were no curtains on the windows and boards in the steps were broken, but that was not Lucy's fault—surely Johnny should have mended the steps, but it seems the novels had got Johnny too, not that he read them, but Lucy didn't get the right sort of meals and Johnny had lost heart, so he couldn't be expected to mend the steps. Lucy came to the door in bedroom slippers and a Mother Hubbard wrapper, and her hair was in curl papers, though this was late afternoon. She was very glad to see us, and took us into the little parlor, where the furniture wore grey linen dusters, and the pictures were crooked on the wall. But her house was warm; and from the bare window looking out on the street, we could see the blue waters of the harbor, and our big white boat waiting for us. Lucy made a cup of tea for us and served us biscuits, "boughten biscuits," but lovely to the taste. Lucy was very sweet and pleasant, and told mother she was late with her housecleaning this Spring, but she was going to get right at it as soon as she finished the book she was reading—such a lovely story about an orphan who was the real heir to her grandfather's millions. But do you think her uncles would let her have the money?—they had laid traps for her in every way, and now they were plotting with the gypsies to steal her, and her so young and sweet and innocent. Even the old gypsy woman was better than her own uncles, and had come by night to see Dolores—that was the orphan— to tell her not to drink—

Mother interrupted Lucy there just when it was getting interesting, and asked for Johnny, and Lucy said that Johnny was the "same old tupenny bit."

I liked Lucy. She had a cat too, a big furry one, black and white, which lay on the top of the sideboard among the newspapers.

We stayed until our boat gave its deep-throated whistle to warn us that one hour had gone, and then mother hurried us out. I wanted to find out about Dolores, the orphan, and what it was she mustn't drink, but I never knew.

The boat carried us as far as Duluth, and again we climbed a hill—this time to find a store, for we had to carry our own food on the train. I had ten cents of my own too, which was causing me some anxiety. I bought maple sugar with it, and rued my bargain immediately, for there were many other things I would have preferred, but maple sugar was the first thing offered to me, and I did not wish to hurt the clerk's feelings.

Hannah was indignant with me for letting my money go so easily. "We have better maple sugar than that with us," she said. "maple sugar is no treat, anyway, when we can make it ourselves."

"I like this," I said, "look at the scallops around the edge, and I think it will have a different taste from ours!"

"You haven't much sense," Hannah said, and I knew

it was true. But I stuck to my bargain and pretended I was satisfied, remembering Aunt Ellen.

The train journey from Duluth to St. Boniface passed like a flash. If there were pullmans on this train, they were not used by us. We slept very comfortably on the seats, for we had pillows and blankets. Our only trouble was that the car was crowded, but I slept very well for a man across the aisle offered to take me, for he was alone in the seat, and made a nice bed for me on his buffalo coat. Mother was afraid he might steal me and so did not close an eye all night, but no such thought kept me from my slumber. I asked him to please waken me when we crossed the Mississippi, and I told him boastfully, I fear, that I could spell "Mississippi," and proceeded to do so, and having gone thus far in making a contact with the great waterway, it was only natural that I should want to see it. He promised to waken me, if he could stay awake himself. He said we would cross the river in daylight, just about daybreak, but he would find out for sure.

I was pretty drowsy when he gently stirred and called me, and I knew it would be a chance of a life-time. He told me we would be on the bridge in a minute. It was in the dull gray of a misty Spring morning; discolored snow lined the yellow clay banks, and the great current of water billowed and threshed and churned its way under us, as the train crawled slowly over the bridge. The air was full of its clamoring roar as my friend held me up so I could see through the clear glass in the top half of the window, and I flattened my nose on it, in my eagerness to see all I could of the turmoil below me.

"I know what it is like," I said, when the train had passed the last trestle, and began to pick up speed on the level track, and I was crawling back into the fur coat.

He expressed his readiness to hear.

"Soft soap," I said, "when it is just ready to boil over and folding up from the bottom."

"I have never seen soft soap," he said, "where did you see it?"

I wanted to tell him about the leach with the black pan under it, but my eyes were heavy with sleep, so I just waved my hand across the aisle. If he wanted information, there was the original soap-maker: she could tell him the story of soap from the beginning.

CHAPTER VI

WE ARRIVE

WE arrived in St. Boniface at night, a close hot May night with no moon. There seemed to be no place to stay, so we crossed the river in a row-boat. Timoleon Tait's ferry did not start to run until later in the season. The seven of us, with our hand baggage were packed in the boat, and I remember trailing my hands in the cold water, which seemed very nearly up to the edge of the boat. We found a hotel that would take us in and let us spread our bedding on the floor, every bed being occupied, and here, sleepy and tired we lay down. But when daylight came, and my mother saw what sort of a place we were in we made a hurried exit. She must have been greatly shaken at the sight, for she imparted to each of us a great desire to get out. I think it was probably her first sight of old and unashamed dirt. The bill was fifteen dollars.

Our next place of sojourn was a delightful one—a tent on the river bank, where all day we could see the activities of both the Red and Assiniboine, for our camping-ground was at the junction of these two rivers. Many other settlers were camped there, and we were welcomed by the older residents and every assistance was given to us. Before three days had gone by we had a floored tent, with a stove, home-made table, a clothesline and bunks around the sides of the tent, and knew all the other families. My mother set to work to wash the bedding, bit by bit, for the memory of that one night in the Browse Hotel had to be purged away by soap and water and the high bright sunshine of the river bank.

We were not overlooked by the purveyors of Winnipeg. A butcher's cart came down to us twice a week with beefsteak at seventy-five cents a pound, and an enterprising dairyman led two cows through the encampment and sold milk at thirty cents a quart, cafeteria style. Land agents with pockets bulging with documents swarmed about us.

Our great excitement was the river boats passing on both rivers; some side-wheelers and some with the propeller behind, great red and white boats churning the muddy water of the river into creamy foam. The landings were made by throwing out a cable, when the boat had come as near to the shore as the water allowed and letting off the deckhands called "Roosters," who tugged at the cables and drew the boat to shore. The landings were accomplished in torrents of profanity, directed toward the Roosters who worked away patiently and without resentment; one of our tent-neighbors said the captains seemed to be even-tempered men, always in a rage.

We were three days in the tent when Will came with our cousin John Clarke, a young man about Will's age, who looked like him too, and when these two sunburned young fellows in their high boots, with whiskers on their faces came in, and hailed us as their own and we knew that we were all together again, our happiness was complete. Now let the hurricane roar, we were here! We had reached the Red River and the world was ours!

I remember lying in bed in the tent trying to keep awake when Will was telling about the time he had spent at the Junction of the Assiniboine and Souris, that terrible winter of '79-80 when the frost split the trees wide open, and they cracked like pistol-shots, and the northern lights pink and gold, and green, waved and fluttered in the sky like curtains hung on a clothesline on a windy day. The stove was kept red-hot but even so his back was freezing while his face burned. And the wolves circled and howled, and snapped their hungry jaws outside the tent, some so near to him that he never ceased to be frightened they would get an ear or a toe, and the two ponies died, although they had made a shelter of logs for them, and covered it with spruce boughs, but they had breathed the frost into their lungs. . . . After that no one spoke for so long that I fell asleep.

But most of all we wanted to hear of the land Will had taken for us—a half-section for himself and one for father, and a quarter for George, all together. Ours was section 20, township 7, range 16, and Will drew a diagram to show us how the sections were laid out, drawing in the running stream that cut through our farm, and circled to make a perfect building site.

Oxen had to be bought now, and two wagons and some place had to be found for us to live. Will's plan was for the family to stay in Winnipeg while he and father and George would take part of the furniture and drive the hundred-and-eighty miles, build a house with the logs he and Macdonald had cut down and dressed, and then come back for us in September, before the cold weather came.

Mother wanted to keep us all together and go on. We could live in the tent while the house was being built, but Will was afraid of the mosquitoes, lack of good water and the general discouragement which might fall upon us. So a house was found, five miles from Winnipeg at Saint James. It was a big, old house with a smoking chimney and a tragic history. Its owner had been shot through one of the windows and the mystery had never been cleared up. The great attraction for us was the fine garden, already ploughed and ready for planting, and this was set with seeds before the men left for their long journey.

Beside us was Sir Donald A. Smith's house, "Silver Heights," a beautiful manor house, surrounded by lawns and flowers and white trellised arbors, with long gabled stables at the back of the grounds. Often in the evening many carriages turned in at the gates, phaetons with wide fenders, covered carriages with lamps on the dash-boards carrying brilliantly dressed people to dance in the great ballroom on the second floor, and on these nights Hannah and I, who went to bed early, would hang half-way out of our room window, listening to the ribbony notes of the violins playing the Blue Danube Waltz and watching the swaying figures of the dancers. We named them and wove romances around them giving them as happy destinies as we thought they deserved. They drew better fortunes from us on the nights they forgot to draw the blue velvet hangings, thus preserving for us a good view of the enchanted ballroom. Sometimes we fancied that proposals of marriage transpired before our eyes in the alcove, and we rehearsed the scene with words of our own making. "Lorelie—may I call you Lorelie? Your love-liness has haunted me since first you crossed my path— and not one peaceful hour have I known since then, so now I must, and will know my fate. Is there a spark of hope that you might grow to love a rough warrior? Nay do not shrink!"

To which I, as Lorelie, made reply with downcast eyes and blushes mantling my snowy brow, "How do I know—I am so young—so ignorant of the world—Sir Hector, I have so lately left my lessons."

Then we had another scene where Lorelie wept and confessed she loved another, one of humble birth, and Sir Hector promised to seek out the handsome herd-boy and make him his heir; so her father's objections would be removed. Whereupon Lorelie fell at his feet and em-braced his knees and cried until Sir Hector, although a little stiff in the back, stooped and lifted her and wiped her tears with his own bandana handkerchief, drawn from the tail of his coat with a crack like a whip-lash. Hannah had invented this scene, to show off her trick of snapping a handkerchief.

Our first intimation of the evil character of the house was brought in by Jack, who said the boys he played with

wouldn't come in for there was a curse on the house, and
a ghost in the attic that moaned in the night.

Mother did not seem to be worried over either the
curse or the ghost.   Hannah and I were greatly thrilled
to be living in a house that had a ghost—that was something surely and we were not afraid, not at the moment
for night was a long way off and the sun was shining.
Anyway, Mother said a person who had a good conscience
need not be afraid of ghosts, even if there were ghosts,
which she did not believe.

But one night there came a storm.   The wind came
down on us, with sudden fury, bending the poplar trees
across the windows, and shaking every loose window in
our house.   We used only two rooms downstairs and two
upstairs, for, having sent all the furniture we could do
without, on the wagons, we were managing with the scant
necessities.

We were all downstairs when the gale struck, and at
first we watched the tossing trees and the rolling clouds
from the front windows.   Suddenly the whole house burst
into groans, rolling higher and higher and then dying into
agonized whispers.   We turned from the window in a
panic of fear.   Mother stood up and listened with her
brows drawn down and every sense alert.   Then she shook
her head and went out into the hall.   The sounds certainly were coming from upstairs.   We were sure it was the
ghost, or a collection of ghosts, but not a word was spoken
until mother announced her intention of finding out.   We
formed a procession, Jack walking ahead carrying the
lamp.   Mother followed with an ax, Lizzie, Hannah and
I fell in, I did not want to go, but it would be worse to
stay behind.

The moans did not belong to the first floor but came
from the attic, rising and falling with every gust.   A
blaze of lightning blotted out the yellow lamplight, leaving us almost blinded.   There was a door to the attic,
always locked, but mother had all the keys with her.   She

found the key, unlocked the door and opened it. A rush of wind put out the light.

"I think I know what the trouble is," she said; "there's no ghost."

"I'll go down and get the matches," Jack volunteered, and I thought it was very brave of him. But mother did not need a light.

"Never mind, I'll go up and close the windows, the lightning will show the way. Don't be afraid, it's nothing!"

We stayed below and heard her steps on the bare floor. There were continuous flashes of lightning. In a few minutes we heard her coming and her voice had a note of victory. "Nothing at all," she said, "just bottles in the windows with their necks turned out, and when the wind blew it roared in and out. I let the windows down, so we'll hear no more groans."

We went down the stairs and back to the kitchen, where a cheerful fire burned in the stove and the lamp-light never looked more welcome. "I think I'll have a cup of tea, and you may have hot milk," mother said, "and we'll sit down a while and read our book. It's not late yet and we don't feel like sleeping."

The storm went on but the sounds in the house had settled down to what night sounds should be when the rain pours down, and the wind is riding the trees. And we had a fine long evening following the fortunes of the "Scottish Chiefs."

Before the men of the family had left for the West, a farm for sale was offered to us, Louis Pruden's farm on the river-bank—four chains wide, as all the farms were, and four miles long—laid out in this way to provide river frontage for everyone and to make it possible for the houses to be close together. The price was sixteen hundred dollars, which was about all we had after the oxen, waggons and supplies were bought. We could buy it on easy terms, and Will saw possibilities in the venture.

"We could sell it in a year and double our money," Will said.

"This land will be sold for town lots in ten years," father said, who was favorable to the project. "Winnipeg will be one of the great cities of Canada, and nothing can prevent it."

But mother stood firm. "Let us go on," she said. "Let us go to an all-white settlement. There are too many jet black eyes and high cheek-bones here. I like them very well when they belong to the neighbors' children, but I would not like them in my grand-children. We came here, John, for the children's sake, not ours, and we'll do our best for them every way."

I couldn't see why she objected. Indian Tommy was the nicest boy we played with, and the McMullen children were all right too. Indian Tommy's mother worked in the kitchen of Silver Heights, so quite often he came over and played with us. He could whistle like a meadowlark and climb any tree on the place, and after he lost his two front teeth, he could spit right through a knot-hole in the fence.

Indian Tommy's mother did not like another woman, called Mrs. Baggs, because Mrs. Baggs said Indian Tommy's mother had never been drunk in her life and she had been roaring drunk once in Winnipeg. This started the quarrel, and when they fought on the river bank, Tommy took me over to see it, and all would have been well if I had not brought home the news, but unfortunately, I did. Naturally I was glad to see my friend's mother win and chase her enemy, almost into the river. Something told me, though, as I went on with my story that I was not "getting my audience." From then on, I was not allowed to go out of our own grounds unless Hannah or Lizzie was with me.

But there was good fun in playing inside, when Hannah would play with me. We climbed the poplar trees which were just the right size for a lovely game that Hannah invented. We had two trees that were near enough to strike when we got them teetering and then the game was to see who could first knock the other one down. It was a lovely game and its name was, "Biting the Dust."

Mother and Jack attended to the garden and it responded with a prodigality of growth which must have warmed their hearts. Rich black soil for a seed-bed, with plenty of rain and warm sunshine, made the plants grow with great vigor, and I believe this kept mother's spirits high that summer more than anything else, for she must have had her times of loneliness. The mosquitoes were like all the plagues of the Old Testament but no matter, the hoeing and weeding went on, for these rows of carrots, beets, onions and potatoes would all be needed in the long winter that lay ahead.

CHAPTER VII

ON THE TRAIL

WHEN the first of September came, we began to watch the Portage road. Our men might come any day now. Mother had a pound cake made and set away in a crock, and the bread supply was not allowed to fall below three loaves and the stove got blackened every day.

One Saturday evening, as the sun was going down in a wine red mist, I saw two ox-wagons come over the rise in the Portage road, beyond the McMullen farm. I was sure it was our wagons, but I had been sure so many times before and utterly disappointed when the wagons went past, that I watched and said nothing. I was the only one on guard at the moment, and I hoped every one would stay where they were so I could have the "scoop." I wanted to run down to the road, but I had done that before and there was no luck in it. So I turned my head away and counted fifty before I looked. They were still coming! I counted another fifty and with masterly self control, refrained from sound or motion even though I could see a red ox, with a red and white ox, a red ox with a black and white ox. It must be them! I had to stuff my sun-bonnet into my mouth to keep from raising the glad shout. At last the first wagon turned in—and I lifted the alarm, which brought the other members of the family flying. They thought I had been stung by a bee Jack said afterwards, and then, to lift forever the bad name which was sometimes urged against me that I never did anything without being told, I dashed out into the back-yard to pick up chips for the fire, but in the general excitement my good deed was not even noticed.

Father and Will had come, leaving George behind to look after the place. . . .

However the evening had one bright aspect. There was so much talk, I sat up unobserved until ten, by making myself small, and quiet and I heard that we must be on our way in a week, and that father said he was glad we had not come with them in the spring, for between the smoke of the smudges and the mosquito bites there wasn't much to choose, and that we were going to get a pony and cart for it would save the oxen, and be a quicker way of getting around, when we got home.

There were trips into Winnipeg, to buy supplies and I got a pair of stout shoes with copper toes, so big I had to pad my feet below and around with newspaper. I would grow into them!

The Sunday before we left we all went to church, walking the mile to the little English church of which Mr. Pinkham was the rector. We had attended there all summer and Mr. Pinkham had come to see us. We said goodbye to the friends we had made: Mr. and Mrs. Armstrong, Mr. and Mrs. Buckley and the Tait family—Mr. and Mrs. Robert Tait, Herbie, Ellen and Addie. Addie was a little older than I, a tall girl with reddish hair, who always had money and seemed to me like a princess in disguise. I think she bought candy every day at the store and in the mixture, when hard candies with a centre like flour paste appeared she threw them away. Ah me! I would have been glad of them, but of course, I couldn't take Addie's "leavings," so I heaped scorn on them too, but it was hard to forget them, in the candyless years that followed.

We left on Monday morning, early, with the poplar leaves stirring in the light of the rising sun. It was a glorious morning, with a smell all its own, dead leaves, ripening again, coffee and bacon, new boots and something else, maybe just adventure, the magic of the unknown.

The garden from which every last vegetable had been taken lay ruffled and tossed like an unmade bed. We were all ready to start when father declared the garden would have to be levelled and raked. There was some dissension about this, but it was done.

"Sure, and it has served us well," he said, as he raked the stalks into a windrow, "and it is only common civility to leave it smooth and in order for the people who come after us. . . . I'd rather cheat a person any day, than cheat the land."

We had two wagonloads of "Settler's Effects,"— which was a broad term that included anything from a plow to a paper of pins. The little oxen, Jake and Brin, went first, for theirs was the lighter load of the two. In their wagon, wrapped in canvas and tarpaulins, were the things that would not be needed on the journey, flour, bacon, dried vegetables, extra bedding, chairs, tables, boxes of clothing. In the covered wagon, which the big oxen drew were the necessities for the days of travel, bedding, dry wood, frying pans, pots, clothing, ox harness, whiffletrees, a neckyoke, tools, spades for digging out mud holes, an ax, ropes and chains, and one bed made up and ready "in case of sickness."

Never had I experienced as great a moment as came to me, when the oxen's heads were turned west on Portage Avenue and the long trail received us unto itself. I felt that life was leading me by the hand and I followed on light feet. We would travel with the sun, until we came to that flower starred prairie where no stone would impede the plow; where strawberries would redden the oxen's fetlocks; where eight-hundred acres of rich black soil was waiting for us, and a running stream would stir the cat-tails in the current and I would have a little boat on it, with white sails and on hot days I could wade in its cool waters, and there would be shady pools and big trees, where I could build a seat and go there and read, when I learned to read, and it would be far enough away from the house, I could not hear any one calling me, and it would be almost the same as having a room of my own. . . .

We walked as much as we could, riding only when we

got tired. I believe my mother walked all the way, for she liked to have her eye on the whole procession and she could only do this from the rear.

It was hot when the sun climbed higher in the sky, but there came heavy banks of clouds that gave us periods of shade and the faithful oxen plodded on, at their own unhurried pace. Wild geese passed into the south to remind us that winter was on our heels, but nothing could dim the radiance of that day of high adventure.

White-washed, Red-river frame houses, set in wide farm yards, well back from the road, stacks of hay and fields of ripe grain with men cutting it down with reapers, and in some fields with sickles and cradles—then long stretches of meadows, growing brown with autumn and then more houses. Over all the odor of wild sage, and golden rod, that grew beside the road, and in the air flights of crows and black-birds visiting the scattered grain fields, and sitting on wire fences, like strings of jet beads.

I wondered how these people could be content to stay on their little farms when there was better land ahead. Perhaps they did not know. Will had said their land was too heavy with gumbo and alkali to ever make easy farming, but they liked living close together with the river at their front door; and had their little circle of friends, and simple pleasures.

Part of the glow I felt in beginning this journey, came from the sense I had that we were well dressed for the occasion. We had dark print dresses and straw hats, lined with the same print as our dresses and banded with a fold of it, dark gray ribbed woolen stockings, hand knit, and good stout boots. Then we had olive green coats, made of homespun, mother's own weaving, with smoked pearl buttons. I remember these coats well, as well I may, for when I grew out of mine I stepped into Hannah's and when it proved inadequate, I got Lizzie's, so that olive green homespun with pearl buttons was my portion in coats until I was fifteen years old. My Aunt Ellen had made them and they were good-looking coats.

The bad roads began at Baie St. Paul, a great swampy place, dreaded by all prairie travellers. We met there, a tragic family who had turned back, discouraged and beaten. It was the wife who had broken down. She wore a black silk dress and lace shawl and a pair of fancy shoes, all caked with mud. She would have been a pretty woman if she would only stop crying. She hated the country, she sobbed, it was only fit for Indians and squaws and should never have been taken from them. Her two little girls were crying too. They had broken their garters and their legs were a mass of mosquito bites.

Mother was very sorry for their distress and tried to calm the weeping woman.

"You're not dressed right for a journey like this," she began. "No one can be happy going through mud in a fine silk dress and thin kid shoes."

"But these are the oldest things I have," she protested tearfully, "and I don't care if they do get spoiled."

"But your shoes are not comfortable," mother said, "and they are no protection to your feet, and you should have made yourself some print or gingham dresses."

"But I can't! I never made a dress in my life, mother always did my sewing,"—and from her eyes came another freshet. "I want to go back to her; she never wanted me to come, but I thought it would be fun, and Willard was so crazy to get land of his own, but he can get his job back at the store."

Mother's zeal began to flag, "Take her back," she said to Willard, "she's not the type that makes a pioneer."

Willard nodded his head grimly, "I see that,"—he said.

Mother invited them to stay and eat with us, for we were stopped for the noon meal and while she was making a bannock in the mouth of a flour sack, Will fried the bacon and made coffee; and Lizzie put Balm of Gilhead salve on the little girls' mosquito bitten legs and mended their garters.

"Poor Willard," mother said, as we saw them drifting down the backward trail. "He'll go on selling papers of pins and yards of tarleton, but all his life he'll dream of the yellow wheat fields that might have been his and his heart will wither with longing. But he made the mistake many good men have made—he married a painted doll, instead of a woman."

"She's a pretty little thing too," my father said, looking after the wagon receding in the distance—"did you ever see a neater ankle?"

At High Bluff we bought a pony and cart, a Redriver cart that had not a nail in it, and whose wooden axle had never known the soothing touch of axle-grease. It rumbled and mourned, and creaked, and whined, as it turned protestingly. We bought the pony from a Methodist minister there, the Reverend Mr. Bray.

Ten miles was a good day's travelling. One day we made only one mile.

At Poplar Point we camped beside the home of Chatsworth people, who had left our neighborhood years before. Mother had written to Mrs. Lance, but no reply had come, but Margaret Lance was the sort of woman who would not write and mother was not offended. Margaret Lane she was before her marriage and the belle of the country side, who could have married any man she wanted; but mother said, "you can go through the woods and go through the woods and pick up a crooked stick at last." So when Johnny Lance came back from the North West, black as an Indian, and his hair hanging down to his shoulder, bragging that he had come to pick out a wife to take back with him, Margaret Lane, (engaged to be married to Billy Spicer, who owned the farm next to her father's), spoke right up and said she would go. Everyone thought it was a joke, but in a week they were married and away—and word drifted back that Margaret

c

said it was the best day's work she had ever done for herself.

We knew they were now living at Poplar Point, so we would go to see them when we were so near.

They lived half a mile from the trail, in a long log house on the bank of a creek. We stopped our wagons on the other side of the creek which was running swiftly under the rough bridge and waited there on the bank opposite their house, while mother and father went across the bridge and up the bank to the house, attended by three barking dogs.

When Mrs. Lance came out of the kitchen door, there was a flurry of wings in the farm yard and hens and ducks raced toward her. Watching from the wagons we saw the meeting, though we could hear nothing above the uproar. A few black haired children came out of the house, the eldest boy vainly trying to quiet the dogs. There was a large duck pond on the side of the creek next the house, where a flock of ducks were feeding, but they, hearing the commotion, climbed out of the water and waddled up in a body to find out what it was all about, making raucous comments as they went.

We were taken into the house and there we saw that although Mrs. Lance had not written she was expecting us. The kitchen table held a fresh baking of bread, and after the greetings were over, the eldest boy was sent out to catch and kill two chickns.

I remember the pattern of their farm buildings. The house was on one side of the creek; and the hen house and stables on the other. When we asked why they had built them this way, Mrs. Lance said she thought it best to keep the animals across the creek by themselves and while she said it, a hen and chickens walked in the door of the kitchen. "We keep her in the woodshed," Mrs. Lance said, "she's late with her chickens; this is her second flock and I'm trying to build them up before winter. It's just time for her boiled wheat and she knows it."

The hen cackled and stormed, sounding a hawk-alarm when she saw us.

Mrs. Lance apologized. "She doesn't like strangers," she said, "but don't mind her, she is really a very friendly hen when she gets to know you."

On the top of the high oven a tin milk pan lined with hay contained three young ducks that had been drenched with rain, Mrs. Lance said, and had nearly died, but if she could just get them feathered out before the cold weather, they would be all right.

"Don't you find it a long way over to the stables, down one hill and up another, with the creek to cross?" mother asked, "how do you manage in the spring when the water is high?"

"Oh! Johnny has a raft and it never lasts very long, maybe a week—he likes it—" she said, "Johnny does like a bit of excitement, and the boys are the same. He's so fond of animals—and he likes them around him. He'd have the house full of them, if I would let him. . . . I don't believe we'll be long here, there's people coming to settle near us and he doesn't like to be crowded."

We made our camp across the creek and stayed that day and night. Mrs. Lance roasted chickens, boiled potatoes and filled our food boxes to overflowing, when we left.

Johnny himself arrived home in the afternoon, with a bag of wild fowl—he had been away shooting on the marsh, and gave us a riotous welcome. Why couldn't we stay a week, and go shooting prairie chickens on the plains? They were as thick as you ever saw black birds in the oat fields in Ontario, and so tame, it was a crime to shoot them.

We could not stay. The weather might break any day and we were only half way on our journey.

"Well, the North West is the place to live," Johnny said, as he drove the hen and chickens out and shut the door. "The Garafraxa would choke me now, if I went back. A man needs freedom! That's what drove me out, and will drive me out again. It's different with women! They never had freedom and so never miss it. I'll have to sell this place pretty soon and move on. There's been two or three land lookers around this summer; wouldn't you like to buy this place John and settle down, and we'll go on to the Souris? It's about time for us to move isn't it Maggie?"

She shok her head.

"The trouble with me is, I won't take dictation from anyone," Johnny said. "Over here two miles away they're startin' a school. That will mean taxes and what do we need a school for?"

"What about your children, don't you want them to go to school?" mother asked indignantly.

Johnny was pressing tobacco into a black pipe, with his broad thumb.

"My boys can get all the education they need from me," he said. "And what good is it for girls? Makes them want to read books, when they should be patchin' quilts; Maggie here, would be a happier woman if she couldn't read at all."

Mother untied her apron before she replied to this.

"The only thing we live for is our children," she said in her Scotch voice, "and if we fail them, we have failed altogether. Every child has a right to an education and if you do not get that for them, you have cheated them."

"You're movin' the wrong way," he said, "if its education you're after. There will be no schools out west where you're headin', for years. It will be like the bush in Grey County forty years ago when my folks went in. The schools came too late for me, and when they came, I was too big to go, but I don't know as I mind. I've done all right. One generation gets missed out in every new settlement, and you'll find that out too. The thing is not to get too much education in the next. It makes too wide a gap. I don't want my kids to get feeling they know more than I do; not that it would hurt me, but it wouldn't be good for the kids. You women are all the same—all for learnin', but I want my boys to stay with me, and this is one way to keep them. Ignorance holds families together."

"You don't mean it Johnny!" mother said at last. "No one could be so selfish as this, or as foolish" . . . .

"I do mean it! Look what education does for people! A man in the Portage forged a cheque and is in jail for it, a good fellow too, would he have done that if he had never learned to write? He had an idea he was smart— knew a little more than the rest of us. And if you do read a newspaper—what do you get? Murders, horse thieving, devilment of one kind or another. What good does her readin' do Maggie, here? Upsets her that's all. Gets her feeling too big for her boots."

That was too much for mother to stand. "Johnny Lance!" she said, "yu married the prettiest girl and the best liked girl in Sullivan County. She jilted a good man to marry you—and she has roughed it with you, in this new country, and put up with you, done without things, and met all sorts of hardships and you would begrudge her the little bit of pleasure she gets from reading a book when her day's work is done and you want to move on again, thinking always of your own wishes, your own pleasure, and not of your family. I wonder at you, Johnny!"

"You got me wrong, Mrs. Mooney," he defended, good-naturedly, "I don't begrudge it to her, if it did her any good, but I claim it don't. She reads in a paper that a man stole horses in Winnipeg and got away, and she's runnin' out all the time countin' ours. Or she reads a story about a man that left his wife and took up with a younger woman, one with yalla hair and I see her eyin' me, and I know she's afraid she might lose me. Thats' what I mean. My claim is it's a mistake to know more than you need to know; and that's why I like animals so well. They ask no questions, tell nothing, have no ambitions or regrets, or complaints, and take things as they come."

Mrs. Lance was making motions behind his head, and no more was said.

Before we left, Mrs. Lance defended her husband's wild talk.

"Johnny just talks to hear himself, but he doesn't mean it. He feels bitter about not ever being to school and covers it up by pretending he does not care. He's a good man to me, Lettie. I don't regret giving Billy Spicer the go-by. I'd have had an easier life, maybe, a good house and near town, but Johnny suits me, for all he's rough in his ways and he likes to talk big. He's a child in some ways, would rather be scolded than not noticed at all. He just loved having you pitch into him. I couldn't let you go thinking that Johnny is mean, for he isn't. He voted for the school and wants the boys to get an education as much as I do. I think most men take a little knowing, Lettie."

They promised to come to see us some summer, when the roads were better. Distances were long in the early eighties and friendships languished in the long silences.

The weather broke the day we left the Lances and the real trouble of the journey began. Fortunately there were many travellers on the road and the mud-holes were the drag nets which brought them all together. Sometimes it took three yokes of oxen to draw a wagon out of a bad spot and even then the long grass beside the road had to be cut and thrown into the slippery, gummy mud to give the oxen a foot-hold.

The men wore long boots of leather and overalls of brown or blue duck, but I do not remember seeing any rubber boots. If the holes were not deep, Hannah and I were left in the wagon for our small weight would not make much difference. But it was like a nightmare to see the oxen go down, down into the mud, sprawling helplessly in its treacherous depths. But they did not get excited as horses would have and they did their best, without urging. In the worst part of the road we were fortunate to have Lord Elphinstone and his traders on the way to Fort Edmonton, and they gave assistance to all the wagons on the road. The traders who had been travelling the trail for years, were always serene and cheerful and said the road was not as bad as it used to be, and that no wagon had been actually lost in the mud for quite awhile.

We stopped at another friend's house, and made our camp in the yard. They were Chatsworth people too, who had come the year before. They had a little girl just my age, named Abigail, a pallid child with faded hair, who seemed browbeaten and sad. She sat stonily silent in a little rocking chair hardly moving, and yet her mother and the older members of the family, often reproved her. "Abigail behave!" is all I can remember of any of the conversation. Hannah and I played the "Abigail behave," game many times, adding interesting variations. I liked to be Abigail, and added to her air of sadness, by letting my hair fall over my eyes and looking cross-eyed while Hannah shouted at me to "behave." Our nice game fell under the ban at last for "mocking is catching," and "people who make faces will find they cannot change back, if the wind changes."

I had a nightmare one night on the trail, when the whole world roared around me like a bursting sea. Only it was a sea of mud, black and greasy, licking me under. All night long, or so it seemed to me, I fought against it, unable to cry for help, and the next day I was not able to walk and so was put in the wagon, which lurched and groaned and writhed over the rough roads.

My head ached and I was very miserable. Every jolt of the wagon increased my pain, although I was packed in between pillows, and everything that could be done for my comfort had been done. I was quite sure my last hour was aproaching, and I was going to be buried by the trail, like Linda. We had seen a little grave marked by a board taken from a wagon box, on which the name "Linda," was printed in white chalk on the green paint. A handful of blue fringed gentians, faded and withered lay on the fresh black earth.

I did not mind dying if it would stop my head from beating—I would be glad to die! The ground would be cold, but it would lie still. Maybe they would take me back and lay me beside Linda.

The wagon suddenly stopped and someone picked me up. Maybe I was dead. . . . Now I thought I must be, for I felt no pain. I had only a great desire to sleep.

"Better let Willie carry her, John," I heard mother say, "she's quite a good weight and your shoulder may ache again."

I felt myself being comfortably laid on my father's broad shoulder.

"Her, is it? A good weight? Poor child! I could carry her to the Tower of Hook. She's just the weight of two dried lamb-skins."

I opened my eyes then, but the light dazzled me and I was too weary to talk. I drifted down into a deep sea of contentment but vaguely through my dreams, I thought of Linda under the blue flowers at the side of the trail. I hoped she liked her grave and did not mind the dark, and I was sure God would send an angel for both of us, before the winter came. If this was dying, it was far nicer than riding in the wagon.

Vaguely through my dreams I could hear my father singing:

> "Shule, shule, shule, agra
>   It's time can only aise me woe
> Since the lad o' me heart
>   From me did part,
> Schedate, avoureen, schlana,
>   I'll dye me petticoat
> I'll dye it red,

And through the world
I'll beg me bread,
I wish in me heart
That I was dead . . . ."

I roused at that, and squirmed in sudden fright.

"Don't say that, dad," I called down to him. "I don't want to die, now!'

"No more did she!" he laughed. "No one does, though it's often said."

"Maybe we shouldn't say it though," I was wide awake now. . . . "Does God know we don't mean it?" I asked fearfully.

Oh, God knows right enough. He hears a lot that He lets go in one ear and out the other. He knows we all like to rave once in awhile."

I settled down then, relieved and satisfied. God wouldn't take a short turn on me. He wouldn't even remember what I said. God was like Lizzie and good at forgetting.

CHAPTER VIII

COMPANIONS ON THE WAY

AT Portage la Prairie we stopped at the Hudson's Bay store and bought further supplies: beans, flour, bacon, salt, nails, duffle, moccasins, a keg of syrup (Golden Drop), dried apples, soda, pain-killer and yellow oil. It was a big room with a rough lumber floor and blue with tobacco smoke. A sunburnt trader had come in and was getting toothache drops. His face was swollen so much one eye was completely shut. He had come from Fort Macleod and he asked us about the roads. He said the road west was not so bad, now, if the rain would hold up. Indians in their blankets stood at the door of the store, not saying a word to anyone, and from their mask-like faces no one could tell their thoughts. No doubt they resented the influx of white settlers and the carts loaded with fur, passing on their way to Winnipeg. But the buffalo was gone, their best friend, source of food and clothes, so perhaps the struggle was over, now that the battle was lost. I hoped they did not mind. Portage la Prairie had a newspaper at this time called the *Marquette Review*, and there was also a planing mill, from which lumber was shipped out on the three river boats. We knew the boats quite well, having seen them make their way up and down the river, when we lived at Silver Heights. They were the *Cheyenne*, the *Marquette*, and the *Manitoban*.

Before we left Silver Heights, one of the neighbors there, a Mrs. Armstrong, gave us a little dog, black and white with collie markings, and on the journey he occupied a wooden keg nailed to the back of the wagon, and slatted over to keep him in, but with spaces between the slats to allow him to look out. He was a cheerful, friendly little fellow with puppy-blue eyes and white markings splashed back from his mouth, giving his face a pansy-like expression.

My joy in having such a pretty little pet, and the brightness of his face seen through the slatted mouth of the keg, helped me to keep my copper-toed boots passing each other, as I walked behind the wagon. The miles grew long and heavy sometimes even to my young feet. But little "Watch" helped me to forget the toils of the journey. Sometimes too, he ran beside me, guided by a rope from his small leather collar, for, being a foolish pup, there was always danger of his getting under the wheels.

One day Hannah and I went into the wagon for a ride, and when we came back, we found the pup was gone. One slat had come unfastened and he had evidently fallen out.

A desperate situation faced us! The day was threatening rain; great purple thunder clouds were rolling up from the west, coming right toward us. The nearest water was four miles away, and the wagons must be kept moving to reach the water, if possible before the rain came. Every minute now was precious. We knew that.

We took hurried counsel, and decided there was only one thing to do, and saying nothing to anyone, ran back on the road we had come. We must find little Watch. We had to find him. Children who have many treasures may regard them lightly, but our love for the little dog was a passion.

Lightning split the dark clouds and a few big drops fell around us. Rain would fill the ruts and holes in the road with water, and what chance could there be then for a fat little pup only three months old? Hannah watched one side of the road and I the other, and we ran and called.

We were afraid to look back. If we were being called it was better not to know it!

I do not know how far we ran. The rain poured down in silver rods, and thunder circled around us, but for once I was not afraid. We prayed as people do in their sore need, surely God would help us; little Watch was so little, and so sweet. He couldn't be left to die!

Suddenly ahead of us, we saw a glint of something white in the tawny grass beside the road and joy clutched our hearts. Hannah dashed ahead and picked him up. He was alive and not even frightened; he had moved off the road and was sitting up waiting for us. He seemed to know we would come.

Then we both began to cry. But it was not because it was raining and getting dark, and the wagons were far out of sight. We cared nothing for any of these things; we had our dog; we were rich again, and our tears were tears of joy.

We began the return journey, running as fast as we could. . . .

Suddenly behind us came the sound of wheels, and a trader in a light wagon drawn by bay horses drew up beside us.

"Where are you off to, kids?" he questioned.

We told him. He helped us into the wagon over the front wheel, and we sat on the high spring seat beside him. He trotted his team when he heard the whole story.

"We'll get you back to your folks as soon as we can," he said, and his voice had a strangeness about it. We had never heard anyone who talked like him. He gave us a blanket to wrap around us to keep off the rain.

We met a man on horse-back who drew up beside the wagon and asked some questions about a man with a black team. Our friend was sorry, but he had not seen anybody. We were afraid we were going to be delayed and were wondering just what sort of a reception we would get when we rejoined our family. Well! Anyway, we had the dog.

Soon after we got away from the man on horse-back we saw someone coming, swinging a lantern, and we were glad to see it was Will. Will would not blame us. He got in the wagon too and we were soon at the camp—I do not remember any unpleasantness.

That night the trader camped beside us, and had supper with us. He had a little oiled tent which fitted under his wagon. Mother asked him to have breakfast with us, but when we got up he was gone. Some days after we heard that the United States police had sent two men on horse-back to look for a desperado, who had shot a sheriff in Montana. When last seen he was driving a black team.

Horse teams were rare on the trail and we thought of our trader. Mother refused to think evil of him. "His horses were bay," she said, "and anyway he was no desperado; he was as nicely mannered a young man as you will meet anywhere, and besides he was good to the little girls."

After we reached home we heard that a settler near Portage la Prairie had his team changed one night. He had bay horses, and one morning he found a black team in his pasture. But they were better horses, so he said he wasn't complaining.

We often thought about our friend and hoped he was safe.

CHAPTER IX

The First Winter

It was a warm clear day with blue shadows toward the end of September when we left the main road, and turned southeast on the Yellowquill trail toward the Assiniboine River. The muddy roads with their terrors were past for we were now traversing a high sandy country with light vegetation, and raspberry brakes. The blue sky had a few white clouds that held the colors of the sunset. The hills around were pricked with little evergreen trees. The oxen sensing the nearness of home, stepped livelier and everyone's spirits rose.

The wagons had to be locked going down the long bank of the river, and at the bottom we came face to face with the clear, zinc-blue water of the Assiniboine. Willows hung over the stream, whitening as the wind turned their leaves, and just above the water, on a dry grassy bank, a fire was soon burning and the black pot boiling. We had a tin stove which held two pots, and a bannock was soon cooking in bacon fat, and the smell of coffee hung pleasantly over the camp.

The river water, clear and soft, gave us all the opportunity of a bath, and with a change of clothes, peace and contentment came down upon us with a great feeling of thankfulness. The little black cow "Lady," who never needed to be hobbled at night, "let down" her milk that night as if she knew her long journey was almost over.

In the early dawn we forded the river. The big oxen drawing the covered wagon, and driven by Will, went first and when we saw them safely climbing up the opposite bank, it was easy to get the little oxen to take the water. The pony cart came next and the cow followed.

72

She had all the intelligence of a good dog and needed no guidance.

We crossed just above the junction of the two rivers, the Souris and Assiniboine, for though the waters are low in September we thought it best not to risk the added volume of the Souris. The Souris was a pretty little stream with deep pools connected by an amber current that twisted around the sand-bars. Both rivers had good hard gravelly bottoms.

And so the last barrier was passed.

I don't believe any of us knew what strain this fourteen-day journey was on my brother Will. He was only twenty years of age, and on him, the responsibility of bringing us out to this great new unknown country, had fallen. I have heard him say that when he got the wagons over the Assiniboine, knowing there were only seven miles more of easy travelling, a thousand years rolled off him.

We reached home at noon of the day we forded the two rivers and found George all ready for us, with a fine pot of potatoes cooked.

No one could fail to be thrilled with the pleasant spot that Will had found for us. A running stream circled the high ground on which the log house stood. Away to the south, hazy in the distance, stood the Tiger Hills; to the northwest the high shoulder of the Brandon Hills, dark blue and mysterious, enticed the eye. Near the house there were clumps of willows on the bank of the creek and poplar bluffs dotted the prairie north of us.

Before we were unloaded from the wagons, mother was deciding the place she would plant the maple seeds she had brought with her from Winnipeg, the hardy Manitoba maple.

The log house had a thatched roof, made from prairie hay and was not chinked, but it had a floor of rough lumber brought to Currie's Landing on a river boat, and one window facing west. One window might be thought insufficient for a house that must lodge eight people, but light and air came in unbidden through many openings; indeed how to keep out the cold became our great problem. We brought a real stove with us and pipes and the first day saw it set in place and mother could then begin her bread, real bread, made with a Royal yeast cake, to displace the soda bannock, cooked in bacon grease, which had been the backbone of our diet on the journey.

The weather favored us; for a long fair autumn gave us an opportunity to get ploughing done and a good stable built for the oxen and Lady. Cattle have been wintered outside in Manitoba but my father believed it was too severe a strain for any animal, and the winter that followed justified his fear.

I remember the pleasant autumn weather, with blue veils over the hills and the long clear moonlight nights, with the light shining in through the unchinked logs, over the bed, where Lizzie, Hannah and I slept.

The stove stood in the middle of the floor, with a long L-shaped length of pipe running to a tin chimney, with a spark arrester in the roof. We had home-made bedsteads made of poplar poles and spread with planks to hold the feather ticks, and with plenty of bedding and pillows we slept very comfortably. Sometimes the howling of the prairie wolves drove away sleep and caused me to shudder with fear; there was something so weird and menacing in their shrill prolonged cries, which seemed to rise and fall in a rhythm which brought them nearer and nearer. Just how terrible their wailings could be, we were destined to know all too soon.

I have spoken of the great love we had for our little dog, and the place that animals fill in the lives of lonely children, but I have not said enough about "Lady," the little black cow. She was a graceful, gentle, intelligent little animal, and had supplied us with milk and butter all summer. On the trip she followed the wagons without being tied, sometimes stopping for a mouthful of grass by the roadside and then hurrying on to fall in behind the procession, and at night when we camped she got her oats when the oxen got theirs; and by this means she made the long trek of a hundred-and-eighty miles without losing her fine sleek coat.

She was particularly my mother's pet and every scrap of food from the table was saved for Lady, who relished cooked potatoes, crusts of bread, or a bit of turnip, and was partial to anything that was sweet, and often for a special treat, was given a slice of bread, soaked in syrup.

She wandered the prairie at will, though never strayed far, and came home running if she heard a wolf howl, her fine big cairngorm eyes wide with fear. Before the stable was built, she spent the night close beside the house, and often in the stillness I was glad to hear her regular breathing, close beside me, on the other side of the unchinked wall.

It was in December; Lady was still milking and that precious quart of milk night and morning was a welcome addition to the porridge breakfasts. The stable had been built, a three-sided building whose sod roof was covered with prairie hay, two stacks of which stood on the north to give more shelter and in this, the four oxen were tied every night and Lady went in and out as she liked.

The hay stacks were fenced with poplar poles to keep out the oxen for it was thought wise to save the hay for the time when the deep snow would prevent them from getting at the prairie grass.

The thirteenth of December came and with it dark tragedy. Will who had gone out first, brought in the bitter word. Lady was dead! She had caught her horns in the fence and in trying to extricate herself had fallen and broken her neck.

We were eating breakfast when Will came in, and I was pouring milk from a glass pitcher on my porridge when the black blow fell. We cried out that it could not be, and hurried to the place of horror! There she lay, cold and stiff with horribly staring eyes. No warm place under her now to warm bare feet; no gentle regular breathing. It was my first sight of death and it shattered

something in me that could never be replaced, a sense of
security maybe. Now I knew that there was always a
grim possibility, a shadow that can fall on the brightest
day. A sinister presence unseen, but none the less real.

Years afterwards, the Rev. Isaac Newton Robinson,
a Methodist minister held revival meetings in Northfield
school and during one of his appeals quoted the words,
new to me then,

> "O sinner think
> Of the feeble link
> Between you and the grave."

I knew what it was. Lady alive, breathing, warm
beloved Lady with her soft brown eyes and sweet breath,
who came to us when we called her and followed us like a
dog; and then the ghastly misshapen bulk, cold and stiff
with blind glassy eyes, that made no response, no motion.

The ground, iron hard with frost, could not be dug
to bury her. So the men drew her away behind a
poplar grove and we all cried again, as we watched that
melancholy procession moving over the snow, the little
dog marching behind barking.

And the nights that followed were terrible when the
wolves fought and cursed and cried over her and we
had to hear them, and see them too, for it was clear
moonlight and they seemed to come from the four corners
of the world, snarling, snapping, hungry ghouls, grey,
lean and terrible.

It was on one of these nights that we saw for the first
time the Northern Lights in all their majesty and awe-
some beauty, and it was not only in the north that they
flickered and flashed, and rolled and marched, for their
bright banners ran up into the highest parts of the sky
right over our heads. If we had not been in such trouble
over the death of Lady, we would have loved all this color
and movement, but there did not seem to be any kindness
in the sky in spite of the pale green and rose and lilac

streamers fluttering and dancing like long lines of fairies' petticoats hung out to dry on a windy day.

I tried to think that what I saw was really great companies of little angels out having a game of "Crack the Whip," all dressed in their lovely dresses, bright and shiny, and that the crumpling sound I heard was the rustling and cracking of the silk as they swung together, but I could not get far with any thought as pleasant as that, with poor Lady lying out under the moon and the wolves fighting over her.

Long after the last bone of Lady was gone, the wolves still came back on the moonlight nights hoping that some other evil thing had befallen us, and their cries were so horrible that I had to sleep with my head under the pillow instead of on it.

Mother wrote her friend, Mrs. Edward Lowery:— "Our first Christmas was not very happy because we lost our nice little black cow. . . . I can't tell you how I miss her. . . . . She had winsome ways, coming to the door and shoving it in with her nose if it wasn't latched, or rubbing the latch up and down, reminding me it was milking time. I had great hopes of Lady! She was going to establish a herd for us, all having her gentle disposition, but that's past! You know I do not cry easily but that morning I did. Just for a minute, and when I saw I was breaking up my whole family, I had to stop, though I would have been the better of a good cry to ease my heart, but when a woman has children, she has no freedom, not even the freedom to cry.

"Lady was more than a cow to us. She was a pleasant companion. Poor Will felt it terribly. He always knows what I feel better than any of the others, and he kept saying: "Don't cry, mother, I can't bear to see you cry! Just as soon as the snow is gone, I'll go to the Portage and get two cows—he will too, poor lad, tramping every step there and back. But there can never be a cow like Lady—. We're all well now, the little girls had sore heels; blood out of order, no doubt, not enough variety in their food, but salt and water healed them in time. The snow was six feet deep on the level, but Willie has snowshoes. He and George got out. We have come through well so far, and will have a garden this summer. There's a great comfort in a garden. It's heartsome to see things grow. There are neighbors coming too, a family from Renfrew. That is good news!

"I get worried sometimes about my own health and wondering what would happen to the little girls, if I should be taken. Boys can always get along but it's a hard world for girls; sometimes I blame myself for coming away so far. There's no doctor closer than Portage, which is eighty miles away. I can't say this to anyone but you, I don't blame Willie; he is a good boy, if there ever was one. It's at night, when every one is asleep and this great prairie rolls over, so big and empty, and cruel. John is as happy as a king, never thinks of anything beyond to-day, so long as he has a place to grow potatoes! He has a field now for his pigs—I never can like pigs, dirty squealing brutes, never satisfied, but we'll be glad of the meat next winter, and will have some to sell too, if there is anyone to buy them.

"Much love to all of you. We'll see you again some day, God willing. John sends his love too, we speak of you often and all the dear friends."

But the trials of that long first winter were not ended. In March the snow fell continually, it seemed, and with the wind shrieking over the plains, packing the snow in drifts as high as houses, we were entirely shut in. It was in this time of isolation that my eldest sister took sick, with a heavy cold, that in spite of turpentine and goose oil and mustard foot-baths, went steadily on through chills and fevers, until it seemed that she would die. She had reached a state of coma, her jaws were locked, and her eyes though still open, did not see. She lay, with her two long braids of bright brown hair, beside her little white face, a tired young traveller, ready to drop out of the race.

My mother, who was a wonderful nurse, had tried every remedy she had, but there was not one flicker of response. Hannah and I were doing what we could to get meals ready, but on this worst day of the storm, no one wanted to eat. It was like a horrible dream. The storm tore past the house, and fine snow sifted through the walls.

Mother came out from behind the quilts which hung around Lizzie's bed, and sitting down in the rocking-chair buried her face in her hands.

"I'm beaten, John," she said. "I can't save her! I am at the end of my resources!' '

Her shoulders shook with sobs and it seemed like the end of everything. No one spoke. Behind the quilts, that labored breathing went on, hoarser and heavier.

"My little girl is dying for want of a doctor, in this cursed place—that never should have been taken from the Indians. . . .

"The Indians have their revenge on me now, for it's tearing my heart out, to see my little girl die before my eyes. . . . We shouldn't have come John, so far—so cruelly far—What's money?—What's land? What comfort can we have when we remember this—dying for want of a skilled hand—the best child I ever had. Her willing little feet and clever hands will soon be as cold as iron. The fluid is rising in her lungs, and I can't stop it, only a doctor could drain it off and give her a chance."

My father tried to comfort her. "You've done all anyone could do, Lettie; don't give up, you always said you wouldn't give anyone up while they were breathing. You're tired woman dear, tired and discouraged, but maybe she's right at the turn now, who knows?"

I couldn't stand any more—I got my coat and cap and mittens and slipped out. I could get to the stable and stay in with the oxen for awhile. The house had grown horrible to me.

When I got out I waited in the shelter of the house for a lull in the storm; the cold struck my face like a lash

and seemed to sink its teeth in me—but it gave me a
savage relief too. I didn't care if it did strike me! I
would face it! I would take its blows! I made my way
against it to the stable and stood watching the turmoil of
snow; there was no earth and sky now, just one great
rolJing confusion that cleared for a moment, then thickened and rolled and screamed past. I couldn't think of
anything only that Lizzie was going to die, and we
couldn't do without her!

In the lull of the storm, I could see perhaps a hundred
yards across the creek, and over the drifts I saw a man
approaching. My heart turned over with joy, and I ran
back to the house, bursting with the news.

Someone was coming on snow-shoes.

He came in hastily shutting the door quickly behind
him to keep out the storm. A big man in a fur coat; one
cheek was frozen but he had a handful of snow to rub
it out.

"I heard you had a sick girl," he said, "and I have
some medicine in my bag. I am the Methodist minister
who has just come to Millford. My name is Hall—
Thomas Hall."

"You are as welcome as an angel of God," mother said
solemnly, as she rose to meet him.

From the moment he entered the feeling of the house
changed. I saw the fear vanish from mother's face. She
was herself in a moment, taking his coat and cap, setting
a chair for him beside the stove, and putting on the tea
kettle.

When the chill was gone from his clothing he went to
see Lizzie and felt her pulse. "She has a good strong
heart and I believe we can pull her through; she has youth
on her side and God always helps," he said.

I could have knelt at his feet and worshipped him.

For three days he stayed with us, taking charge of
the case like a doctor and when he left, Lizzie was able
to speak and could drink beef tea. She made a complete
recovery in the next few weeks.

CHAPTER X

Spring Came at Last Bringing Neighbors

WHEN the spring came, Will walked to Portage la Prairie—eighty miles and brought back two red cows, and from these our herd grew. They were just cows; that gave milk and ate grass, chewed their cuds and switched off flies; and in season bore their young, wabbly little sprawlers, but they could not take Lady's place.

Perhaps, in fairness to the two cows, I should say they were over shadowed by another factor. Will brought home a cat at the same time, a black and white cat, named Philip, a gift from Mrs. Sutcliffe, who had a stopping house on the Portage Plains.

Philip was a full-grown cat, bearing on his portly person, evidence of hardship and struggle, tips of ears were gone, and a crook in his tail gave him a swagger in his walk. But he would purr, when greatly pleased; and he walked abroad in search of gophers. The little dog Watch, who had not seen a cat in his life-time, let one loud and distressful yelp when he saw Philip and the battle was on.

Hannah and I undertook to allay the ancient grudge between our two pets, trying to reason with them and bring them together amicably. On the dog's part, there was a desire for reconciliation ever after he had been clawed and bitten, but Philip's only medium of communication with little Watch, continued to be a spit with elevation of back fur! He remained a mean-tempered arrogant old rascal, as long as he lived. But he was furry and soft and would purr, and we bestowed on him a large measure of unrequited affection.

The house, which was to receive a family from Renfrew, stood about three miles from our house, and all that first long winter, it served as an emblem of hope to us, across the snow. It was a square frame house, built by Mr. Naismith and his brother-in-law, Tom Dunfield, who had returned to their home in Renfrew for the winter.

One day we saw wagons arriving and great excitement prevailed. We had neighbors! It wouldn't be long until we had a school, life had begun. While we speculated and talked and wondered, mother set a batch of bread and took me with her and went over to meet the strangers.

Mrs Naismith had the loveliest straw-colored hair done in braids around her head, and when she made a cup of tea, she served it in cream china cups with rosebuds. The family were all boys except one little girl, the baby, a very pretty little thing with big blue eyes like her mother, and the same wealth of golden hair. The boys were shy and would not play with me, but Minnie let me sit beside her in a big black rocking chair, which had a log cabin back and cushions, and my heart overflowed with joy to know there were children so near. And I know my mother was never so lonely again. Mrs. Nasmith, next to my own mother, will always typify the pioneer woman to me, calm, cheerful, self-reliant, and undaunted.

In 1882 we built our house; logs had been brought for two winters from the bush, squared and made ready and there came a great day when the neighbors gathered, men and women and the house went up, with great good will. The men gave their help freely bringing their own axes, and planes, and saws; and it was an occasion of excitement and pleasure. In Ontario, "barn raisin's," were often accompanied by liquor drinking, and sometimes accidents and fights occurred as a result, but there was nothing of this, at ours. My mother was strong in her belief that liquor was one of the devil's devices for confounding mankind; and anyway there was no liquor in the country at that time.

But there was a long table set in the shadow of the

old house; where roast chicken, potatoes, turnips, custard pie, currant buns and big pots of tea, cheered the workers.

I remember the "raisin'," not only because it was a great event, as a new house must always be, but because it was on this day that we were given one of the good gifts of my childhood. Mr. and Mrs. Naismith, brought us a pup, a lovely black and white pup, half Newfoundland. We knew that their dog had pups, we had seen them, but we had not even hoped to get one, for we had one dog, and pups were so precious and in such great demand, they were not casually asked for. But was this little fellow welcomed? I spent the day of the raising carrying him in a basket, so afraid I was that in the excitement someone might step on him; we called him "Nap," and he grew to be a beautiful dog, the best loved of any dog I ever owned.

The house was a great joy to us, a clean new lumber-scented house, with a big room downstairs, a bedroom for father and mother, a real stairs, and two bedrooms above, and a large kitchen with two windows and a pantry. It still stands, bent a little by the heaviness of years, but its beams have held and the corners still split the winds. It is a tool house and workshop now on my brother's farm, but to me it is a storehouse of happy memories.

The first summer, flower beds were made in front of the house, round beds, in which mignonette, portulaca and balsams were planted. The beds were edged with buffalo bones, from the piles which lay along the creek. The buffalo had been gone only a year when we arrived. and the bone piles indicated the places where Indians had held their feasts. Arrow-heads of bone, and occasional broken bows with thongs of rawhide rewarded our search. Most magnificent were the beaten paths leading to the water holes, still called "buffalo runs" where the hoof marks were almost as clear as the day they were made.

It was sad to think of the buffalo, and how they had been killed, so wastefully, by the hunters from American cities, and yet, the buffalo had to go if the country were to be opened up for settlers. Some of the people believed the Indians had destroyed the buffalo, killing them, and using only their tongues for food, but that was not true. The Indians could not possibly have exterminated such great herds. The American hunters had done it, selling the hides in Minneapolis, and the meat too. No doubt they considered them their own buffalo, even if they had come to Canada looking for better feeding grounds.

The last buffalo had been seen the year before we arrived, but I held to the hope that I might some day come over the top of a knoll and see the dark brown, curly breasted, heavily set animals, with their great shoulders and small hindquarters, feeding on some grassy meadow.

The Indians still had bags of pemmican, after 1880, which is buffalo meat sun dried, and beaten to a pulp and mixed with berries, probably saskatoon, or cranberries, and pressed into bags; it was a black, hard mass, with bits of hide and hair in it, for the squaws who made the pemmican were not always particular. Still pemmican was hearty fare, and on the prairie in the cold winter, not to be despised.

The buffalo was a fat animal, and in the roasting of their meat, there must have been great supplies of fat, which the Indians allowed to burn in the fires. My mother's frugal Scotch heart was grieved when she thought of this waste, and she often wondered why the Indians did not use some of the fat to grease the wooden wheels of their carts, and so prolong their usefulness, and end the weird groanings and dismal creakings of the protesting axles. But maybe the creakings and whinings were liked by the red men, and made the music of the trail for them.

In 1884 there was an effort made to gather up the bones for fertilizer, and five dollars a ton was paid for them in Regina, Saskatchewan.

CHAPTER XI

THE HEN-HOUSE DOOR

OUR flock of hens, little and big, numbered twenty-six in the fall of 1882, and they were comfortably housed in a tidy little log hen-house with a pitched roof made from wide rough boards. One window let in light and air, and the door, fastened with a wooden button, had to be closed each night to prevent marauding mink or weasels from entering. Living beside a creek has its disadvantages, for these blood-thirsty little animals that lived in the clay banks, menaced the lives of our hens.

One night in December the blow fell! For by some subterranean passage weasels had made an entrance to the hen-house, and in the morning the twenty-six hens lay dead on the floor, each with her throat slit. The weasels had gone the way they came leaving our poultry project in ruins.

It was a severe loss, but we recovered from it, by the kindly help of our neighbors the next spring. I think Mrs. Naismith organized the chicken shower which established once more our feathered industry.

One lovely June day, when the prairie was at its best with buttercups, and wild peas, the neighbors came from the four corners of the compass, our four neighbors, each with a box in the wagon and in each box was a hen and chickens, and strangely enough, each hen bore a resemblance to the kind doner. Mrs. Nasmith's hen was a fine golden yellow one with black markings. Mrs. William Johnston's sturdily built Plymouth rock, iron gray and placid. Mrs. Ingram's a graceful little white hen, and Mrs. Burnett's a coal black with shining eyes. We called them: Nancy, Mary, Georgina and Annie, after their owners, or rather, we tried to apportion to them these names, but mother suppressed the suggestion. She said the names of respectable married women were not to be lightly bandied about a farmyard.

A plank floor was put in the hen-house and other precautions were taken against mink and weasel, so our flocks grew steadily after that. The next year we had a pond made for ducks and they grew and multiplied.

Shutting the hen-house door became one of my chores. At sun-down it must be closed for every decent hen goes in as soon as the shades of evening fall. When we later added a few turkeys my cares increased. Turkeys know nothing and care nothing. Death has no terrors for them. Rain kills them when they are young so they walk out in it every chance they get, piping their melancholy little notes; and so far as lies in them, they resist rescue. I always felt it was a low trick to set a hen on turkey eggs.

Of all fowl, hens are easily the most intelligent. There is a core of real good hard sense in every hen, and in addition to this, some of them are distinct personalities.

The yellow hen given us by Mrs. Naismith had the misfortune to freeze her feet one winter. She was a born rover and once had to spend the night out and it was a cold night too. We found her on the sheltered side of the hen-house in the morning, with her feathers fluffed out and her temper equally ruffled. She blamed everyone but herself for what had happened.

We brought her in, applied coal-oiled rags to the frosted toes and gave her a bran mash with pepper in it. She recovered from her hard experience but the ends of her claws were too badly damaged and poor Nancy found she could no longer scratch.

The next spring, she became a problem for she wanted to hatch. She was shut up in a box; she was tethered by a cord, to one of the little maple trees; she had fluffy skirts put on her legs, which take up the attention of some hens and make them forget their maternal urge. But Nancy could not be distracted. She demanded her rightful place in the community. Why should she be deprived of the joys of family life, because she had lost a few toes? She kept up her agitation, until mother gave in and let her have six eggs, and peace reigned for twenty-one days.

Then Nancy stepped off her nest with six chickens and led them straight to the kitchen door and noisily applied for relief.

She couldn't scratch up any seeds for them, of course, but we had to let her think she was doing it. Many times a day someone had to take bread, soaked in milk, or boiled wheat out to Nancy. If not, Nancy walked in at the kitchen door with her six trailers and raised a disturbance. The only way to keep her out was to supply plenty of provender. All the other hens were afraid of her, and she had full right of way at the water pans. She couldn't fight with her maimed claws, but I have no doubt she had a retentive memory and a scurrilous tongue.

We all liked her, so no one minded giving her a hand with the chickens. But when they were feathered out, she began to steal chickens from the other hens, just to show the world, that she was as good as the best. No one knew how she did it, or what inducements she offered, but she increased her flock to ten and before the season was over had adopted two lumbering young turkeys whose real mother had tired of them.

It was a sight to see her sitting over her brood at night, with the vacuous faces of the young turkeys sticking out through her feathers.

She couldn't hold herself on the roost, so we made her a box with a little bar across, just high enough to lift her slightly off the floor. She managed to stay on this by leaning against the back and side of the box, and was comfortable, I think. She was never quite reconciled to the low seat, when all the other hens had gone up to roost and sometimes flew up and tried to balance herself on the roost, but she couldn't manage it, with her poor little stumps of claws.

The hen-house door was a profound influence in my

childhood. Once I forgot it and wakened in the dark middle of the night with a sickening sense of guilt! The weasel might have come! Or a mink! Every last hen became suddenly dear to me, a thousand times more precious than ever before—now that I had betrayed them. And Nancy, poor Nancy, sitting on the floor, she would be the first to feel the weasel's tooth!

I got out of bed and carrying my boots in my hand crept down the stairs. The slightest sound would waken mother so I went as softly as a weasel too, but the steps in the stairs squeaked and by knees cracked like pistols.

But I got out, closing the door like a thief, and crossed the yard; the night was as dark as the inside of a cow, not a star even, and quiet as a tomb. It was a cold night too in the fall, but I was so frightened I felt nothing. If the hens were all dead, I might as well die too, like the Roman generals who ran on their swords when they lost the battle.

I knew I was near the door and was feeling for it with both hands when suddenly I stumbled over something warm and furry. It was Nap, precious Nap, the dog, who ordinarily slept in the straw stack. He was guarding the door.—Good old Nap!—He was trying to cover up my misdeed. I went in to see if everything was safe and felt on the roosts. Sleeping hens stirred drowsily as I ran my hand over their hard little feet. Evidently all was well. Nap had saved them—and me. I felt for Nancy on the floor, and got a re-assuring peck from her, sweet as a hand shake.

I made my way back to the house so relieved I could have danced for joy, but I could feel the cold now, piercing through my factory cotton night dress.

Responsibility is no doubt good for a child, for one has to learn sooner or later to take it. The hen-house door was my first big assignment and certainly left its mark on me. For years after I grew up and was away from the scenes of my childhood, I would waken from sleep in a panic of fright. Had I closed the hen-house door?

CHAPTER XII

SOCIAL ACTIVITIES

FIVE miles north-east from our farm, at Millford, on the Souris river where it was joined by Oak Creek, there was a flour mill owned by Major Rodgers, who had brought with him a colony of young men from Peterboro, Coburg and Port Hope in 1880. The boarding house was run by Mr. and Mrs. George Motherwell and Mrs. Motherwell's sister, Maria Somers; and the store was owned by John Brown, late of Owen Sound. William Turnbull, a Scotchman, had a blacksmith shop, and John Wheeler, an Irishman, had a cobbler's shop.

The mail came from Brandon, for in 1888 the Canadian Pacific Railway was extended that far, and at least once a week, usually on Saturday, the mail man reached Millford, with his welcome bags. It was a thirty-mile drive so arrival in the winter was naturally uncertain and the subject of many wagers. Would he come at all? Would be come Friday? Or Saturday? Before noon? Or afternoon? The petty cash of the boarding house changed hands each week, according to the mail man's arrival. One sour old fellow, a true pessimist, put his twenty-five cents each week against all takers that the mail man would not get through at all and twice during the winter of 1882 raked in all the stakes.

There were dances in the boarding house in the winter evenings, when the two long board tables could be shoved back to the walls and the bracket lamps turned up as high as they would go without smoking. My brother Will and George went to the first one, but mother sternly held out against Elizabeth's going. She was only fifteen years old and much better in her bed. But when Will put in a plea for his young sister, and Lizzie had just made for herself a beautiful wine-colored cashmere dress with a cream lace collar and cuffs, (material sent by Aunt Ellen) mother began to weaken. I know now how she felt but then, none of us could see any reason for her reluctance.

Lizzie went and no doubt made a sensation. She was a pretty little girl, very slight and graceful, with two great braids of glossy brown hair, bright brown eyes, fair skin and high color, a sweet voice and ringing laugh which set the dimples in her cheeks. Hannah and I were bursting with pride when Will and George and Lizzie set out, all in their best clothes and their shoes done with lamp-black and tallow. They drove the oxen, in a sleigh and were well covered with blankets and robes.

After that the weekly dances became a feature of our lives, and though Hannah and I were years removed from any such exciting pleasures, we planned ball-dresses, and selected jewels, for ourselves, with a fine prodigality, and wore them, according to our own testimonies with devastating effect. Every eye in the room was on us we said, when we entered the ball-room, and mothers of marriagable daughters turned pale with envy when they saw our dazzling beauty. What chance had their pallid daughters now to gain the hand of Lord Ronald, and Lord Elphinstone? We gossiped too, unmercifully, about our rivals, and disposed of their matrimonial chances, in stinging words. Lady Mary Manners was a "chit" from school. The Duchess of Trent dyed her hair, and the Countess of Whifford's two daughters, though stiff with jewels, could never grace a baronial mansion, for one had an evil temper, and the other one was bow-legged.

With the opposition thus well out of the way, the Mooney sisters were ready to concede their own election. . . . Each night after we had gone to bed, we carried along the story through endless episodes.

The pup given us on the day the house was raised grew into a fine big dog, and when he was a year old,

I had him well broken as a sleigh dog. Each Saturday in the winter, I made the journey to Millford for supplies for the week, and the mail. The *Family Herald* from Montreal brought the world to our door. We knew that the boundary of Manitoba had been changed and enlarged, but that made little difference to us. A lot of good that would do us! A million acres of jack pine and jack rabbits added to our territory! But any news of railway extension kindled our hopes. Bitter denunciation of the Canadian Pacific Railway's insistence on its monopoly was on every tongue, when it was known that American companies were willing to come, but the Government at Ottawa had promised the Canadian Pacific Railway Company they would have no rivals for twenty years. No one blamed the Premier of Manitoba, honest John Norquay, who, Conservative though he was, was fighting his political friends at Ottawa, on behalf of the people of his province, who far from the one line of railway, were finding it hard to market their crops. The matter of interprovincial transportation rightly belonged to the Government at Ottawa, under the provisions of the North America Act; but teamsters on the long trails, cold and tired, were not disposed to consider fine points of law. They wanted a shorter haul to market.

My father, who was a staunch Conservative, became the apologist for Ottawa and the Canadian Pacific Railway. He pointed out the expense the Canadian Pacific Railway Company had incurred in building a coast to coast line; and what about it, if they did get all the odd number sections for twenty miles on each side of the railway, and a twenty-year monopoly. What use was raw land anyway? And if American companies were allowed in they would soon own us, lock and barrel. The Government saw this danger and wanted to keep us British.

Later when the Canadian Pacific Railway's branch line was built from Winnipeg to Glenboro sixteen miles straight east of us, my father said that was near enough. Who would want a railway any nearer? "Sure, you can

D

go and come in a day," he said, "and what more do you want?"

But the younger members of the family were not satisfied so easily, and annexation with the United States, as a solution of the deadlock over the delay in railway construction, became the topic of conversation around the nail kegs and sugar barrels in John Brown's store in Millford, or any place where the neighbors gathered.

The great event of our first three years was the building of the school—two miles from our farm, a government school, for the upkeep of which a tax was placed on each acre of land, and ten dollars a month was given as a grant from the Provincial Government. I would be ten years old that fall and I was deeply sensitive about my age and my ignorance. Hannah, who had been to school in Ontario and could read newspapers or anything, was willing to teach me, but I would not be taught. I was going to be a cowboy anyway, so why should I bother with an education? I could count to a hundred and I would never own more than a hundred head; all of which was a bit of pretense on my part, a form of self-protection.

One of the neighbors, lately come from England, had a boy my age who could read. Not only could, but did. Even brought his books over when his family came to visit my family and read. He stood in the middle of the floor and intoned like a curate, page after page from some dull book all about plum-cakes at a school-treat, and my mother took the occasion to deplore my state of ignorance. "Just listen to Frankie! And he is no older than you are. Now don't you wish you had let Hannah teach you—a big girl ten years old, who will not learn anything."

My heart was hot for revenge and it came, when Frankie came out to play with me.

Frankie ran crying to his mother when I landed my first blow on his neat little features and when he sobbed out the story of his injury, I reached new low levels in the social scale. No one could defend my action; even

Lizzie admitted it was a pretty low thing I had done—
to actually strike a visitor, but when it was all over and I
had been made apologize, I was still glad that I had done
it, it gave me such a glorious sense of relief. Lord it
over me—would he?

Philip, the old black and white cat, had a rival, a
sweet little silvery grey kitten with white paws and
breast brought by Will and George one day when
they came home from the Moggey farm on Oak Creek.
The Moggey family had lately come from Owen Sound.
We called it Sylvia, after the heroine of a story that was
running serially in the *Family Herald*, and she was the
prettiest little thing we had ever seen. Hannah wrote a
poem to her:

> "Hail Sylvia, sweet and frail
> Snowy breast and arching tail,
> Whither cometh thee to bless
> One poor family's loneliness,
> Princess in a feline dress?"

She slept on a pink quilt which covered our bed,
and when she lay a lovely ball of silver fur, in the centre
of that quilt Hannah and I often went to feast our eyes
on her loveliness. But again came tragedy.

Old Philip, tired of hearing this young interloper
praised and sung, killed her one evening. He grabbed
her when she was drinking from her saucer and shook
her. It was all over, before anyone could speak. One
shake and the tiny neck was broken and grief broke over
us in an overwhelming flood. Having accomplished his
evil purpose, Philip fled and was not seen for days.

For weeks afterwards, I believed she would come
back. I couldn't make myself understand that death is
permanent; surely with all the cats in heaven, God would
send a good trusty angel down with Sylvia for us, when
we loved her so much. I often tiptoed with my eyes shut
into the room where our bed stood with my heart beating

like a hammer, expecting, hoping, praying that the soft ball of gray fur would be curled up on the quilt. . . .

We buried her on the sunny slope that ran down to the creek, under a silver willow, whose shiny gray leaves brought back the glorious sheen of our little friend's coat. We sharpened a shingle and drove it in at her head, with a small stake at the foot, marked S and on the shingle Hannah wrote, with a carpenter's pencil:

"Here lies dear little Sylvia Moggey,
A thing that died oh far too young,
From a bite from Philip Sutcliffe
Philip bit her on the tongue."

He didn't exactly bit her on the tongue, he shook her roughly, but we couldn't put that in a rhymne; we had tried hard to tell the exact truth, even sought help in this honest endeavor. Try it, if you think it is easy! But what did it matter? She was dead.

To the sunny southern slope, where the wind turned over the silver leaves with a gentle sound that broke my heart afresh for it made me think of Sylvia's gentle purring, I often went to lay a flower on her grave.

Hannah pointed out that it was strange how often I was overcome with this desire just when the dishes were ready to be washed. We had high words over this, and in the end I set up a grave for myself and wrote my own verse or at least composed it, for I couldn't write:

"Four dear dogs—they died alone,
Noboody saw them, or heard them groan,
There they died by the drifts of snow
While the wind rocked their tails to and fro."

Hannah did the writing for me but under protest. She knew I never had four dogs and so naturally had not lost them; that I had created them merely to cut them off in their prime, and she said a person shouldn't lie, even in a epitaph, but in that contention, I found out afterwards that she was in a hopeless minority.

CHAPTER XIII

The Church and the School

In the summer of 1882 the church at Millford was built by volunteer labor, though the expense of the material was met by the Missionary Society of the Methodist Church of Canada. Rev. Thomas Hall, the good angel who came out of the snow storm to us, the March before, had the full qualifications for a Missionary, for he could do anything.

Under his guidance the church was ready for occupation in the fall of the year, when a great Harvest Home Festival opened the church activities of the Millford district, and every resource of the neighborhood was brought to the success of that event. Mrs. Naismith did not even withhold her rose-bud china.

On a bright September afternoon when every person within a circle of ten miles came, and the field around the church was black with wagons, ox teams and a few horses, the church was dedicated to the "services of God and humanity."

The first couple married in the church were Roman Catholics and Mr. Hall used the sign of the Cross at their request in the ceremony, which led to some criticism, but my father defended Mr. Hall and said as Christian people we should never forget that the cross was the sacred symbol of our faith. "Many a time," he said, "when I was on the Ottawa and our raft was nearing the rapids I crossed myself with the Catholic lads on the raft. It helped me to remember that God was with us even in the high water."

The first funeral in the church was that of the minister's little boy, his only son, Wilbur, a handsome little lad of three with bright golden curls; who died in the spring of '82 when the wild anenomes were spreading their blue carpet over the prairie. We made a blanket of them to cover the plain lumber coffin, by opening a new gunny sack and sticking the stems of the flowers through the open mesh. The church was full of their sweetness, that hot spring morning as we sat and listened to the solemn words of the burial service, and when the little coffin was lowered into the grave on the hillside and the clods of earth fell on it, it was with a softly muted sound.

A Sunday school was started in the little church at Millford and a Mr. Calverly became the superintendent. Mr. Hall had three preaching places and so could not be at the Sunday School. We drove to church which was held in the evening, but it was a long walk to get to Sunday school in the afternoon, a five mile journey each way.

Great excitement prevailed when Northfield School was finished. We heard that the teacher was a man, who had taken a homestead at Pelican Lake and had been teaching near Winnipeg, and the school would open one Monday morning. I had a new pair of boots and dark gray hand knitted stockings and a homespun dress, some of my mother's own weaving, which Lizzie had made up for me. White lace was frilled in at the neck to keep the flannel from scratching me and, as my hair was shingled, I needed no hair ribbon. The dress was gray and red in small checks. I wished I could have some "boughten," material for my dress, I was sure I would be the only girl at school with a homespun dress and, I was. I think mother had been somewhat hurt with us because we all preferred "boughten" goods. It was in vain she told us of how long the homespun would wear.

I can't remember why Hannah did not go that first palpitating day. Bert Ingram called for me and we set off in the gloom of an October snow storm. The Ingrams who came from Woodstock, Ontario, were our nearest neighbors, living one mile west of us on section eighteen. Bert had been to school in Woodstock, and was a real man of the world in my eyes. He had a tailored suit of gray tweeds, knee pants, a tweed coat with pockets and a leather belt and a skull cap. He carried a pea shooter, too, and said if the teacher gave him any lip he would sock him in the eye. Bert was two years older than I, and reading and writing and number work held no terrors for him.

We hesitated for a minute at the fire-guard,—the one improvement made on the school property—six furrows of plowing to check a possible prairie-fire. School was in; heads showed at the two windows. The question of whether we should walk in, or knock held us up. It was settled for us, by the teacher rapping on the window in a way that suggested speed, and we went in.

The teacher sat behind a desk of unpainted wood; and when he said good morning he smiled at us, and asked us our names. Bert told him, his and mine too. By this time, I did not know mine.

He told us we could sit together, until he got the classes arranged. I was too shy to look around at the strange children, but I was surprised to know how many children there were. I wondered where they had all come from. There were fifteen or sixteen.

In front of us sat Annie Adams, dressed in a lovely navy blue cashmere dress, with red piping and brass buttons, and she had two long brown braids with a red ribbon braided in them, and a bow on the nape of her neck and one on the end of each braid. Not only that, but had a circular comb in her hair and a red one at that. I felt naked and ashamed with my round shingled head, destitute of ribbons, or any place to put a ribbon. Annie had every piece of equipment, a provident child could think of. The frame of her slate was covered with red felt and her slate rag, a piece of white cotton had a herring-boned hem and a heavy glass salt cellar, filled with water indicated a source of moisture. She even had a pen-wiper.

The teacher was finding out what we knew, and looking at the books we brought. When he called me to come up to his desk bringing my books, I had nothing to bring, but a battered old "Second-part" Ontario Reader and a slate with nothing on its frame. I could tell of no school experiences at all, "I cannot read," I confessed miserably.

He smiled at me again, and said, "Never mind that, you'll soon learn."

"I am nearly ten," I said, determined to tell all.

"Good!" he said, "a very good time to begin school; you'll be reading in three months." I looked at him then and the compact was sealed. I knew I would be reading in three months. I knew my burden of ignorance was going to be lifted.

When I went back to my seat, I did not care how many bows or combs Annie Adams had. I did not mind my homespun dress. Something had happened and a new world had opened before me. Another door had opened!

When I went home all I knew about the teacher was that his eyes were gray with green pebbles in them, and that he wore a lovely brown knitted coat, (we did not use the word sweater) and that he had said I would soon be reading.

The following spring we had our first Inspector, Dr. Franklin of Portage la Prairie, and he came without warning, just a knock at the door and he was in, a fine looking tall man, with a brown mustache and side whiskers, and a black frock coat which impressed us deeply. I had not seen one before. Dr. Franklin had started a Young Ladies' Seminary but when the direful effects of the real estate boom of 1881-'82 began to be felt, the young ladies were forced to return to their homes, and the seminary languished. Dr. Franklin then accepted the position of Government Inspector of Public Schools.

I remember him with gratitude. I was in the Second Reader then, and able to read. We were reading for him the lesson called "The Faithful Dog," and when my turn came the story was approaching its heart-breaking climax, where the traveller, having shot his dog thinking he had gone mad, rides on and then suddenly remembers the saddle bags left behind in his haste, and gallops back to find them safe with the dog, who had crawled back leaving blood drops all the way, and now lies beside them, dead.

I mired down before I got that far and could not either see or speak. It was an awkward moment, and some one in the class laughed, and my humiliation was complete. Dr. Franklin reached over and took the book from me, and said "Very well read little girl! That's really too sad a story for a school-reader,"—then to Mr. Schultz, "Here is a pupil who has both feeling and imagination, she will get a lot out of life."

And at that I cried harder than ever.

Soon after Northfield School was built there came a new settler to our district, a Mr. Frank Kinley who took up a homestead just east of Mr. Naismith's. He was from Prince Edward County in Ontario and had been a church worker all his lift. He canvassed the neighborhood to see the state of our spiritual life and found that only a very few of the children went to Millford Sunday School regularly and he suggested that we start a Sunday school in our own school house.

The people welcomed the idea and money was subscribed for papers and soon the opening day came. Mr. Schultz, the teacher, gave his hearty support and under his direction the school house was tidied up, wood-pile straightened and everything made ready .

I don't know how it was arranged for the school room was very small; but there were four classes organized. My sister Lizzie had the little girls. Mrs. Ingram the bigger girls, and Mr. Naismith and Mr. Kinley the two classes of boys. Mrs. Ingram played a little organ, sent, I believe from a Sunday school in Ontario. Mr. Kinley had sent for the Sunday school lesson helps and each of us was given a Quarterly with a red and white cover.

Hymns appropriate to the lesson were given in these and the music, so we learned the lessons in prose and verse. In the day school each morning we read first the lesson and then the daily readings. So when Sunday came we were rooted and grounded in the scripture for that day and the Bible stories flamed into reality with us. Rehoboam and Jeroboam walked with us as we crossed the prairie with our dinner pails and we had long discussions on what would have happened if better counsel had come at the call of the young king. We could see how jealousy ate up Saul and the story of his throwing the spear at David was so well dramatized one day at noon that Billy Day nearly lost an eye.

Mr. Schultz gave us composition exercises and memory work from the Scripture lessons too, and the Bible became to us a living book over-flowing with human interest. Mr. Schultz went home each Friday night, fifteen miles south to Pelican Lake, but his support of the Sunday school was a great factor in its success.

Mr. Kinley was a tall thin man, with light blue kindly eyes and a hesitating way of speech. His wife, a faded little woman, was an invalid and had not walked for years. Each Sunday, he carried her into the school room, wrapped in a fur coat, even in the hottest weather and deposited her in a rocking chair, kept there for her use. From her veils and mufflers her sweet little withered face looked out at us with a little hopeful bitter-sweet smile, which often made me want to cry. It must be terrible to be helpless! But Mr. Kinley's honest face beamed with love, when he spoke of her. She was the guiding star of his life, he said.

Sometimes, when he reviewed the lesson at the close of the Sunday school session, in his painstaking way, the school grew restless. We had very little sentiment and he had an irritating way of saying the same thing over and over, and usually before the school was dismissed the order was lost.

One day, I heard two of the teachers discussing the situation with him. "I often wonder if the children are getting anything out of the lessons," Mrs. Ingram said, "We try so hard and yet they seem so inattentive. I watched my class to-day and not one was listening, they were looking out the window, fumbling their books, pinching each other, whispering. I declare, I am about ready to quit."

"Oh no!" Mr. Kinley said earnestly, "we won't quit, I don't believe they are as inattentive as they seem. They may forget what we say now, but they will remember it in years to come. . . . Anyway, we owe them a duty, no matter how they receive our teaching, we owe it to them, we, whose hearts have been touched with grace, we must not eat our bread alone."

I was about eleven when I heard this, and it opened another door for me, that gave me a glimpse of a heavenly country here on earth. If "no one ate their bread alone," we could have a glorious and radiant world here and now, a bright and happy world! There would be joy and gladness and singing in it, with plenty of work for everyone, but it would all be happy work; there would be no bad tempers, or tattlings, or scoldings, or ox beating, or ugliness. . . . I saw it in a flash, in a radiant beam that shone around me in that moment, and I experienced a warming of the heart that has never altogether faded even in my darkest hours.

That week I told the other children as we sat in the shade of the wood-pile playing "knife," what I had heard, and how I felt about it, and we agreed that we would give Mr. Kinley a surprise and this would probably please him more than the mustache cup we were saving up to give him for a Christmas present. We would listen when he reviewed the lesson and we wouldn't stir, not so much as lift a finger, and he could talk as long as he liked. The first Sunday, we sat like graven images, every eye on him, and all went well, only Bennie Rothwell, began to laugh. We had been afraid of Bennie, but Joe, his brother clapped a handkerchief over Bennie's nose and rushed him out, and Mr. Kinley in his larger charity thought it was a nose bleed.

CHAPTER XIV

PICNICS

THE spring of 1882 is remembered by all Manitobans, for two reasons: the great floods that turned the peaceful rivers and streams into raging torrents of water; and the great real estate boom that convulsed the city of Winnipeg.

The flood concerned us closely, for even our own shallow Spring Brook swollen by the spring thaws, and rains, ran from bank to bank and had to be crossed on a raft. The Souris River at the junction of Oak Creek, where the little village of Millford stood, had widened into an inland lake which filled all the lower level of the valley. Cellars were full and there was grave danger of complete inundation. As it was, there was no way of getting down to the store and post office, but by the use of a boat. The valley had three levels and Millford stood on the second with a high bank at the south running up to the plain above.

Major Rodgers' boats were used to cross the flood, and there were plenty of idle men in Millford to man them, for the flood had risen above the level of the mill, thereby stopping its operations and carrying away its warehouse. The mailman still made his visits from Brandon, though irregularly, because of the high water. When anyone appeared on the high banks of the river a boat was dispatched from the store to see what was wanted, and the boats from Winnipeg still brought supplies to Currie's Landing. No one suffered for food.

I remember the flooded creek below our house with great delight, and all the excitement of seeing the home-made raft pushed out in the whirling current when George and Will, with long poles worked their cumbersome craft over to the other side, losing much ground in the crossing, so that they landed some distance down stream. However, that did not matter. But they had to pull the raft up on the opposite bank, making due allowance for a rise in the water line, since the creek rose each night with the melting of the snow. Having crossed the creek at home, they walked the five miles to Millford, where a still greater flood had to be crossed, but the rowboats made this an easier accomplishment; I would have liked to go with them, but I knew that was a vain hope. However it was exciting enough to watch for their return, and to be the first to see them a mile away on the snow-patched prairie, with their grain bags on their backs. I was sorry when the current of water in the creek fell to its normal size, but no doubt the older people were relieved.

While we were concerned with the floods, the real estate boom in Winnipeg which had begun the fall before, gathered momentum with the coming of spring. Weird tales of the excitement drifted out to us. We knew that American, and Eastern Canadian speculators had flocked into Winnipeg and that money was flowing like the swollen waters of the Red and Assiniboine. People were sending money to these men to buy them lots, and the whole population had caught the fever. Lots sold and resold, without having been seen or surveyed. It was a strange and hectic time, when even sensible people were caught up in the whirlwind of speculation. We heard of real estate offices opened in livery stables; money kept in tin pails and baskets, weighed down with horseshoes; and people making a hundred dollars a day selling lots that they had never seen. We knew we had made a mistake in not buying Louis Prudens' farm. We could have sold it all for building lots, and become wealthy, beyond a doubt. Mother refused to believe that fortunes were being made so easily, but we believed it, my sister Hannah and I. Consequently, we spent many happy times, after we had gone to bed, dressing ourselves in

silk attire, and outfitting riding horses in brocaded velvet
saddles and jewelled bridles, and doing ourselves very
well in the matter of riding-habits. I had a yellow plume
on my black velvet hat that swept the horse's withers,
but Hannah corrected me on that, by telling me that I
would be facing the wrong way on my horse, if the plume
reached the withers; she said "rump," was the word I
should use, but I stuck to withers. "Rump," was a horrible word, applied only to cattle and had nothing to do
with a well-curried horse turned out to carry a lady.
I would sacrifice the plume rather than us it.

About the middle of the summer the boom broke, and
the investors awakened out of their dream. It was a
hard blow to the young country. Every one seemed to
have lost money. The Eastern speculators went back,
angry and disillusioned, blaming the country for their
losses. There is no doubt that this spectacular boom, and
its complete collapse, marked the beginning of the ill
feeling between the East and the West.

We suffered from it, too, in finding that the machine
companies had pushed up their prices, and that immi-
gration had suddenly ceased. However, we still had a
ready market for all our surplus crop; wheat, hay,
potatoes, but we were resentful of the fact, that the West,
through no fault of its own, had been given a black eye!

Our first community effort was the holding of a picnic,
on the first of July that year. I think Frank Burnett was
the originator of the idea. Frank Burnett had been a
stockbroker in Montreal in 1879, but having read Butler's
"The Great Lone Land," he began to think of making the
venture of coming West. This intention was strength-
ened by listening to a lecture by Thomas White, of the
Montreal *Gazette,* (afterwards Sir Thomas White) who
had made the trip in 1878, and written many articles on
it for his paper. So in the same year that we came West,
1880, Frank Burnett, his wife Henrietta, and their two
small children, Nina and Frank junior, made the journey.

I have heard them tell the story of their arrival in Winnipeg, in March of that year, with a capital of eight-hundred dollars and a great optimism, born of inexperience. They bought an outfit, and started for Prince Albert. It was a wild undertaking, for Prince Albert was at least six hundred miles distant, and with the outfit they had, they could never have made so long a journey.

Fortunately when they reached Pine Creek, which was about thirty miles from the junction of the Souris and the Assiniboine rivers, they heard that my brother Will, and his friend Macdonald, had lived that winter in a tent at the Junction getting out logs for a house, and that they had taken land in a fertile valley. Mr. Burnett resolved to go and see this country. Leaving his family at Pine Creek, he pushed on with his pony cart. When at last he arrived, and saw the country he decided to go no farther. Here was deep, black loam, excellent drainage, three running streams, the Souris River, Oak Creek, and a little creek we afterwards called Spring Brook. The Tiger Hills formed the southern boundary of this fertile area, which was thickly studded with timber for firewood, and there was the additional advantage to Mr. Burnett of being able to buy logs for a house from Will and his friend.

The first summer Frank Burnett, and his two brothers who had come from England, built a double log house, partitioned by a log wall in the middle, and in it the five adults (James Burnett had brought his family) and the six children lived for two years. The women had had no pioneering experience, and it must have taken all their resources of courage, and fortitude to endure that first terrible winter.

The Burnett house was about a mile and a half south west of ours, and like ours was built on the bank of Spring Brook. Farther south on the creek in 1881, William Johnston and his wife built a house, and later Robert Park came and put up a house, and went to Portage la Prairie in the winter of 1882 and brought back a wife.

Settlement went on apace after 1882, and soon we had, much to our delight a real neighborhood. The settlers were at first all Ontario people, except the Burnetts. Bob and Charlie Johnston, two young Englishmen came in 1883, and took up a section two miles straight west of our farm naming their place "Clonskey," and by that name it is still known. C. Gardiner Johnston, (Charlie) was for many years a well known shipbroker in Vancouver.

Frank Burnett, who was a natural leader, began to talk of a picnic early in the summer of '82, and he thought we should hold it at Millford, beside the river. There could be tables set in the shade of the poplar trees, seats constructed and a clearing made, which would make a permanent picnic ground.

A committee was formed and a program of sports arranged. There was to be a baseball game, married men versus single men; a pony race, an ox race, a slow ox race, and foot races. I was hoping there would be a race for girls under ten, or that girls might enter with the boys. But the whole question of girls competing in races was frowned on. Skirts would fly upward and legs would show! And it was not nice for little girls, or big ones either, to show their legs. I wanted to know why, but I was hushed up. Still, I kept on practising and tried hard to keep my skirts down as I ran. I could see it was a hard thing to do. In fact, I could see my dress which was well below my knees, was an impediment, and when I took it off I could run more easily. I suggested that I would wear only my drawers, (we did not know the word bloomers) I had two new pairs, held firmly on my "waist," with four reliable buttons. My suggestion was not well received. Then I wanted a pair of drawers made like my dress; for that would look better than white ones with lace. Lizzie thought this a good idea, but mother could not be moved. There was a stone wall here that baffled me. Why shouldn't I run with the boys? Why was it wrong for girls' legs to be seen? I was given to understand that this was a subject which must not be spoken of.

Mother was very concerned about food for the day. "Don't I wish I could make half a dozen good juicy pies!" she said. "There's nothing a man likes as well as a pie, but with no fruit, no eggs, no pumpkins, its hard. Still I am going to think out something. . . . Well, one good thing anyway, is, there will be no whiskey drinking to spoil everyone's fun. We won't have that trouble for a while for there's no whiskey in the country and if everyone felt as I do, there never would be any. I've seen too many nice times spoiled with it. Drunken men fighting and swearing in the street, and their women crying and trying to separate them. It was awful sometimes in Chatsworth, no fun for anyone, just bad times."

The picnic day was the loveliest sort of a day; bright and warm, yet cooled by a gentle wind, and the prairie on July the first with its sweet brier roses in massed bloom was a sight to remember. The buds were deep crimson and the blossoms graded in color from that to pure white, according to their age. Orange lilies were just beginning their season, and being scarce were much prized by the young hunters. The strawberries had been killed with the frost in June, and having no fruit had sent forth a great crop of leaves. Saskatoon berries were reddening on their branches but would not be ready for a couple of weeks yet, though their unripe state did not keep us from trying to eat them; but their tastelessness dulled our enthusiasm.

Down by the river the tables were set, and benches from the boarding house brought down for seats. There were raisin-buns and cinnamon rolls, curled like snail shells, doughnuts, and cookies, (ginger and molasses) railroad cake; lettuce cut up in sour cream, mustard and sugar, cold sliced ham, home cured, and mother had made half a dozen vinegar pies, using her own recipe. The filling of a pie is rather a delicate matter when you have no fresh fruit, or eggs, but she made her filling of molasses and butter, thickened with bread crumbs, and sharpened and flavored with vinegar and cinnamon. Her one regret was that she had not the white of an egg to make a frosting, but we had no hens that year.

The great surprise of the day was the box of oranges that came from Rapid City, and a great bunch of bananas just as it came off the tree, held up before us by John Brown, the storekeeper. There were not enough to give one to each person, but we all had a piece, and what a disappointment that first taste of a banana was! It tasted like white flannel to me. But there were people there who enjoyed them, and that made me wonder. Bob Naismith did not like his bit either, but Mr. Burnett told us bananas were an acquired taste, and explained what that was: "One grew to like them," he said, whereupon Bob and I, with this encouragement made another assault on the saskatoon berries.

But in the barrel of supplies from Brandon was a wooden pail of chocolates, bell-shaped, black grocery chocolates, thinly coated with this new delicious substance, and filled with white cream candy, which was soft, but not sticky. Two of these were our portion and having eaten one, and found it to be like something one would dream of, but never taste, I tried to keep my second one to help me to meet some of life's vicissitudes. I might be crossed in love, as the years rolled on, or lose my character, or my money, and I knew this piece of magic, held tightly in my hand would comfort me, for one moment at least, though all the world went wrong. But looking at my treasure I discovered it was melting and spreading and oozing out between my fingers. So, to save it I had to eat it. But I made it last as long as I could; and licked my fingers so hard I almost took the skin off them, in pursuit of the last drop of this unbelievable sweetness.

The seats from off the wagons were set around the place where the baseball game was played. The ball was a homemade yarn ball, and the bat a barrel stave sharpened at one end, but it was a lovely game, and every one got runs.

There were enough provisions for supper. So we

stayed on and ate again, and were sorry to see the sun
going down in the west. There would be chores to do,
cows to milk, and pigs to feed when we got home, but
no one cared. It was so good to get together. I believe
my special joy in the day was to see my mother so happy.
She had on her brown poplin dress, and because of the
bright sun, wore a wide straw hat instead of her bonnet.
Under the trees, at the table, she took off her hat, and
her pretty brown hair curling over her ears made her
look as young as any of the women. It was so good to
see her talking and laughing, and making light of the
hardships of the long winter. I suppose she was the
oldest woman at the picnic, though she was not yet fifty,
but a new country belongs not to age but to youth, and
mother seemed to advise all the younger women, and
become a mother to all of them in their family cares.

At the supper, the men began to tell why they came to
the Northwest, (Easterners still called it that) and in
almost every case, it was to get land for their boys. One
woman spoke up and said, she wanted to come because
she and her husband had too many relatives in Paisley,
and they couldn't buy a fanning mill, or a neckyoke, or a
black pot, without the relatives knowing, and they would
be sure to get a "dig" about it from some of them, and she
dare not buy herself a hat, even though it was with the
butter and egg money, for some of Jimmy's relatives
would say that Jimmy would die in the poorhouse, because of her extravagance.

Everyone laughed, and there was more fun about
relatives and their inquisitiveness. And I remember one
man said he hoped coppers would never come into use in
Manitoba, for they had been a curse in Ontario. Mr. Hall,
the minister then spoke up and he hoped they wouldn't
either; they were hard on the churches, but they served
one good purpose, they made it possible for Scotch people to be generous. I knew my mother wouldn't like that,
but she laughed with the others.

Coming home as we did at last, in the purple prairie

twilight, we were very tired and happy, with the pleasant evening sounds around us, drowsy birds softly twittering, the distant rumble of wagons, dogs barking, cattle lowing, the western sky still barred with crimson, and bright edged clouds above us; we were sure that no neighborhood had ever had a happier picnic.

"We have good neighbors, John," mother said, "friendly, jolly people. What a blessing! I thought I'd never find neighbors like the Lowerys, the Congers, the Charltons, and the Littles and the Blacks and Carsons, and Kingsburys, and Hemstocks; but these will be just as good to live with—and its just as Mr. Hall said, picnics give us a chance to get acquainted. . . . It did my heart good to see Frank Burnett and George Motherwell bite into the vinegar pie. In another year we'll have hens and I'll make some lemon pies that will melt in their mouths. Step up the oxen, George, the sun is down, and 'twill be nearly dark before we are home, and the cows will be at the bars, wondering where everyone is."

Then the conversation turned to Mrs. Dack, the woman who came west because of her numerous relatives. Mother thought it was a queer way for her to talk of her relatives, and maybe she was extravagant, too, certainly her hat with its plumes looked very dressy. . . . Anyway it would have been better for her to let Mr. Dack do the talking, when there were so many strange men present.

I couldn't see why, but I knew enough not to say so.

The next year, 1883, we had a picnic in the same place, and we had a horse race that year; for the settlers had added horses to their equipment. Our boys wanted to run Kate, the smarter one of the team we had just bought, but mother was against it. "A work horse isn't cut out for racing," she said, "and you have no saddle to ride her. Just let her stay where she is, I never saw any good come of horse-racing, anyway." There was a brass band from Brandon that year, and ever so many more people, Oak Creek people and some from Brandon Hills.

Mrs. Frank Burnett's sister had come from Montreal and her city clothes and colored parasol gave a real impetus to dress styles among us. Her picnic dress was of factory cotton, trimmed with knife pleating, and her hat, a red straw turban. She was tall and graceful, and looked like a picture in Godey's Lady Book.

Having experienced how lovely a picnic can be, we came to this one, with great expectations. Some of the print (white ground with blue and yellow dots) brought from Chatsworth, was made into dresses for Hannah and me by Lizzie's skilful hands; I can see them yet, and smell their pleasant starchy smell. They were made with a tight "body" buttoned down to the waist behind, and a full skirt. The plainness of the "body" was relieved by a graduated frill which ran over the shoulders, wide at the top and tapering to nothing at the waist, and referred to as "wings."

The band from Brandon, with their great brass instruments, drove into the picnic grounds in their big democrat, with red rosettes on their horses' collars, and when they alighted, coming swiftly down over the wheels, we were pleased to see how young they were. It was just a boys' Band that had come to play for us. Nice, fair-faced hungry boys, who came over to the tables declaring they had been thinking of this meal all the way from Brandon.

They played: "Rule Britannia," "The Maple Leaf," and "God Save the Queen," in a perfect torrent that shook the ground. I had never heard a brass band before and it affected me powerfully. It seemed to change everything while its billows passed over me. The bandsmen went up the hill to the ballground, where the races were to be held, and we ran after them determined not to miss a sight or sound of these young magicians. Even the distribution of oranges, bananas and chocolates did not alter the focus of my mind. Though I did eat my banana, a whole one this time, the taste had not yet come.

The women were having their visit down at the tables. The baseball game went over noisily, and the horse race was not nice to watch for one horse was ridden by a real jockey in a red cap, and he beat his horse from one end of the half mile to the other, with a short black-snake whip, and I was glad he did not win.

In the slow ox race, our black and white Jake was entered, and I was glad no one would beat him; for one rule of that race was there would be no whips or switches. Each man would ride his neighbor's ox, and endeavor by words or entreaty or hand slaps to get the ox to move as fast as possible. Some one could run behind the ox and push him or slap him, and some one could go ahead with a pan of oats to coax him. The slowest ox would win the race, and the prize was a box of raisins from Read & Callendar's store; and as our Jake had won the race the year before, we were hoping he might again. Jake was a placid little ox, very gentle and knowing. He could push open a door with his nose, and although he was never seen hooking any animals in the farm yard, he was recognized as the boss of them all. He was oddly marked with a black back and white sides, the black part making almost a perfect blanket. His face was white with two black eyes, giving him a rakish look. He had been washed for the occasion and was received with applause when he was led out to the road where the race would take place. Jimmy Sloan, who worked for one of the neighbors would ride Jake.

Just then the women came up the hill, Mrs. Dale wheeling her baby in the carriage. We had been watching the baseball game, but I ran over to Mrs. Dale's carriage to see if I could wheel the baby. Being the youngest of my family I had never had the care of a baby, so it was a treat to me to wheel a carriage. Mrs. Dale gladly relinquished the baby, and I kept the carriage moving as I watched the slow ox race forming at the far end of the field. Little Jake took his place with the other four oxen. And the word was given!

The race began, and the fun was on. In spite of entreaties Jake kept his pace. He merely shook his ears, but refused to quicken his steps. The people cheered and shouted, and three of the oxen began to trot, Jimmy Sloan waved his straw hat, from side to side, ki-yi-ing like a coyote to frighten his mount.

Suddenly, I saw Jake dart forward with a bellow of pain—he began to gallop like a wild thing, and threw his rider in his frantic lurchings. He was coming straight for the end of the field, still bellowing—A horrified silence fell on the people. What did it mean? Had he gone crazy? He was making straight for the shelter of the trees, where I stood with the baby carriage. . . . My heart turned cold with terror! Some one was screaming! He changed his course a few feet from me, and crashed into the brush! As he passed I saw that his white side ran with blood!

The picnic broke into an uproar. Jimmy Sloan had used spurs! The race was spoiled—All the fun had gone out of it. Then the truth came out. Jimmy Sloan had been drinking. He would never have done this if he had been himself; there wasn't a better boy in the country than Jimmy Sloan.

I couldn't walk; my knees had gone weak, and my memory of the picnic is confused from that point. I know Mrs. Dale came running and her face was white and sick looking. There was great indignation, high voices and excitement. Who had brought liquor to our picnic?

There was to be a dance that night in the boarding house, and the Band was supplying the music. Lizzie and George and Will were going to stay, but I think only Will stayed. The whole temper of the day was spoiled. Jimmy Sloan was not hurt when he fell. I heard some one say something about a drunk man's luck. But the picnic had gone raw and sour, and broke up in disorder, suspicions and accusations.

That night behind the boarding house there was a "stand up and drag out fight," between the Canadians and the English, for the Band boys had brought a supply of liquor from Brandon, and every old grudge, under its influence came to the surface. One man had traded off a spavined horse to an Englishman, who had believed the horse to be sound. Another Englishman had jumped a Canadian's claim, when the owner had gone to Winnipeg. Every old grievance became suddenly inflamed, and there were heads smashed, noses broken, and at least one chewed ear. There might have been more serious happnings but for the intervention of Frank Burnett.

We had no picnic the next year.

That was my first direct contact with the liquor business and coming so early in life, it left a mark. The maddened ox, blind with pain, coming bellowing toward me and the baby asleep in her carriage—that was my nightmare for many years and still holds an allegory which has not lost its meaning as the years go by. I know there is a pleasant aspect of this matter of drinking, and when many people think of it they see the sun-kissed vinyards, where the grapes hang purple and luscious, and the happy people sing glorious songs of praise, for the wine that cheers their labors, and warms their veins. Some think of how it loosens the tongue and drives out self-consciousness, and makes for good fellowship when people meet. I think of none of these things. I remember a good day spoiled; peaceful neighbors suddenly growing quarrelsome, and feel again a helpless blinding fear, and see blood dyeing the side of a dumb beast.

CHAPTER XV

THE WAY OF THE TRANSGRESSOR

THE prairie summers were delightful.

The cool, dewy mornings with a sunshine clear as cellophane; langurous afternoons with heat waves quivering the skyline, every blade of grain and grass growing and every bird singing; clamorous evenings with the cows coming home and the teams coming in from the fields, waggons rumbling and dogs barking, dishes clattering; light of day dulling down into the long purple twilight, and the short swift night so soon streaked with dawn.

The prairie was never stingy with its flowers, from the furry-nosed blue anemones that pushed the snow aside in early April to the wealth of golden rod and purple sage, and blue fringed gentians that embroidered the headlands in the fall. Between these, bloomed buttercups, marsh marigolds, trilliums, wild vetches, wild roses, tiger lilies, lady's slippers—yellow as June butter and sweet as honey, and if you knew where to look for them you could find the purple blooms of great size and of orchid-like beauty. In some places these were sold at the stations to the travellers on the trains.

The peak of the year came in harvest time when the ripening grain made golden squares and bands on the prairie, and blue haze shrouded the horizons, and the dewy nights distilled all the fragrances of the field. I loved to listen to the sibilant whispering of the ripening grain billowing and dappling in the wind, and to watch the dark blue flowing shadows cast by drifting clouds. From the time the grain began to turn to gold in early August until the stooks polka-dotted the fields, the whole countryside throbbed with color and movement and sound.

There was a great pride in my heart, when I saw the cultivation of our farm increasing year by year. We had taken fields of grass and turned them into fields of grain. We had brought the seed and soil together.

'I had walked proudly behind my father, in the clean new furrows in my bare feet, as he broke the new sod on our farm, and as the coulter cut the sod, and the share turned it over, I knew he was doing something more than just plowing a field. I knew there was a significance in what he was doing, though I had no words to express it. I knew this was what the land had been waiting for all these long years. It was for this that the rain had fallen on it in summer and the snows had covered it in winter. It was for this the grass had grown on it, withered, and grown again, that some day someone would come and claim it, not for himself alone but for all people, claim it in the name of humanity and press it into humanity's service, stamping and sealing it forever with the broad signature of the plow.

But there was a shadow on my happiness too. From the time the grain was high enough to be eaten by the cattle, someone had to keep them out of the fields for we had no fences at this time. Before the school started, I was very glad to be the herder. It was much nicer to sit outside with good young Nap beside me, than stay around the house, where there was always dishes coming up to be washed. But when I started to school and got a taste of learning, and swept through the Second Part and the Second Book and arrived in the Third Book, and was able to stand by Annie Adams in her blue cashmere dress and brass buttons, her hair ribbons and covered slate frame, all in the first year, how was I going to survive, if I had to stay at home and keep the cows out of the grain? But someone had to do it.

Hannah was a wizard at learning, and in two years was by far the best student in the school, and would soon be able to write for her second class certificate; she must not be held back. I knew that, I knew too, that when she got through and was able to teach, she would help me. I was very proud of Hannah, as we all were, Mr. Schultz had said she was the best student he ever had.

But when in the morning, I saw Bert Ingram and Hannah walking up the trail on their way to school, when I set out across the creek driving the cows ahead of me to the pasture, on the School section, the darkness of the pit was in my soul. I had a little brown arithmetic with me, a slate and pencil and I would lie on my stomach on some green knoll, and work long division problems and Hannah would mark them for me at night, and tell me what happened all day, but that did not dry my tears.

I had a great friend and advocate in my sister Lizzie who freely gave her opinion that a pasture should be fenced for the cows, so I could be able to go to school. This was done at last; a fine grassy field was fenced in along the creek, and I enjoyed a brief season of freedom, but unfortunately a dry season came that year, stunting the grass, and the cattle had to be driven to new places, to supplement the pasture, and again I had to be the herder.

No one prayed more earnestly for rain that I did, in those stifling hot days, when an insolent sun came up in a cloudless sky, and glared down on us all day, as it rode the heavens in sublime indifference to our needs. I wore boots without stockings, a print dress and a straw hat, a home-made straw hat, (Mrs. Naismith had shown us how to make the braid with seven strands of oat straw) and mine was really a small umbrella in width, held fast under my chin with elastic, making a fine circle of shade around me.

There were times when I hated the cows and could have drowned them gladly, for I felt that they were cheating me of the one thing I most wanted. My work was all so endless; only at night, when they all lay asleep behind the pasture bars, was I free, and what good did that do me? They held me a prisoner as truly as any one was ever held by prison walls and I could see life passing by me. There could be no release until the harvest was gathered and threshed and the fields were free then to all comers. But looking ahead that far seemed an eternity.

A heavier blow fell on me too that summer. I had taken the cows out to the east end of the School-section and let them join the neighbor's herd. The School-section (No. 29) was vacant land and I could have left them there, but for the danger of their sneaking back to our oat field into which they had once bolted when I was bringing them home. Having tasted the young oats, they were not likely to forget. Cattle never forget anything. So I had to stay.

I was busy reading Collier's History, with Nap beside me lazily snapping at flies. The sky was cloudy, with a promise of rain, in the northwest, where thick dark clouds were piled on the horizon. Rain would save the country, if it came now, for the grain was in the shot-blade but with the intense heat, was yellowing. Rain would bring up the pasture too, and ease the mental strain from which everyone was suffering. My people were getting edgy, and cross, with this sorry business of waiting and hoping and being daily disappointed. To-day, I had been glad to get out and away by myself, and as I sat on a knoll, reading about King John and the barons, I wondered about the common people of that time, and what they were doing and thinking while King John and his nobles battled at Runnymede. Maybe they did not know anything about it, nor cared; perhaps, that was the fate of common people, to go on raising crops, doing all the drudgery, paying taxes, fighting when they were called out and, always letting some one else decide big questions.

Mr. Schultz had said something like this one day, when we were having a history lesson and he told us about the Peasant's Revolt in Germany and how one-hundred-and-fifty thousand of them were slaughtered, by advice of Martin Luther, because they dared to ask for certain simple privileges, like leaving the farm on which they were born. Hannah and I didn't mention this at home, for we knew Martin Luther was the father of Protestantism and so somewhat of a god. I was sorry to hear this about Martin Luther. I had thought better of him.

The fires of rebellion in my heart were fanned by the agitation going on now about the railways, and the men at Ottawa giving away our railway rights without consulting the people of Manitoba. Frank Burnett, who lived near us had been over talking to my brother Will, and telling him the farmers must organize to strengthen Premier Norquay's hand, or we would be no better than the serfs of Russia, moved about like pawns. I didn't know what pawns were but I got the drift of the argument. I knew the Government at Ottawa had promised the Canadian Pacific Railway Company that no other railway would be allowed to come into Canada for twenty years. American companies were ready to come, but they could not get permission. We wanted them, and needed them. It was our country! We were doing the work, but we were powerless! We were the common people! I grew indignant as I read the history and saw how little the people ever counted, and longed for the time when I would be old enough to say something.

But my business at the moment was to acquire knowledge. Knowledge unlocked doors and gave liberty. I had to plug at these books, snatch every minute I could, and let nothing divert me. Hannah would soon have her certificate; she would get a school and earn money to hire a herd boy and set me free. Perhaps I could go to Brandon and work for my board and go to the High School there, when I was ready.

Mr. Schultz had come to see me, the night before, and had praised my work. My heart was still light as I re-called his wonderful words. "Nellie," he said, "no one can hold you back—no condition can defeat you—if you keep your health; remember no one can really hurt you, but yourself." I turned that over in my mind, not quite sure of its meaning.

I may have been so absorbed in my own thoughts that I did not notice that Nap had left me. The cows were contentedly grazing in the lowlands by the creek, where wild pea-vine and goose-grass mixed with the prairie hay, afforded them excellent pasture.

I was roused by dogs barking, and a sudden stampede of the cows; instinctively I ran toward them calling for Nap. Then I saw that two dogs, Nap and old Jack, the terror of the neighborhood were running the cows toward the creek, with the whole herd in confusion and panic. One of the young heifers was bellowing with pain and fright, as the big black dog hung to her tail. I cried and called, racing with all my speed. The thing I dreaded was happening! The black dog, belonging to one of our neighbors had sneaked up on the cows and Nap had joined him, in his bad work. Tail biting was the unforgivable sin in a dog! Two of our heifers were carrying short tails now and Nap had been the cause. He would be shot if it happened again, and it was happening! He wouldn't have done it if this black brute had not started the chase. . . . I must reach him . . . make him hear me, before his teeth closed . . . . oh! if some of the cattle would only turn on him, he would come to his senses—I reached him at last, and flung my book at him, but not before he had swung for one horrible moment on the big cow's tail. He fell back when at last he heard me, and came crawling to me, abject in his misery. He knew as well as I did what he had done.

The cattle had crossed the creek, and surged up the opposite bank, taking refuge in the trees and stood there panting and terrified. The black dog had disappeared. I went among them trying to quiet them. The neighbor's cattle had separated from ours when the attack began, running toward their home and I did not know whether any of them had been bitten or not.

I could have killed Nap, I think, in that moment, when I saw the damage he had done to the big cow. A beautiful two-year-old heifer was the other victim and her tail was badly torn by the fangs of the black dog and she was in such a state of fear that I could not get near her. The big cow let me wash her tail in a water hole below the hill, and I tore the frill off my petticoat for a bandage, but I could do nothing for the heifer, who still raced and bawled with pain.

Then I proceeded to deal with Nap, who had come back to me. But how could I go on thrashing him, when he lay at my feet and took my blows? I dropped the poplar stick, sick at heart; why should I inflict pain on a dog, who would pay for his one crazy moment with his life? No one could beat a dog who was going to be shot; who might not see another sunrise.

I flung myself down beside him in an agony of grief, and thought my heart would break with its load. I was sorry for the wounded animals and I was sorry for Nap; and sorry for myself, and it seemed that my little world had come to a sudden and tragic end.

The cows gathered around me in excitement; it's a wonder some of them did not step on me, but I didn't care, if they had, nothing could hurt me any further. I had gone beyond hurting. When my grief had spent itself, I sat up and looked around me. The cows had drawn back, and stoood in a circle looking at me. Nap huddled against me, with his ears flat against his head, and his eyes on the ground—the picture of guilt. He tried to lick my hand, but his bloody jaws were terrible to see. I took him down to the creek and washed him carefully, leaving no outward trace of his misdeeds on his coat. He was lamb-like in his gentleness; even whimpered a little to try to get a kind word from me. But I steeled myself against him.

There was a bachelor neighbor who lived near, where

we were then and I decided to go over and get some salve from him. I knew I could get my hands on the heifer when she quieted down, and perhaps her tail could be saved. . . . Nap walked along behind me, and came into the little house at my heels. Jack Thinn was out, but his house was not locked, of course, and I found the very thing I wanted, a little jar of balm o' Gilead salve, the kind my mother always kept on hand. I hunted for a clean rag, but all I could find was Jack's white shirt and I knew that was sacred for funerals and the Twelfth of July, but I did find strings which would help me to fasten the bandages.

I left a note, Jack's pen and pad were on the stove, telling him I would bring the salve back. When I came back with the salve Jack was home; he had been making hay on the river flats, and he had the kettle on the fire, to make a cup of tea, and asked me to drink a cup with him, but I had to get back to the cows.

"That black brute should have been shot two years ago," he said, when I told him what had happened. "He took the tails off two year-old calves this spring. Now any dog that will run a calf is not a dog at all—he's a low bred cur. They keep him because he can kill wolves, and they get the bounty, but I hope your dad insists on him being shot this time. He's and old brute anyway, and has done his mead of evil."

Not once did it occur to him that Nap might have had a share in the bad work, and a plan came to me . . . . though I knew it was not the way of truth. No one had seen the dogs—no one knew. . . . I might be able to save Nap.

Jack was talking still.

"Drink a cup of tea, Nellie, you look like a ghost, just look at yourself in the glass!"

That was not easy, too many flies had been there ahead of me, but I could see my face was blood stained and dirty. "Better wash your face before your mother sees you—or

you'll give her a fright. . . . I can see the cows from here
—they're all right."

I think he saw I had been crying, and being too much
of a gentleman to embarrass me by noticing it, he became
highly jocular. "Gosh, Nellie, you look as if you had
been in a fight . . . are you sure you didn't bite the cows?
I knew you were pretty mad about having to stay home
and mind them, but I never thought you'd break right out
and bite them like this, and blame it on the old black dog."

I didn't see much fun in Jack's railery, but I knew the
kind motive back of it, so I washed my hands and face,
and drank a cup of tea gratefully.

He offered to help me with the cows, but I knew I
could manage them more easily alone. When I got back
to them I fund some of them were were lying down, and
some were cropping the grass.

My mind was in a turmoil. I wondered if I could
save Nap. He would never have chased the cows, if left
alone. The death of the old black dog would be a good
thing! A dog that would chase yearling calves had no
license to live. . . .

I tried to straighten out all the strands of evidence.
But could not be sure. A lie was a lie, no matter how
justifiable it seemed and there was a knot in the skein,
of my reasoning, which would break the thread sometime.

There was no other way. . . . I would have to lie to
save him. I could not expect mercy for him, if the truth
were known. Bob-tailed cattle would not sell for as much
as animals with their tails; and the poor brutes surely
needed the full length of tail to whisk away the flies. . . .

I knew it would be a great grief to my father too, to
have Nap shot for he loved every animal on the place.
Of course, if he had seen Nap with his teeth in the big
cow's tail and heard her bellow with pain, he could have
shot the dog himself, but for that matter so could I, at
that moment. Mother would take the practical view, and
set aside her feelings. The dog was a danger to the

E

cows—so the dog must go, no matter how fine he was in other ways, and that would end the matter.

The cows walked ahead of us quietly and I had plenty of time to think my own bitter thoughts. Even the sky was unfriendly now. Not a cloud remained of all the thick dark ones that had been piling up over the Brandon Hills promising rain. Another dry day with shrinking ponds and withering crops, would not improve tempers, that had been pretty brittle when I left in the morning. So there was all the more reason for careful talk on my part to prevent a flare-up.

I would have to lie, clean and straight. There was no other way, and I wouldn't tell a soul. . . . I did want to tell Lizzie; she would have been so sorry. I wouldn't put any share of this load on her or anyone else. I'd have the decency anyway to keep it to myself. I would do my own lying. . . .

The cows stopped to graze on a little low spot that was still green, so I did not hurry them. The big cow was eating now, but the heifer paced restlessly through the others, bawling and switching her tail. I rubbed her head and talked to her, trying to soothe her, but her big soft eyes were still full of terror. I suppose it was the first pain she had ever felt, and she didn't know how to bear it.—Strangely enough none of the cattle were one bit afraid of Nap. I don't believe even the big cow knew that the crazy barking fury, with teeth of fire, that had hurled itself on her was any relation to the friendly furry friend who went in and out among them every day.

All the family was at home, when I drove the cattle into the pasture and put up the bars. I told my story and it was believed. My father declared he would go over to our neighbors the next day and ask that the black dog be put out of the way.

It was my brother Jack who pointed out the weak spot in the case.

"They'll say the dog was at home all day. They probably think he was, and every one knows Nap has bitten tails too, and what's to stop them saying it was Nap that did the damage. No one saw it but Nellie and they know she's so crazy about Nap, she might lie to save him."

"Now that's enough!" mother interrupted. "There isn't a person in this neighborhood that wouldn't take Nellie's word."

I thought I would choke with humiliation and shame. Fortunately, it was dusk in the kitchen, so they couldn't see my face, but I was afraid they would hear my heart beating.

"Poor child, it has been a hard day for you," mother went on, "you did well Nellie to get the salve from Jack Thinn, I must give him some more—I am glad I made plenty in the spring when the buds were on. I don't know anything else we can do—I think you can compel them to shoot the black dog, John. Isn't it queer that he never goes for any of their own cattle? They keep him because he's a wolf killer. I would hate to quarrel with a neighbor . . . but what can we do?"

Father did not go at once to deliver the ultimatum in regard to the dog. He kept putting it off, for he could never do a disagreeable thing. "Maybe the tails will heal up," he said hopefully, when mother declared she would go herself, if he didn't.

I was utterly miserable; made more so by the fact that my story was not doubted. I had had a good name, and had thrown it away.

Nap was blithely indifferent. He even went away to my brother Will's place and stayed for days, leaving me alone to take the cattle out, and that hurt me. Here was I, blackening my soul for him, and a lot he cared! I suppose he felt a sort of dog-remorse for what he had done and felt easier in his mind when he was out of my sight.

CHAPTER XVI

MEN, AND MACHINES

THE rain saved me, at least for the present, for the next day, all the deceptive clouds that had marched across the sky withholding their rain, came back apologetically and gave us full measure. For three glorious days, without wind or lightning, a steady rain fell in silver spears straight into the ground and the withering crop lifted its head and revived. Indeed it made a wonderful recovery for when the rain was over, there came a strong ground heat that lifted the plants, filled the heads and began the process of ripening.

The whole temper of the neighborhood changed, and my troubles seemed to have had a happy deliverance.

Even the two wounded cows were more contented and were now on the way to recovery. The gashes had closed over, and the heat had gone out of them. I wondered if I could escape as easily as this, and if my prayers could all be answered in this magnificent way. It seemed very generous of God, if it were true. But I had my uneasy moments. There was a stern Puritanic part of my conscience that told me I had sinned and I would suffer. "Without the shedding of blood there is no remission of sins!" Had not that been the golden text, the very Sunday after? What did it mean? But the excitement of the coming harvest, seemingly secure now, drove away my gloom; and a great event was about to break, in the effulgence of which, all other considerations paled. We were going to get a binder.

After the rains, an agent canvassed our neighborhood, a sleek brown-whiskered fellow who drove a brown team, in a top buggy; and came first to see us for he was an Owen Sound man. The Company was offering a

special concession to any neighborhood that would buy
six binders. An expert would come and set them running,
and repairs would be left with the blacksmith in Millford.
Three-hundred-and-forty dollars was the price, and the
payment would be spread over three years. . . .

We had an old reaper, bought secondhand and with
it we had cut the two former crops, but it was
inadequate for the eighty acres of wheat, that lay
across the creek, turning yellow now and dimpling in the
gentle wind. The land was clean and strong, and not a
weed broke the symmetry of the even heads.

I never say my father happier. "You brought us to
a bright land, Willie," he said with emotion, one night
as he looked at the ripening grain. "After grubbing
and hoeing and picking stones and pulling weeds—that
field brings tears to my eyes. This crop will give us a
footing, please God!"

It was in this state of reverent expectation that the
machinery agent broke in and the binder was bought, and
the great day came, when it was drawn from Brandon.
The neighbors went up together and six binders came in
a procession, great red and white machines with carriers
of white canvas.

That very night, Billy, one of our horses (we had just
one team) became sick, and that threw a cloud over the
rejoicing. But we made light of this to each other. Billy
would be better in time to do his share on the binder; we
had arranged to hire a horse from one of the neighbors,
and in another year, if this crop came off, as it looked
now—we would have another team. We had a good yoke
of oxen, fine big blood-red ones—a perfect match.

But Billy's sickness went on, and developed into a
low fever, which held him to his stall for six weeks, and
that was how we had to hitch Kate with the Oxen. Our
neighbor's horse met with an accident before we started
cutting by getting caught in the barb wire of the pasture
fence, so the first day of the cutting was robbed of part of
its glory. But, with a fine day of cloudless sky, velvety

air, sweet with the rich scents of ripe grain, bergamont and golden rod, we refused to be cast down. Kate was hitched beside the oxen and although she gave every evidence of hating her work-mates, the binder was put into action; the wheels turned, the knives bit greedily into the yellow stalks, the canvas carried them aloft; they fell into the bundles and were tied by the binding twine and dropped on the stubble. Will drove the binder and the sheaves were set into stooks by Jack and Father. George was working for a neighbor.

The first round was accomplished with difficulty for Kate could not accustom her pace to the slow steps of the oxen, and could not refrain from nipping them. But this was remedied by checking her head up, so she could not reach them. The second round was better, but the third round the knotter broke—a casting was faulty and snapped off—and each sheaf was thrown down loose, and a piece of idle twine with it. . . .

Father wanted to go on, he would bind the sheaves the old way, anything was better than to let the grain stand, for it was dead ripe and every minute was precious, but Will thought it would be better to go to Millford and get a new knotter. The agent said there would be "parts" kept there and it would save time in the end.

In Millford, he found there were no knotters, so he had to push on to Brandon, thirty miles away, and could not get back until the next morning. So the first day was lost.

Kate made the trip to Brandon, gallant Kate, with her ears back and her head up. She was a quick traveller and evidently never tired. With a couple of hours rest, after coming back from Brandon she went on the binder again, leaning over to take a bite at the ox nearest to her, to let him know that, though she might be a little tired with the long hours, she still had her pride. I do not know how many times Kate was driven to Brandon through the night that harvest, but I do know that she showed no sign of weariness at any time.

The story of that binder is a story of grief and the others binders were no better. Everything went wrong, someone was on the road to Brandon nearly every night for the parts left with the blacksmith were not sufficient for the demand. The costs were mounting too, for the Company disclaimed all responsibility for breakages.

In fact the Company from its office in Winnipeg assumed no responsibility at all, for anything. Their work was done, when they got the notes signed. But they did write letters. My face burns as I write these words, thinking of the insults they hurled at us.

I remember one lovely day early in September when at least it seemed that we had replaced every part on the binder that could possibly break, and all day it had been working well. Hannah and I carried out the afternoon lunch as usual. The big pot of tea, hot buttered biscuits, and on this day we had a fine cranberry pie (with the pits in) just out of the oven, juicy and sweet.

The binder was working so well every one was holding their breath, and almost talking in whispers. I think it was the first whole day the binder had worked and the night was not yet!

We like to carry out the lunch for everyone was glad to see us. Even Kate was glad for it gave her a half hour release from her despised companions, while she ate her green oats in peace. There was no comment made on the binder's fine performance. Irish people are superstitious about talk; it can breed mischief. "If you are doing well, say nothing." . . . .

We laid out the meal almost in silence. "It looks like the end of the field to-night," Jack said, as he wiped his hands on his overalls. "It's full moon and that means we can work a little longer. If we can see till half past eight, I believe we'll be done."

My father was sixty-nine at this time, but he was strong and well, and worked as long hours as the boys. He had a great love for the fields, and in harvest time, it seemed he was never tired. He was busy now rubbing out a head of wheat.

"Sure, and it is a grand country that can grow forty bushels of this to the acre. Look at how plump it is and hard, and yellow, packed in its little case, neat as a baby's fingernail. . . . It's great to be alive on a day like this, with enough to eat, and a bed to lie on. If it were not for this touch of rheumatism in my knees, I believe I could work all day and all night too, at as nice a job as standing sheaves on end for the sun to shine on. . . . Rest yourself, Willie lad. . . . There's always another day, and it will be a good one by the look of the sky. . . ."

"There's always the danger of frost," Will said, as he ate hastily. The trouble with the binder had put lines in his young face.

Hannah and I waited until the binder started. We would carry the sheaves for father for a while to save him the stooping, and as we worked he told us stories of Ireland. He was talking of the Rock of Cashel that lies on the plains of Tipperary, " 'The Divil's Bite' it is called," he said, "and that's what it is. The Devil had come to Ireland to make trouble but the blessed Saint Patrick was there ahead of him and he could do nothing with the Irish at all, at all, and he saw he might as well go home to England. But before he went, such a rage came on him, he took a bite out of the hill for spite and made off with it. But he had bitten off more than he intended, and to hold it was pulling his back teeth out, so he dropped it just where it lies on the green plains of Tipperary, and up above, you can see the place it came from."

Suddenly the hum of the binder ceased! and we waited in suspense. Had something gone wrong? We hurried around the end of the field and saw to our dismay that Will was unhitching.

The tongue of the binder had snapped. There was no reason for the break, for no extra pressure had been put on it. There was an old crack in the wood, smoothed down and painted over, but there it was! Anyone would know it would break sometime. . . . Jack ran to the house to get two boards; maybe it could be mended to get the field finished. Will stood looking at it without saying a word. He whistled through his teeth as if he were cooling his lips. Father looked at the break and broke into a wild Irish denunciation of the Company, checking himself in the middle of it to pat Will on the shoulder and say: "take it aisy, lad."

Someone was coming across the field. It was Jack Thinn bringing the mail. "Trouble again," he called across the stubble, "one of the axles of mine broke—we worked only two days this week and my grain is shelling. Tom Aylsby has gone to Brandon for a new wheel. I brought over the mail. I see the Company has written you a letter, Mr. Mooney. Nice letter writers aren't they?"

Will opened the letter and read, I remember this sentence: "Every part of our machine is tested by experts, but no machine can do good work in the hands of a bungling operator, and unfortunately we cannot supply brains, our business is machinery."

That night the sun set clear and cold, and at dawn the next morning came the frost that caught the standing grain.

Two years afterwards when at the Harvest Home Festival in Millford, one of the professors from the new college just opened in Winnipeg, came out to preach on Sunday and to lecture for us on Monday night and in the little church there were gathered all the people of our community. The Reverend Doctor, with his great gifts of oratory, had warmed our hearts and many an eye glistened as he dwelt on the opportunities of higher education that the new college made possible for the boys and girls of to-day.

"The best crop in this fertile valley, so favored in its rich soil and abundant rain-fall is not your number-one-hard wheat, or your seventy-bushels-to-the-acre oats, or your white-faced Herefords, it is your boys and girls with their bright faces and eager minds. . . . You came here from your comfortable homes in the East for their sakes, not your own, and now, dear friends as the Lord has prospered you, we know we can depend on you for support in this great new enterprise."

The people were nodding their consent and the doctor knew he had his audience.

"I am glad to be able to tell you that we have received heartening messages from people outside our own Province, especially from Eastern sources. And you will be interested to hear that one of the first subscriptions and a generous one too, came from the ——— Machine Co., of Toronto, whose name I see on many of your machines."

Oh! oh. . . .!

There was an intake of breath in the church, and the atmosphere curdled and soured like new milk in a thunder storm. The people squirmed in their seats and their faces changed. Inadvertently the kindly old doctor had run his hand across old wounds that bled again:—I remembered the letters. . . . "We cannot supply brains, our business is machinery."

Coming home in the wagon we discussed it. Liza, (Mrs. Ingram's Liza, brought from Woodstock) who happened to be riding with us gave us her description of what had happened in the church. Liza was the best berry-picker in the neighborhood and could find berries where the ordinary person saw nothing but leaves, so Liza drew her illustration from her own sphere of activity:

"That church was like a berry-bush," she said, and everyone hushed to hear what was on Liza's mind for she seldom spoke at all. "A berry patch with raspberries hanging bigger'n thimbles everyone pickin' and eatin'! Nicest berries they ever saw. Then at the same minute, everyone, not one or two mind you, but everyone bit into a raspberry bug!"

Before I leave this part of my story, I want to pay

my tribute to Kate, the horse who worked beside the two red oxen with such contempt for her humble helpers. Her bones lie deep in the soil of the farm she helped to make in the Souris valley, but her memory will endure as long as any of our family are in the land of remembering.

Billy and Kate were our first horses, bought from Arthur Robinson, Mr. Schultz's brother-in-law, who lived near Hilton in the Tiger hills. Billy recovered from his long sickness and lived to be a very old horse, a patient cheerful steady horse, whom anyone could drive, but Kate was the real personality. Not that she was a likable horse; for she was never in good humor, and lived in a state of continual ill-temper, with her ears laid back on her head. But she was a horse of iron nerve and will. My father explained her bad temper by saying she couldn't help it. She must have been teased when she was a colt.

She was never tired, and never sick a day in her life. She lived to be twenty-five years old, and for the last few years had to have her food chopped, for her teeth were gone. But not her temper! The colts in the pasture never made the second mistake of being familiar with her for she lost no opportunity of taking a nip out of any horse that came near her, except Billy her mate, for whom she had a real affection. I can remember how they stood with their necks crossed in the pasture.

Billy died first, and soon after Kate grew too stiff to leave her box stall. At the last she would not lie down, for I think she knew if she lay down she could not rise again.

One day when my brother Jack was in the barn he heard a sound from her stall like a long sigh and hurried over to see what was wrong. Her hind legs had given away and she was sitting on her haunches with her eyes glazed over. Kate had come to the end of the long furrow, but she died as she lived, with her head up and her ears back!

CHAPTER XVII

LIMITATIONS

ONE Sunday at church I received a great message of comfort from Mr. Hall, the minister, when he read the passage from Revelation that describes the outcasts from the heavenly city:—"For without are dogs," he read and I sat up with a shot through my heart. Dogs. . . .! I supposed he meant bad dogs who bit tails. "Sorcerers and whoremongers," I didn't know any of them. . . . I did not know what the words meant, "murderers and idolators," and then I got my message of comfort, "whosoever loveth and maketh a lie." My heart sang with joy. . . . I was not in that list, for though I had made a lie, I had not loved it. God, who knows everything would know I had not loved it. I lied because I couldn't help myself, but I did not love it.

I had my mind almost made up to tell Mr. Hall in the fervor of my happiness. I craved absolution. But I got no opportunity then, and as my exaltation faded caution came back. This matter was between God and me, and I would not widen the base. . . . Poor Mrs. Dick Walters was a lesson in keeping one's mouth shut. Everyone knew what had happened to her. At the revival meetings, held by Mr. Hall at his Souris City appointment Mrs. Walters had fallen under conviction of sin and had confessed a mishap in her girlhood. She was only seventeen when it happened, but as the result of her confession her home was broken, her husband had cast her off, not that he wanted to, but he felt he had to prove his manliness to his neighbors. So he put her out without a dollar. He was a coarse, cursing, rough fellow, but he couldn't live in the house with a woman who had sinned! She had reared her eight children and worked like a

slave; had been patient and kind, a good neighbor—
everything a woman should be. She was working now in
a hotel in Brandon and her family was lost without her!
Oh, if she had only kept quiet no one would ever have
known, for the Isle of Skye is a long way from Manitoba,
and thirty years should be long enough to expiate any
sin. I shut my lips tight when I thought of her and resolved that I would never go to a revival meeting as long
as I lived.

But I experienced a great lightening of my heart that
day in church. If God understood, what need I care? I
hoped now I could forget it.

Threshing time came on and I was back at school,
and working in a feverish joy. The days were mistily
bright and odorous, full of the glamor of autumn. The
two-mile walk was a progress of beauty—the grass crisp
beneath my feet, the sky blue overhead and the Tiger
Hills mauve with mystery. Hannah had told me stories of
English history and recited poetry, as we walked and I
had never had a happier time. I was getting on; we were
all getting on. The big crop had not turned out as well
as it had promised, but there would be no lack of food
and clothes. Indeed I never thought of these things. My
heart was so full of the overwhelming thirst for knowledge, I did not place much value on material things,
though I did look forward to a time when I could earn
money, wear well-cut clothes, red in color, and have a
pair of gold cuff-links with a horse's head on each one.
No one could ask for more than that from the powers of
this world. I was well contented with my lot in life, especially now since my conscience was clear.

One day we had the "Miller o' the Dee," for our reading lesson. The king was speaking to the merry miller,
telling him how fortunate he was to have plenty but not
too much, and no worries with councillors, advisers,
foreign powers, wars, taxes and the other entanglements
that come to vex a king. I was in the Fourth Book then,
running neck and neck with Annie Adams and only a few

marks behind her. That day Annie missed a word in spelling, "blythe," it was, and when I reached the head of the class, a dark wave of anger kindled the fair cheek of my deskmate. Annie liked me in my place, but my place was not ahead of her, as we stood before the teacher's desk. It was the first time I had reached the dizzy heights of being at the head of the reading class and I may have been offensively proud. Anyway, I was heading for punishment.

When we went out to play Annie handed me a sore blow: "You needn't be so pleased about getting ahead of me. I let you spell me down because I am sorry for you. I don't know how you can bear to come to school, wearing your only dress. Everyone knows you have no Sunday dress now, and this one is getting too short for you."

Ah me, it's the truth that hurts! and I reeled under her blow. But when I recovered I tried to think of something that would be a crushing reply. I thought of something too in the next period and I would say it to her when school was let out, and I knew how I would say it too. I had not listened to the serial stories in the *Family Herald* without learning something. I would draw myself up to my full height and with a curling lip and a flashing eye hiss out the words. I could hardly wait for the time to come, so well prepared I was.

"You"—I would say. "You—dare to taunt me with my lack of raiment! What are dresses anyway, but things that perish, you, who would clothe the body and starve the soul. What do you know of the Scottish Chiefs or the Tales of the Border?' '

By noon my anger had cooled, I couldn't say it. It was too deadly and anyway, I knew I would have a nice new dress as soon as threshing was over and mother went to Brandon; and besides I knew something else. I was going to Brandon myself when mother went. Maybe that would hold Miss Adams!

I would let it go! I would have my revenge another way! And I would never let her see the top of the class

again. Miss Adams' sun had set. I told myself grimly,
she would rue the day she taunted me!

The girls at school, Annie included, were doing fancy
work at noons crocheting lace and doing wool-work for
table mats on corks with pins, and I was seized with a
desire to create something beautiful too. It looked quite
easy and I got a hook from Lizzie and a spool of white
thread and was all ready to go when I made a painful
discovery. It was not easy at all. I could not get the
right crook in my little finger, and I seemed to have no
way of making the stitches of uniform length. The
veteran fancy workers who were now doing intricate
designs in Gordon braid, raised their eye-brows as they
watched my frantic efforts. I put my tongue out too,
which was always a sign with me of mighty concentration. But I could not make a scallop that had not a
bulge and the thread soon lost its snowy hue. It was hard
to take the things they said as they talked over my head.
Even Annie's little sister Maude who had just started to
school could do the mile-a-minute pattern. There was
only one thing I could do.

I renounced all forms of handwork; and plunged into
the regular work of the school with greater diligence;
though my heart was sore at my defeat, I professed a
great disdain for lace trimmed petticoats and drawers.
Plain ones for me. Underwear should be neat but not
gaudy! And how I studied my spellings, drew maps and
memorized all the poetry in our readers; and recited
with gestures one Friday afternoon:

"The heights by great men reached and kept
    Were not attained by sudden flight,
But they, while their companions slept,
    Were toiling upward in the night.
They did not leave their reading books
    To fool around with crochet hooks;
They did not slight their history-notes
    To make lace for their petticoats;

But step by step they did advance
 And gave no thought to coat or pants!
So let my steps be ever led
 Away from wool, and crochet thread;
And let my heart be set to find
 The higher treasures of the mind."

I did not get clear away. The crochet squad were not deceived by my high resolves. Little Maude Adams tried to comfort me by telling me her mother knew a woman once who couldn't crochet or do any fancy work either and it was all right. She couldn't help it. Her father and mother were cousins.

CHAPTER XVIII

RETRIBUTION

A FEW nights after this, something happened that made me forget the head of the class, my high resolves, the new dress, or the trip to Brandon.

I came home from school, changed my one dress into an old gingham which had been Hannah's, and ran out to dig potatoes for supper. I liked digging potatoes; maybe, because I was not often allowed to do it for father liked to dig them himself, but he was helping the Ingrams to thresh. It was lovely to see the big ones rolling out of the ground, and to keep from cutting them with the hoe required some skill. The straw stacks gleamed like piles of pure gold on the faded stubble; the grass was tawny and crisp with autumn; and the cattle could run now anywhere they liked and I was free— free until the crop grew again, and that was a long time.

Suddenly it occurred to me that I had not seen Nap. He had not come to meet us at Kennedy's corner as usual. A man was coming up the bank of the creek, it was Jimmy Sloan, the waterman of the threshing outfit. He came running up from the creek where he had been filling his water tank from the big pool. The threshers were working at Mr. Ingram's; but Jimmy still came to the big pool on our farm for water for the engine.

The increased crops had shelved the old-fashioned horse-power machines, and a new steam thresher owned by Billy Ferguson of Glenboro had come into our neighborhood.

"I think your dog is in trouble, Nellie," Jimmy called to me, "I saw him this afternoon fighting with a boar, that belongs to Jack Thinn. I tried to get him away, but

Nap seemed to think he should finish the fight. He was pretty badly chewed but game for more."

"Where is he?" I asked, distressed at the thought of Nap being hurt.

"Across the creek, on the ploughed field they were," Jimmy said. "But I don't see anything of them now; maybe Nap has come home, though, has he?"

"No, he hasn't come home! Take in the potatoes Jimmy," I said, thrusting the pail into his hands. "I must find him."

The short October evening was drawing in, it would soon be dark, and I never needed daylight so terribly. Nap may be lying bleeding to death some place where I could not see him. I ran across the creek bed and over to the ploughed field. There were signs of deadly combat; black hair and blood; the ground torn up, I ran and called and listened.

The stillness of evening mocked me, gentle sounds of cow bells, loaded wagons, the distant hum of the threshing machine, voices, cows lowing, geese clearing their throats. A warm breath of air from somewhere quickly replaced by the cool breeze. "O Nap, Nap," I called. "Answer me! Nap!"

I turned back to get Hannah to help me, and crossed the creek farther up, and as I raced over the bank, something caught my eye in the bushes. Something that made my heart skip a beat. It was Nap, a poor bundle of blood-stained fur. He had tried to crawl home and had fallen here, weak from loss of blood.

I knelt beside him in the gray light, and saw, to my great joy that he was still living; but with every beat of of his heart, blood flowed from his breast, torn open by the boar's fangs. He knew me and tried to lift his ears.

I ran to the house for flour, to stop the blood and came back with a milk-pan full, and a roller towel, taken from the clothes line. I put handfuls of flour on his breast, but the red stains came through. Then I piled on all I had and wrapped him in the towel as tightly as I could draw it. He felt horribly limp and lifeless. I ran down to the pool where Jimmy was still filling the water tank with a pail.

"You'll have to carry him Jimmy," I said. "I can't lift him and I am afraid he's going to die."

"I've got to take the water back to the machine," he said, "but I'll come right back. This is my last load for the night. Get a drink of milk for him, if he can swallow, and I'll be back as soon as I can. Now remember a dog can take a lot of killing, and as long as he is breathing there's a chance."

I got a bowl of milk from the milk house, and went back and sat beside him and talked to him in an agony of remorse. Was it for this I had saved him, by lying for him? Saved him from a quick merciful death, to die like this? One quick straight bullet if I had told the truth, and then no more of anything, no pain, no bleeding, no fear, no blinding rage,—just peace and a great darkness and the day ended, his happy dog's day over. But now, he was broken, bleeding, suffering, and I could not save him. He was out of my hands now.

Sometimes I thought his breath had stopped, so faint it was. I wet my fingers in the milk and put them on his tongue, but he made no response. But still I felt he knew me.

"I won't leave you, Nap," I told him and I know he was glad to have me beside him.

Jimmy came back and hitched one of his horses to the stone-boat. I could have done that myself, but there was not a horse or an ox on the place—and all our men were helping at the threshing. Jimmy thought this was easier for Nap than to be carried. We got Nap into the old house, now use as a granary, and put him on a pile of grain sacks.

"You can't do anything more," Jimmy said to me. "Now don't you stay out here, breaking your heart. I'll put this horse blanket over him and you go on into the house. He may live, but I wouldn't count on it."

It was dark in the granary and I went into the house to get a lantern. Mother came back with me, and looked at Nap. His eyes were closed but he moved an ear when she spoke to him.

"I am sorry for you, Nellie," she said, "but if he does die, it will be a relief in a way. I've been afraid he might chase the cows sometime, or the neighbors' cows and have to be shot. When a dog gets a bad habit, its hard to break him. We'll warm some milk and feed it to him with a spoon, and put hot bricks beside him; he's cold from the loss of blood. You go in and warm the milk and I'll stay beside him."

I brought back the milk and held the lantern while mother tried to make him swallow. But the milk ran down his jaws. She shook her head.

"I think he'll be gone in the morning," she said. "Remember, he's only a dog, child, and not many dogs live out their days. If he's living in the morning we will wash the blood off him and dress his wounds, but I don't think it is well to disturb him now."

I nearly told her then, but I knew it would hurt her to know I could lie so stoutly as I had. I couldn't eat that night, nor did I look at a book.—I slipped out again with my coat on, for it was cold in the granary; and I sat beside him in the dark, stroking his head. If he were going to die, I wanted to be with him. I had carried him in my arms when he was a pup, watched him grow into the lovely dog he had been; had him these years for my friend and playmate; we had sat together on the hills and minded the cattle,—he had guarded the hen-house door, when I forgot it—he could all but speak to me; and always knew if I were worried. I would stay with him if he were going to die, but over and above my grievings, I could feel, in the silence of that long night in the granary, there was a power that was working in life, a great unseen power, a law, an unchanging law, and Nap and I, and everyone was subject to it, and we couldn't escape it. I couldn't pray that night. It all seemed so

useless. The power of the law was so heavy, so in-
exorable. Without the shedding of blood there is no remission of sins! And I thought I could change that with
a lie! And some have thought they could change it with
prayer. The laws of God could not be changed. They
were like the multiplication tables. How pitiful we were
in our helplessness, under the law . . . . under the law.
Why had there to be such suffering? And who asked to
be born anyway? I didn't! Neither did Nap! Nobody
did!

Through the window above my head, I could see a
bright star, twinkling in the western sky. I wondered
about it. I wondered if there were people living on it,
and if they were under the law, or if they cared? The
world was so big, and this star was a world too. . . .
It began to blot me out. . . .

It was grey day when I wakened, and a pale light
was draining in through the window. The granary with
its discarded harness, boxes, fanning mill, horse collars
hanging on nails, parts of machinery, took shape. Then
I remembered and looked at Nap; he was still living, but
his body still had a terrible coldness and his eyes were
dim.

I went into the house and lighted the kitchen fire.
Mother would soon be up and she's be glad to have the fire
burning. I put the kettle on; I would try again to get
Nap to take hot milk. She came into the kitchen then.
"You're up early dear, I didn't hear you come down and
that's queer, I thought I heard everything. Is he still
alive?" I nodded. She didn't know I had been out all
night.

The fire was crackling cheerfully and hot porridge
would soon be steaming on the table. Mother's face
looked heavenly to me. I couldn't put it into words, but
some glimmering of life's plan swept across my mind.
Sorrow and joy, pain and gladness, triumph and defeat
were in that plan, just as day and night; winter and summer, cold and heat, tears and laughter. We couldn't

refuse it, we must go on. We couldn't go and sulk in a corner and say we wouldn't play.

The sun swept up over the horizon and all the landscape kindled and blazed. It was a new day and I was part of it.

Mother was taking wood for the fire out of the oven where she had put it to dry. "Now call the men, Nellie, we're all a bit late this morning."

When I came back she was stirring the porridge. The day's routine had begun. The cows were standing at the pasture bars, and the milk pails were waiting outside on the bench, scalded and aired. I was glad of the cows standing at the bars, bawling indolently, just to be doing something, glad I had to go out and milk them. Work! That was life's remedy. Not philosophy or explanations. There was no formula, no answer for the old problems. But we could go on. We had to go on. We were like horses on horse power engines, travelling in circles, not knowing why we were doing it, but just as they were accomplishing something, maybe we were too.

"You look tired Nellie," mother was saying. "You're fretting too much over the dog. I never thought you took anything hard; for you are Irish, like your father, and light-hearted, but you mustn't worry over what you can't help. Animals will fight; their instinct drives them. Nap thought he was protecting us when he attacked the boar. Cats kill birds, just because it is their nature; they are driven by their instincts and they can't be blamed. Nature is cruel, I often wonder why; red in tooth and claws."

When I went outside to milk, I felt better. I never could be gloomy in the sunshine. The morning glow burned in the windows of the Ingram house and came back in a glittering beam. The hens were coming out of their house, full of cheerful observations and when I pulled my milking stool over to the big cow, she put her foot back, and turned her head toward me, with a friendly look in her big eyes. I laid my head against her warm white flank, and was grateful for the comfort of it, and as the milk foamed in the bright tin pail with a rhythmic thrumming, the little cow came up behind me so close, I could feel her soft breath on my neck.

There were bright spots in life's pattern.

Nap did not die. I stayed home from school with him for a week, and by that time he was well enough to walk, but he lurched and swayed uncertainly. He lived on milk for two weeks and had three eggs a day,—but we did not let him know he was gettings eggs, because he might be tempted to help himself later. Billy Smith, the butcher who came once a week from Glenboro, brought him bones, and a new growth came to him, making him a bigger, finer dog than he had ever been. And as I saw this great growth and bounding spirits come back to Nap, my burden of guilt was lifted.

CHAPTER XIX

My First Sight of Brandon

MOTHER, Jack and I went to Brandon the first week of December, on a load of wheat, and for a thirty-mile drive on a heavily loaded sleigh, necessitating a slow pace, it is a cold way of travelling. But with plenty of robes and by running behind the sleigh, occasionally, we managed very well.

It was a bright winter day with new snow, loud with frost. Every fence post and leafless silver willow shrub, every clump of willow wands bordering the streams, every roof of house or stable was edged with hoar frost that glinted and sparkled as the sun rose. The world with its glittering whiteness, blue sky and chiming sleigh-bells, was one glorious come-to-life Christmas card.

I know a verse about a snowy morning, which I wanted to recite to mother, but it is not easy to recite through a woollen scarf and besides I was shy about reciting poetry before Jack, who would think I was trying to show off. Jack had a high disdain for anything senti-mental, and had not wanted to put the sleigh-bells on the horses but mother held firm on that, for sleigh-bells had a significance to her. The winter of the deep snow when she had gone alone for three long and terrible weeks, with snow so deep no one could get through, the signal of release had been young Robert Lowery's sleigh-bells, as he ploughed his team through the snow, and she said the bells of heaven could not be sweeter.

I wanted to recite: "The snow had begun in the gloaming, and busily all the night had been heaping field and highway with a silence deep and white." But I couldn't break through. However, I would tell her about it, when we were alone.

146

It was curious to see what happened to the Brandon Hills, as we travelled nearer to them. From our place the Brandon Hills make a dark blue shoulder that rises abruptly from the plains, but as we approached, this prominence straightened out and become merely a country-side of small hills and shadowy blue valleys with farm buildings here and there, in sheltered places. Columns of smoke climbing straight into the clean air from the houses, and a few cattle circling a straw stack made the only bits of color in this white world.

We reached the Black Creek Stopping house at noon, and had dinner with Mrs. Corbett. Mrs. Corbett had belonged to the Salvation Army in Winnipeg, before she came to the Black Creek, and was rejoicing over the Army's conquest of Brandon .

"Ain't it grand entirely," she said as she served us from the stove, "how well the Army is doin' in Brandon, and I'm tellin' you there's an improvement here too. Harry Lovey—maybe you know him, he drives for Nicoll's big farm—teams every day to Brandon and back, well he's got it, and asks a blessin' at the table here, yes sir, in all the rush and bustle of this room, says Harry in a high hollow voice not a bit like his own, 'Let us return thanks!' and mind you, every head went down.—They say he preached over at Brandon Hills, when the minister couldn't get through, on account of the snow, and them that heard him says he can bate Mr. Cheney all to the devil. Oh, he's a man of education is Harry but it's small use he's been puttin' it to, heretofore. . . . You should go Mrs. Mooney, and take your little girl, when you're in Brandon. She'll never forget it, at her age, she's old enough to take it in too."

"I'll see," mother said in her guarded way. "Little girls of her age are best in bed."

Mrs. Corbett's stopping house was one big room, with one end used for a kitchen, in which stood a great high-oven black stove where Mrs. Corbett with quick movements filled the plates with a cut of roast beef and helpings of turnips, potatoes and gravy. Each man, who was helped took a place at the long table, covered with oil-cloth, where he found everything else he needed.

"Da," Cosbett, traversed the length of the table with a blue enamel tea pot and filled the cups that were stationed at every place. Bread and butter, pickles, biscuits and cheese were set at close intervals, along the length of the table and it took but little time to serve thirty or forty men.

Mother and I were set at a little table near the stove and our plates were brought to us.

"It's a treat to see a woman," said Mrs. Corbett, in her friendly way. She was a tall woman, with a pair of long jet earrings that lashed around her face as she talked. She wore an embroidered Jersey and a short black skirt, and a clean white apron with a pointed bib, trimmed with Gordon braid.

"I saw there was a woman drivin' in and I grabbed my white apron, that I keep here in the drawer of the cupboard. It's women that notice; men just want their vittles and a lot they care who gives it to them. . . .

"And the first thing I thought, Mrs. Mooney, when I saw you, was that I was glad I had the place white washed after the flies were done. If the walls are clean, no one will notice the floors, for floors can be dirtied in a few minutes, but it takes time to dirty walls and no one minds new dirt, anyway."

Mrs. Corbett had set us near to her so she could get a chance to talk, and said so frankly.

"It's a relief to get my eyes on a woman and they come so seldom too. There's pie for dessert, little girl, s don't be fillin' yourself too full of potatoes."

"You can accommodate a great many people here," mother said admiringly, "you are a good manager, I can see."

"Well I do and I am, you might say. You see the lads are all fightin' hungry and that's a great help, though

it's hard on the grub. But they're not nosey, I'll say that
for them."

"Haven't you any help at all?" asked mother.

"Just Da and Peter Rocket over there, and Peter just
scrapes plates and washes them and Da keeps the table
filled and pours the tea. Peter is not as bright as some
but a good lad too. . . .

It's good money, forty cents a meal, women and children free, and glad to see them, and then a stable fee of
twenty-five cents a team, if you bring your own oats.
We're not doing so badly at that, and everyone is pleasant,
poor lads, I often wonder how they are, comin' in so cold
and discouraged with the price of wheat so low; and them
havin' to wait in a line for hours to get it sold."

She was ladling out food on two plates as she talked.
"The farmer is the only man that has to take what he
can get for his stuff," she went on, shouting at us over
the shoulder of a big teamster who stooped down to get
his plate filled and then turned back to get another baked
onion.

"Because there are so many of them all raisin' the
same stuff and instead of helpin' each other by standin'
together and lettin' one man speak for all of them, they
cut each other's throats without meanin' to, but maybe
they'll learn.

Come and get your pie sissy, and a piece for your
mother, here's raisin' and this is dried apple—take the
raisin'; Peter, come here and pour tea, Da's gone out and
the men are lookin' for it."

"I'm washin' dishes," Peter said stolidly, "and I'd have
to wash my hands before I could pour tea for anywan. . . .
wait a minute."

I could see he was a lout of a boy, who could not
even think of two things at once.

There was an impatient rattling of spoons on cups.
So I jumped up and went to the stove.

"Let me do it," I said, and took the smallest pot on
the stove and went down the line.

I could hear Mrs. Corbett's voice above the chatter. "Look at that now, there's a girl with a quick turn, and her not more than twelve years old. I'd be a proud woman, if I had a little girl like that comin' along. By gosh, I like action."

After the men had eaten they sat on the benches beside the stove and soon the room was blue with smoke. "You might as well rest a while," said Mrs. Corbett to us, "there will be no chance of sellin' the wheat to-night. That street leadin' to the elevator is one solid line of teams up till eight o'clock every night. The thing is to get your load in the line and leave it there, and hook up early in the mornin' and if you're early enough you may be able to edge up nearer the elevator. It's a crime the way the grain companies treat the farmers. And the railways and all. Look what happened to Grand Valley! Just because McVickers wanted too much for his farm, when they were lookin' for a townsite the whole place had to suffer. My sister and her man were there, built a house and all; sure the railway would come, they had been promised it, but what of that. . . . The Syndicate was not carin', and changed the station to Brandon. Mrs. Mooney, it's time the women had something to say about things."

My mother shook her head.

"It isn't a woman's place," she said, with her Scotch voice. "Surely, if men can't do these things, there's no use of women trying. It will all come in time, don't you think? Remember the country is young and the men are so busy getting a foot hold."

"Yes, and that's the time women should get into things, and get everything off on the right foot. If I weren't so busy feedin' hungry men and makin' bread and pies in my spare time, I could think out a few things. Maybe you'll do it sissy, when you grow up."

"Maybe I will," I said eagerly, "I'd like to."

When we were in the sleigh again, Mother told me, I should not be so forward. It did not look well for a little girl to jump up and pour tea for strange men. Mrs. Corbett was well able to run her own house; and all that talk about women doing things was nonsense. It's women's place to help the men and keep out of public matters and out of public notice.

"Mrs. Corbett talks too much, and has a certain boldness about her that I do not like, with those swinging earrings she looks like a gypsy. . . . I was not pleased with you, Nellie."

Jack agreed with her. Jack was sixteen and knew a lot. "I felt cheap," he said, when the men at the table were all saying: "Got a new waiter, eh? Who's the kid? Some of them knew too, who you were."

"Well, supposing they did," I said, "I didn't spill the tea down anyone's neck, did I?"

"Nellie, not a word, you're too ready with an answer, your brother is right. You did a bold thing, getting out there where everyone could see you. Though I know you did it on impulse and with a desire to help, but it did not look modest."

"She did it to show off," Jack said, "and nothing else, she likes to be noticed; we made a mistake in bringing her."

The argument was an old one and I did not pursue it further. I could see nothing wrong in what I had done. Why shouldn't I pour tea for strange men? Mother was wrong in her attitude this time, but I would be free some day and I was not going to be cast down over it. I got off the sleigh and ran behind a while and put the whole matter out of my mind.

We came into Brandon from the southeast, passing the great yellow brick Court House, the largest building I had ever seen. The new wooden houses, scattered irregularly over the white prairie looked like children's blocks thrown down in a hurry, only they were all one color, in the pale light of evening, pinkish yellow, the color of human faces. I had wondered how the houses were arranged in a city; were they continuous? or were there gaps between? and if so, what were in the gaps? It bothered me, but I would soon know, so I said nothing.

When we got into the city, we passed down a long street of stores, and other places of business standing side by side. Outside the stores fur coats and fur robes hung, horse collars, and sets of harness with brass trimmings, and in front of one a full-sized painted wooden Indian wrapped in a blanket. Through the frosted windows red lamps shone, and in the small clear spaces I could see that some of the lamps had slashed red tissue paper shades hung over them, and I hoped they would not catch fire. The sidewalks seemed to be full of merchandise, zinc tubs, wheelbarrows, axe handles and so many things that the people had to step into the street in some places, There were people everywhere I looked, nearly all men, in fur coats and caps.

The predominant smell was of lumber, shingles and tar paper and from the time we entered the city, we could hear sounds of building, hammering and sawing; loads of lumber were drawn through the crowded narrow street.

Here was life and color and movement in this great-swarming city, and we would be here for two nights and a day. My resentment faded out, in this new bewildered happiness.

Jack knew his way around, having been here many times the winter before on the grain sleighs. He drove straight down to Pacific Street to the Farmer's Home, a high unpainted new hotel facing the railway track. I liked the location for now I would see the trains. Generally my people stayed at the Kelly House, but there had been some fights and disturbances of drunken men there, and the Farmer's Home, being newer, was considered quieter. We got a nice room, with one across the hall, for Jack, and when we got freshened up a little, went down for supper, to a long narrow dining room, lighted by bracket lamps and a large glass fringed chandelier. The table napkins in fan shapes flared out of heavy water glasses and the table cloth had a red edge.

"Can we go to hear the Salvation Army to-night?" I asked. "I would like to go."

"Don't let her mother," Jack began, "she's too young to be out at night."

"I am too tired to go," mother said, "my face burns with the wind, but I'll see if there's anyone going from here. I'd like you to go, won't you take her Johnny?"—

"I won't go with him," I said, getting in ahead of him.

Jack explained his side of the case. "I don't want her trailing after me. I want to go with some fellows I was talking to at the Stopping House."

The waitress solved the problem. She was a tired, sad young woman, with a drooping face and carriage and I think it was her extreme homeliness that made mother believe in her trustworthiness. She must be a good girl, with a face like that. Her hair was draggled and her mouth sagged. She looked like a doll that had been out in the rain.

Mother always took to homely people or bitter medicines. She had confidence in them. I remember once a doctor prescribed something for her and because it was pleasant to the taste she wouldn't take it. It could not possibly have any virtue.

Bertha, the waitress said, in her sad way, she would be glad to take the little girl, and she was going to the Army. Yes, she was going alone, though she might meet a friend there. But it was all right, she'd be in early, She couldn't get out before half past eight though, on account of having to do part of the dishes.

I offered to help, and Bertha said I could. "She's a nice quiet girl, I can see," mother said, when I came up to the room to get my coat and cordigans. "Now, Nellie, remember, this is a big wicked city, and you're an innocent little country girl, and don't be picking up with strangers. Your fault is you are too friendly."

I had one of the olive green homespun coats with a red flannel lining in it, a great long red scarf that wrapped around me like the Highlander's plaidie, a red toque, with a tassel and red mittens.

Bertha took my hand, and we set out, in fine spirits. There were no street lights, but never having seen street lights I did not miss them. We could see the sleighs of wheat filling the road-way dimly outlined in the frosty starlight.

"It's quite a walk," Bertha said, "but we'll go in and get warmed where the Medicine show is going on, if we can get in."

We went up Sixth Street and then climbed a stairs that creaked and groaned beneath our feet, to a hall above a harness shop.

People were standing at the back of a bright room and we pushed in. It was warm, but not pleasant, for the odors of wet fur and stale tobacco smoke polluted the air. But I wanted to hear what was going on.

A man with a red satin coat edged with gray fur, had a bottle in his hand, and a table beside him was full of similar bottles and a lady, in green satin, sat at a piano, facing the audience.

"Here it is, ladies and gents," he was saying. "The greatest living known remedy, no drugs, no stupifying narcotics but distilled from Nature's choicest, sweetest, most powerful herbs, and bitter herbs and grasses, fed by the dew and rain, and sweetened by the sun, planted on earth for suffering humanity. The old doctor's greatest discovery, Nature's own remedy to rout, dispel, and destroy disease and bring back lustre to the eyes and roses to the cheek, lightness to the step and joy to the heart, bitter on the tongue and purifying to the blood. If the blood is right, you're all right. Don't take my word for it, I'll show you what it does; Miss Lipkin show the tape worm."

The pianist lifted a glass jar from the top of the piano and held it aloft.

"Forty-one feet long, head on both ends and a knot in the middle, and this was eliminated when the second bottle was taken, by a party in your midst, whose name will not be mentioned but can be ascertained. Given up by doctors, as a last resort he tried our remedy—the great swamp root bitters, and to-day is a well man .... leaping and running as one of old. Step up ladies and gents, and spend a dollar on your health. The great health restorer. . . . What is your trouble? It can relieve them all. Floating kidneys, fallen arches, glands in the neck or sty on the eyes, boils, bunions, erosions or eruptions, the ip, the pip, the peesy-weesy, or the gout."

More people crowded in now, and we were nearer the front. The pianist was handing out the bottles and receiving the dollar bills. I had my little purse fastened into my coat pocket with a safety pin. I got it out, and extracted the one dollar it contained. It was the chance of a lifetime!

Putting the bottle inside my coat, I could hold it easily with my elbow and Bertha and I went down the stairs. "Maybe your mother won't like you spending your dollar this way," said Bertha sadly. "Oh but she will," I said quickly. "I'm glad I came, maybe this will cure her. She has headaches you know, it won't freeze under my coat, will it?" Bertha thought not.

We went down the street and came to the Army Barracks where a great crowd of people were milling around the door. Inside a drum beat, and a fife shrilled a tune. Under a street light, a man in blue uniform was leading the singing, clapping his hands together to keep them warm;—"For you there is cleansing in the blood."

A man came up to us and spoke to Bertha. "What's been keeping you?" he said crossly.

"I'll bet that's her brother," I thought.

"I came as soon as I could, Fred, honest I did, we're awful busy now, at the house."

F

Then he noticed me.

"What's this?" he asked, rudely, I thought.

She explained my presense.

"Can she get back alone? Fred asked pointedly, "we can't take her down there."

"I don't want to go Fred, not to-night. You see I got the kid on my hands."

Fred took her arm, and hustled her along, but they talked so low, I couldn't hear what they said. I followed along behind them. We came to a brilliantly lighted hall. Music, violin music, punctuated by drum beats, came out to us and the rhythmic scuffle of dancing feet. The blinds were up and I could see the dancers weaving and passing.

Fred and Bertha hesitated for a minute and I saw her hand him a slender roll of bills. A big sign in the window said: "Gent's $1.00, Ladies, free.

We went in. They had forgotten me by this time, but I followed them in.

There was one man in the middle of the room acting funny like a clown and people were laughing at him, as he snatched at the girls who danced past him. Suddenly he fell on his face and the orchestra stopped and everyone rushed together. They carried him out through a back door and the music began again, and no one seemed to think any more about him.

There were two narrow stairs leading up to a less brightly lighted place above, where I could see people eating and drinking at little tables.

Suddenly, I shrank back into my corner and pulled my toque down over my face. Jack had just come in with two other young fellows and was walking over to the place marked, "Gent's overcoats." Now, I must get out! If Jack saw me, he would feel it his duty to take me right back to the hotel. . . . . I looked for Bertha and Fred but the floor was crowded with dancers and I couldn't see them. Anyway, I could tell the man at the door who took the money, that I was going and if Bertha were looking for me—he would tell her. But I didn't think Bertha would remember anything about me. I had seen girls go into a trance of delight like this when they had a beau.

I made my escape safely for no one took the slightest notice of me. The man at the door cut short my explanations with a wave of his hand.

The air was still frosty and it smelled late. Indeed the street beyond the circle of light looked black and wicked. But I wasn't going to be afraid. There was nothing to be afraid of, and I would know the Farmer's Home when I came to it. Hotels are always open.

The street had a strange look to me as I started out. Still I could ask, if I were not sure,—but I wished Bertha hadn't deserted me.

I started off quickly, I might be afraid but I wouldn't let on I was. I'd find the Farmer's Home all right. It was just over there about a half mile;—not any farther than the cross-ways of the pasture at home. It wouldn't take me long, and I could run when I got away from the lights.

A man was walking very fast behind me, gaining on me. I was getting frightened as his heavy steps drew nearer. There was no use in running. I knew that. If you run, it shows you are afraid.

Then he called, "Hold on kid, I want to speak to you!"

I turned around and he said, "Say kid, don't get scared. Aren't you the little girl that poured tea for us to-day at the Stopping House?"

I hesitated. I did pour tea for men, once at a stopping house, but that was a long time ago, it seemed like a month.

"Yes, I did," I said and waited to see what he wanted. Now, I would know the worst. Maybe mother was right, maybe he thought I was a bold hussy and he could speak to me any way he liked.

While this was flashing through my mind, the man was saying:

"I just thought it was you when I saw you go out

and I came after you. It's late for a little girl to be out alone and there are lots of drunk men around, you might get a scare. Can I take you, wherever you want to go? I'd be glad to."

I thanked him and told him where we were staying. He didn't ask me how I came to be at the Music Hall and I did not volunteer the information.

As we walked along in the darkness he said, "I liked the way you jumped up and gave a hand to-day, at the Stopping House. It was just a little thing but it showed something of your disposition."

"Mother thinks I am too free in my ways," I said. "I do things before I think, but I can't see any harm in being friendly, I like people who are friendly with me, like you are now."

"Keep on being friendly, kid," he said, "It works both ways."

I was really very grateful to him though I did not know how to say it, and when we said goodnight in the circle of light that came through the front window of the Farmer's Home, I got a good look at him, but I never saw him again, and never knew who he was.

The next morning when we went down to breakfast, I saw Bertha making signs at me to come out. She had swung the door out just a little. So I went out to see what she had to say.

"Say, I am sorry about last night. Does your mother know? Oh, that's good, well you know, Fred would have me stay and dance and I only get to see him in the evening and sometimes not then. I was going to get him to have a dance with you. I know it would have pleased you."

"I do not dance at public dance-halls," I said with dignity, "I am quite too young for that."

My voice sounded much more like my mother's than my own. I hardly knew it.

"Fred never wants to dance with any one but me," Bertha went on rapturously, "but he would have done it, if I said so. . . . Did you notice how very handsome he is"?

"I did not!" I said truthfully.

"Oh yes," she said happily, "he is remarkably handsome of the Black Hawk type. . . . I often wonder what he sees in me."

I remembered the incident of the slender roll of bills, that changed hands outside the door, and I wondered too.

"I had not seen him for three days, until last night, and I was worried. There are plenty of women just ready to entice a handsome man away. But he's just the same dear old Fred. O, I am so much happier now, you wouldn't believe."

Her pallid face actually glowed. "You see we are almost engaged. He has given me more than one hint that he is going to propose. We have been keeping company for nearly a year now, and for the last month, we've been keeping close company."

There was a fine shading of meaning there, but it was lost on me. "It's pretty nice for a girl to have a gentleman to take her around, for no nice girl goes out alone. She would soon be talked about, if she did."

Here it was again from Bertha and again I rebelled against it. I would go out alone, any time I wanted to!

Bertha's draggled face, with her drooping wisps of hair, giving me that pathetic drowned look, kindled a sudden rage in me. What fools women were! How terribly dependent on men; and how pleased when some man, no matter how worthless, took notice of them! Bertha was rambling on.

"I often wonder what he sees in me, I am too pale to be considered really pretty, but Fred seems to depend on me some way, and you should see how he bosses me around. Sometimes you'd think we were really married."

She was simpering now and looked more horrible than ever. I couldn't think of anything to say but I was heart sorry for her. I knew, young as I was, that Bertha was a tragedy. The kitchen looked gray and greasy in the bright morning light. The table was full of dirty dishes. There was nothing ahead for her but monotonous work. She seemed very old to me, as I looked at her and I knew that Fred would take her money and break her heart. I wanted to do something about it! Just then the cook shouted at her to stop "chewin' the rag and see who was poundin' the table inside, and who did she think she was anyway?"

I went back to the dining room.

Jack joined us before we were through breakfast in fine humor. He had been up early, hitched up the team, and sold his wheat. Sixty bushels at seventy-five cents a bushel. He counted out the money on the table and gave it to mother.

She was very much pleased with him and praised him for his success in getting the load sold. I thought it was very smart of him too.

We waited until he had finished his breakfast, so we could all go together to do our buying.

"Mother, I got you a bottle of medicine last night," Jack said as he ate his porridge.

"Was it swamp root?" I asked, with a sudden fear. Now I knew what would happen. I had presented my bottle as soon as she was awake.

"Yes, how do you know, it's a new thing."

"Nellie got me one too," mother said. "You're good children to be spending your money on me, but I don't need the two bottles, so Nellie can take her's back and get her money."

"I can't do that," I said, hot for battle. "A sale is a sale, I would have no reason for taking it back."

"You can tell him your brother bought one too, that's all you need to say."

Seeing a storm about to rise, mother implored me to be quiet. "You can do it more easily than Johnny, a young man can't very well seem to change his mind, but it's different with a little girl like you, and the man who sold you the bottle, wouldn't think anything of it. Now don't be so headstrong, I'll go with you,—I'll tell him how it happened."

"Why not use both bottles," Jack said, "I know how she feels about not wanting to take it back."

"No, one bottle is enough to see if it is any good and it won't hurt her to take it back, I don't see why she is so stubborn about it."

It was the old trouble, with the old solution. Always I was the one who was expected to give in.

When we went up to our room to get our things on, to go out, I sneaked down the stairs with my bottle of Swamp Root and give it to Bertha. If anyone in the world needed it. she did; "lustre to the eye—roses to the cheek." I was sorry to see my dollar go this way, but at least the matter was settled.

Neither mother or Jack knew what I had done with the bottle, so we started out for one big day in good humor. I had pictured this shopping expedition many times, and I didn't want anything to spoil it; I hoped mother would forget about it, and to that end, kept up an animated flow of conversation regarding our purchases.

"We'll buy all the men's things first,'" mother said, "I want shirts for your father and cloth to make him a pair of pants, a suit for George and Johnny, and yarn for socks . . . overalls for the hired man. . . ."

She had her list written out and consulted it often, as we went from side to side of the big store. Our parcels were put in a big wooden box and would be left in the store until we were leaving the next morning.

I was going to get the makings of a Sunday dress, but as the piles of parcels grew, I had a momentary fear that there might be no money left to buy it. But I put that aside as an unworthy thought. What my mother promised, she fulfilled, whether of good or evil; I never knew her to break her word so I gave myself up to the enjoyment of the day.

"Don't forget your own dress," I said to her, in a

sudden warm feeling of loyalty to her. I was sorry I had
talked back to her about the medicine. I could have been
more tactful.

"We'll see how the money lasts,"—she answered, looking at her list with her brows drawn down.

"It doesn't matter much about me, I do not have to go
out and the rest of you do."

The dress goods occupied one side of the store and the
rolls of cloth were arranged diagonally on the deep
shelves. So that not only the ends but six inches of the
side of the roll could be seen. The colors were radiant,
such reds and greens, a lovely greenish blue, called electric
blue. I wished we could get that color for Hannah for it
was just like her eyes. Seal brown was what Lizzie looked
best in, to set off her hair and eyes and she was going to
have a cashmere dress of it, trimmed with velvet of the
same shade.

The clerks were very attentive and carried a chair for
mother to sit on as we went around the store. I can't
remember that there were any saleswomen; there were
many shoppers in the store and mother met one of the
women who had been tenting near us on the bank of the
Assiniboine. She had gone to Grand Valley and started
a boarding house but the town was moved to Brandon,
so they were trying to farm, but she hated it. She
had always lived in a town. She had lost little Lucy who
was the baby when we saw them in Winnipeg, but she
was buying white flannel and I knew what that meant. I
thought she ought to be glad, but she wasn't. She had
lost her teeth and looked like an old woman. Mother was
deeply sorry and kept telling her not to cry. No doubt
the worst was over . . . . but, with the callousness of
youth, I wanted to get rid of her—we should get on with
our buying.

The streets were full of men and sleighs. I had
never seen so many people. I wondered where they came
from. Oxen with their hair standing up, with the cold,
like plush, stood patiently waiting, but the poor horses

with their shorter hair and some of them unblanketed, pulled on their halters and blew their breath out in clouds of vapor.

In front of the Kelly House we saw three teams without blankets as we passed, and when we came back to the hotel for noon they were still there shivering and pawing the snow. Mother went in and spoke to the man at the desk about them, and he promised to look up the owners.

"They are somewhere in the House," he said, "and I'll get them. It is a shame to leave their horses like this."

"Look in the bar," mother said, "that's the likeliest place to find the sort of men who would leave their horses to freeze. . . .

He promised again.

When we came out we noticed there were blankets in the sleigh and Jack put them on the horses.

Mother's indignation flamed still higher, "think of that—and yet we call horses brutes. That's what liquor does to a man,—makes him forget that someone is depending on him and many a man has forgotten his wife and family, just the same way."

That night I did not get out with Bertha, for I had to go to bed early, on account of the early start, which we must make. I was very happy over our purchases. There were moccasins for everyone. Mine had a design in blue and red beads with red duffel to line them with; wool to knit stockings; a dress pattern for Lizzie; a new lamp, the biggest one I had ever seen. It would have red flannel in its bowl when it was set up. Writing paper and an envelope of pen points, 292's, and some stubs for Will, who wrote with his pen held between his little finger and the one next to it, in a very dashing way, which I would have gladly copied if I could. There were dresses for the three girls, and mine was the color I loved, a crimson cashmere and the buttons were clouded pearl.

Mother was a very careful buyer and knew that the

best quality is the cheapest in the end. She had a great love for good materials. "Even if your dress is old and patched," she would say, "you can still have pride in it, if it is of good material."

There was only one regret when we got home and that was that she had bought nothing for herself. But she made very light of it. However, the first load of grain that George took in, he bought her a dress length of Henrietta cloth, with passementerie trimmings, out of his own money.

That morning when we drove out of Brandon, with the sleigh crunching the newly fallen snow and the east reddening behind the Sand Hills, toothed with pines along the top, I was in a high state of exhilaration, and even on good terms with Jack, and prepared to admit he was a very smart boy for seventeen. A few rags of clouds idled above the Sand Hills to the east, holding the color of the sunrise.

The great yellow Court House with pale lights shining in half a dozen upper windows, threw its blue shadow over us as we passed and a heavier shadow on my elation, for I knew there was a man in a cell there who was going to be hanged the day after Christmas. He had come home drunk and shot his wife, while she was ironing and he was sorry for doing it. He told the Judge he didn't know why he had done it. I thought of him for many miles, and prayed that he might find peace for his soul, and go into his Maker's presence unafraid. God would understand better than the Judge, and do whatever should be done for him, when he passed over. The liquor business was a curse on people and I had a guilty feeling about it. We were all to blame someway, but this poor fellow was the one who had to take the punishment. My eyelashes began to freeze down, so I knew I had to stop thinking about him, and asked Jack to let me get out and run behind for a while; I said my feet were getting cold.

CHAPTER XX

CHRISTMAS DAY

CHRISTMAS was a jolly time that year. We had spruce boughs, brought from the Sandhills, across the doors and windows, and streamers of red tissue paper and red and green balls, made from tissue paper cut in circles, folded and sewed together. Mrs. Lundy had showed Hannah how to make these, when Hannah had stayed with her in the summer holidays. Mr. and Mrs. Lundy had a store about a mile east of Millford.

I remember particularly the apple-jelly tarts that we had at Christmas and how delicious they were. The apple-jelly was bright red in color, for snow apples were now sold in Mr. Lundy's store and mother had used only the parings and cores for the jelly, and the other part was made into apple sauce. Mr. and Mrs. Frank Burnett, Nina and Frankie were our guests that year. A long table was set and no one had to wait for the second table.

Mrs. Burnett was a pretty woman with hazel eyes and a fair skin and the most beautiful clothes I had ever seen. She had a dolman of smoke gray brocaded velvet and a black grosgrain silk dress with bugle trimming, and a gold bar brooch set with pearls, and ear-rings to match. She was the daughter of a well-known Montreal family and must have found the life she was now living a sad contrast to her life in the city. But she made light of the hardships of the prairie. "If only we could keep the bread from freezing" she complained once. "I cannot make very good bread anyway, but it's worse when it freezes. Even when I wrap it in Frank's fur coat, it freezes." I was not old enough to fully appreciate her gallantry of spirit but when I heard her singing to her children, "Grandpa will come with the Wo-Wo and take us away from the cold," I knew she was singing it to keep up her own spirits too.

Christmas Day has always been flavored to me with the pound cake and apple-jelly tarts of those first days in Manitoba.

The front-room always got a new coat of white-wash on the log walls at Christmas, and everything was scoured as white as sand or soap could make it. The hand-knit lace curtains, brought from Ontario, were washed and starched and stretched on home-made frames, so they would hang straight and reach the floor. Short curtains were considered slightly indecent. The two long widths of rag carpet in bright stripes with orange warp were brought out and laid on the white floor, with the good mats, one hooked and one braided. The home-made lounge had a covering of dark maroon canton flannel and was well supplied with patch work cushions, crazy pattern of silks and satins and two log cabins, one made of "stuff pieces", the other one of prints. There were two book-cases made with spools, painted black, and set with shelves and a "what-not" of five shelves, on which stood china ornaments, a shell box, with a green plush pincushion on the top, apples filled with cloves, and cups and saucers, (honorably retired from active service because of cracks, or missing handles, but with these defects tactfully concealed in the way they were placed), colored glass mugs, and on the top, a bouquet of prairie grasses, set in a frosted glass vase, a lace pattern on deep blue. I remember it well, for I broke it years later, when bouncing a ball, on the floor. Who would have thought a yarn ball would bounce so high?

When the weather got cold, the kitchen stove had to be brought into the big room, and it was a family grief when this change had to be made. If the weather did not come down too hard, the stove was kept out until after Christmas. Later when the storm doors and windows were added, and a bigger heater bought, a fine big barrel of a stove, with a row of mica windows around its middle, through which the coals glowed with all the colors of a sunset, the kitchen stove remained in the kitchen all winter.

But even when the kitchen stove was in the middle of the big room, there was a cheerful roominess about it. The woodbox papered with pictures of the Ice Palace, in Montreal, (*Family Herald Supplement*) when covered with two boards over which a quilt was spread made a nice warm seat and when we got the hanging lamp from Brandon, with a pale pink shade, on which a brown deer poised for a leap across a chasm, through which a green stream dashed in foam on the rocks, the effect was magical and in the pink light the white-washed walls were softened into alabaster.

We had two new pictures now, enlarged photographs of father and mother in heavy oak frames with a gilt edge, done by a travelling artist, who drove a team of mules and carried a few lines of tinware. Every family in the neighbohrood had taken advantage of his easy plan to secure a lasting work of art. You paid only for the frame and received the picture entirely free though this offer might be withdrawn any minute for he was doing this merely to get his work known. He said there was no nicer way to give one's parents a pleasant surprise, and the pictures would be delivered in time for Christmas. When they came, we all had a surprise. We had thought that the seven dollars and thirty-five cents paid for both frames but we were wrong. Each one cost that amount and even at that the artist was losing money. The pictures were accepted and hung on the log walls, and in the declivities behind them were kept tissue paper patterns, news-paper clippings, and other semi-precious documents, thus relieving the congestion in the real archives, lodged in the lower regions of the clock, where notes, grain-tickets, tax receipts were kept.

After the Christmas dinner of turkey and plum pudding, the men sat and talked of the trouble Louis Reil was causing. He had come back from Montana, where he had been teaching school and was now in Saskatchewan, stirring up the half-breeds and Indians and inciting them to make raids on the white settlers.

"Why don't they arrest him now, and get him safely in jail before someone is killed"? Mother was greatly disturbed over the situation. "I can't sleep," she said, "thinking of the poor women there, frightened to go to sleep at night. They say he has given guns to the Indians and there will be another massacre like there was in Minnesota."

Frank Burnett was indignant that the Government had not sent an armed force, just as soon as the trouble began.

"Uniforms would settle the trouble," he said, "the red coats and the flash of steel, a few guns fired and the half-breeds and Indians would know there was law in the country. Riel should be hanged anyway for the murder of Thos. Scott.' '

I wanted to talk. Mr. Schultz had told us about it in school. The half-breeds and Indians had a grievance, a real one. The settlers were crowding in on them, their land was being surveyed over again, and divided into squares like ours. They had long narrow lots, as they had along the Red and Assiniboine, so they could live side by side, and now a new arrangement of land was being made and they were afraid their land was going to be taken from them. When they sent letters to Ottawa, they got no replies.

I knew how they felt. I had often asked for explantations and got the prescribed 19th century dusty answer, "because I say so—that's all the reason you need". How I hated it! And how unfair I felt it to be! The Government officials were treating the Indians the same way.

I knew the government was to blame but I would not be allowed to say it, and if I did get it said, I might get

Mr. Schultz into trouble. Mother would feel he was undermining our respect for authority.

But much to my delight, Hannah came forward and defended the half breeds. Hannah was always listened to when she spoke. She had what I lacked, a quiet and dignified way of expression.

"The country belonged to the Indians and half-breeds," she said in her even voice. "We must not forget that. I know they have made little use of it and must yield it to white settlers, in time, but there's enough territory for everyone if it is handled right, and they could be easily appeased and satisfied."

She told about the new survey, about the delay in getting the patents out for the land the half-breeds had proved-up on, about the slaughter of the buffalo, the Indians' source of food, and clothing.

Hannah was fiftten then, with a fine presence, fair skin, a round face, and fine large greenish-blue eyes, and abundant bright brown hair, inclined to curl. She had been wiping dishes behind the stove and came out with a plate in one hand, and a flour-sack tea towel in the other. Her face was flushed and her eyes bright and to me she looked like Joan of Arc. I was very proud of her, but I knew there was a sudden tightening of the atmosphere. Even now, men do not like to be taught by women, but at that time for a girl of fifteen to presume to have an opinion, was against all tradition. However, Hannah had a prestige all her own.

She went on. "It is not the Catholic church, and it is not Louis Reil, who is causing the trouble—it is the stupidity of the Government at Ottawa, and if settlers are killed by the Indians their's will be the guilt. A few words of explanation, a few concessions and peace could be restored.

"My God"! exclaimed Frank Burnett in real concern, "that's hot talk, Hannah, you've said enough to hang you in some countries. If you were in Russia, you would be shot for a Nihilist, my girl."

My mother was too much amazed to speak. If I had said half of what Hannah had, she would know what to do with me, but Hannah, quiet, dignified Hannah, the image of her own mother, Margaret Fullerton McCurdy, could not be sent upstairs in disgrace.

Hannah went on wiping the dishes with great composure. She had said what she wanted to say and now withdrew from the conversation. Her hearers had heard the truth, and they could take it or leave it. Responsibility had passed from her to them.

Mr. Burnett continued the argument. "I am afraid there is bad work going on at Northfield School", he said. "I gather that is where Hannah gets her ideas. This man Schultz is a German; he has no love for British institutions and is using his position as a teacher to undermine the children's respect for authority. We'll have to look into this. We'll have to call a meeting of the trustees."

My heart stood still. Had we involved our teacher in some trouble that might lead to his losing his job?

They all began to talk; and I could feel a hostile tide of opinion gathering and sweeping ahead of it all good sense and reason and it seemed to me I would have to speak, no matter what happened. Will would listen to me anyway. I went over and stood before him.

"Will," I said, "I want to talk, make them keep quiet."

"Nellie has something on her mind," Will called out in his good humored way. "It is not often this poor tongue-tied child wants to talk, and she should get her chance on Christmas day, of all times."

Mother rose up to protest, but Will waved her back.

"Let the kid talk," he said, "talk won't hurt anyone. It's the things we don't say that hurt us, I know."

Then came the ordeal, when the silence fell on the room. I have faced audiences who were hostile since then and encountered unfriendly glances, but the antagonism here was more terrible, being directed, not as much against what I had to say, as against the fact that I dared to say anything.

I addressed Will, as people air their views in letters addressed to the Editor. "The Government is like the Machine Company, Will", I said. "The half-breeds are dissatisfied with the way they are treated, they are afraid they are going to be put off their farms, just as we were afraid when the tongue of the binder broke, and we saw we were going to lose our crop. The half-breeds have written letters, and sent people to see the Government and asked them to send out someone to straighten out their troubles, just as you, Will, wrote letters to the Company and asked them to send an expert, who would put the binder in good shape. The Government won't answer the half-breeds, won't notice them, won't talk to them—and the only word they send them is a saucy word—"what we will send you will be an army; we'll put you in your place." Just as the Machine Company wrote to us a saucy letter saying that it was our own fault if the binders broke, and they couldn't supply us with brains. It's the same spirit. We should understand how the half-breeds feel. That's all I want to say," and before anyone could say a word, I left the room, glad to get away.

Hannah came out soon after and we went upstairs and took counsel together. "Don't worry", she said to me in her comforting way, "Mr. Schultz is safely away at Pelican Lake and won't be back for two weeks. Two weeks is quite a long time—they'll cool off before that, father said there was a lot of truth in what we said, but they talked him down."

"What did Will say?" I asked anxiously.

"Oh, Will just laughed about us and said we had put the case well, but mother thinks we are in the same class as Guy Fawks who put the stick of dynamite under the House of Parliament, and she says she will go to the trustees herself, if no one else will."

Then I had something to worry over. I begged her

to tell me how this would be prevented. She shook her head, but her coolness comforted me.

"The Lord will provide", she said airily, "Listen! the dogs are barking! Someone is coming."

She thawed an eye-hole in the frozen window and looked out. "'People from Millford", she called back to me cheerfully, "cheer up, brother Ridley—we won't be shot today."

Visitors were never more welcome to us than they were at that moment, for we knew that mother would rise to the occasion and the subject would be dropped for the day, at least.

It was no wonder people liked to come to our house, for mother was never happier than when she was pouring a cup of tea, and serving a visitor with some of her own good cooking.

When she would fall into low spirits, the first few years we were in the country and sit drooping and sad under the pall of loneliness that wrapped us around for many months in the year, Hannah and I used to look eagerly across the waste of snow, hoping we would see someone coming. Sometimes we would climb to the top of the stable to get a wider view; and the one on the ground would solemnly ask the one who had gone aloft, "Sister Ann, Sister Ann, do you see anybody coming?"

Once when I was on the ground and asked the question of Hannah, who was balancing herself on the ridge pole of the stable, she held her two arms up to get the breeze and solemnly replied.

"I see the snow drifting,
   And feel the wind shifting,
 And e'er the sun is higher
   A traveller draweth nigher,
So let our gloom be lifting
   Hence, minion, mend the fire!
 And tell your angel mother
   To cease from idle weeping
And let the tea be steeping."

I never knew whether Hannah made up her rhymes carefully beforehand or like Alan-Bane in the Lady of the Lake, had the gift of minstrelsy. There was no way of finding out either.

I can't remember whether I went down stairs or not that day. For if my mother said she would go to the trustees, she would. She had a sense of duty that would drive her through fire and water. I knew she was wrong this time and that hurt me, for I loved my mother and understood the working of her mind. She was above all things, loyal to her own. Her family, her relatives, her country. She was critical of us, and set forth our faults in plain language, for she was anxious to make us what she thought we ought to be, but if anyone else found fault with us, she would spring to our defence, without question. She saw nothing but virtue in her own relatives or at least admitted nothing but virtue and had a fine scorn for men or women who criticized their husbands or wives to outsiders, or slandered any member of their own family connection. Family loyalty was woven into her life's pattern. "It's an ill bird that fouls its own nest", was her comment when anyone tried to tell her their family troubles.

So it was with her country. Great Britain was the greatest and best and most God-fearing country in the world, and Queen Victoria was the hand-maiden of the Lord. Mother had seen her once in her widow's mourning, driving in an open carriage through the streets of Dundee and loved her with a passionate devotion.

So she would be very high-minded in her visit to the trustees, when she went to complain of Mr. Schultz' teaching, and she might even come to the school and reprimand Mr. Schultz before us all. He would be very polite with her, for I know he had a high regard for her, but the scene would be too terrible to think of. She wouldn't reason, or listen to reason, for her mind was made up. And it would end in a high note of tragedy for she would walk out with her head up, calling on Hannah and me to follow!

And what would we do? Knowing her to be wrong?

And yet how can anyone desert their mother! I knew then what Christ meant when he said that is just what you may have to do if you swear allegiance to the truth. But I knew I wasn't ready for this.

If ever I prayed in my life, I prayed then that the decision would not have to be made, that somehow it would not come to this!

Mother had had one serious illness since we came to Manitoba, an illness that came on suddenly, almost like a "stroke" and I was fearful that the excitement of a visit to the school might bring a repetition, and this dark and stifling fear was on me day and night during the holidays that year, and even when sleigh riding down the steep bank of the creek north of the house, when Hannah and I played out each fine day. I loved the swift rush of the runners over the hard drifts and the impact of cold air on my face, with an occasional spill at the bottom when the sleigh shot on without us, I loved it for it made me, for one brief moment, forget.

CHAPTER XXI

A Visit From the Teacher

WHEN school began in January I knew we were skating on thin ice, the break might come any day and I was so worried over it I could not sleep or eat. Mother was sure I was growing too fast and saw to it that I drank a quart of milk each day, which had no effect on me, except to keep me from liking milk all my life. I was sure she was going to carry out her threat of visiting the school for I never knew mother to break her word. That was another motif in her life's pattern. How I wished she were less conscientious, though I remembered how I gloried in the story of her going to the Settlement School on the Common, where Will attended when he was a little boy, before the Public schools came in Ontario and reprimanding the teacher, a bad tempered old soldier, for his cruelty to another boy. Will had come home in tears because of the unmerciful beating given to his little friend, an orphan boy, who lived with his uncle, and mother had gone in all haste to the log school with fire in her eye and put the fear of death into the brutal teacher. I thought this was a very fine thing for her to do, and I knew she was quite as conscientious now in her intention of protesting against what she thought was false teaching at Northfield.

My general listlessness and lack of appetite diverted her mind and I tried to feel that I was a martyr in the cause of freedom, but I couldn't get any sensation from my state of mind, but a sort of dull despair, and when I was kept home from school, the sorrows of life overflowed my young soul .

I knew Hannah had a better philosophy of life than I had and vainly tried to lay hold on it.

"Don't worry over anything before it happens and don't worry then. Let things happen—if they must, you can't stop them anyway. You're foolish to be losing your time and energy when you should be studying. Work so hard, you can't think."

Looking back at it, I wonder what power nineteenth century parents had over their children and how did they hold it. I was not a particularly meek young person, but I could not stand up to my mother, even knowing that she was wrong.

But one day deliverance came as easily as a sunbeam comes in at a window. I was out tying in the cows and doing up the evening chores, for the three boys were away to Brandon with loads of wheat, when I saw Hannah coming down the snowy road, with Bert Ingram and Mr. Schultz. I wondered if Mr. Schultz was coming in. Had he heard that mother was on the war path, and had come over to see her? I knew she would be polite to him, if he came in—that was another part of her pattern.—"Let it never be said that you were ill-mannered in your own house." I stayed out in the stable until I was all but frozen. When at last I went in, what a sight met my eyes.!

Mr. Schultz sat beside the stove, in the big rocking chair, drinking a steaming cup of beef-broth. He greeted me affectionately. "I came over to see you, Nellie", he said, with his ready smile. "Hannah tells me you are not feeling well and I am a bit under the weather myself, so I came over to get a bit of your mother's good nursing too. I just couldn't go back to a cold house tonight and frozen bread. Newt Thompson is hauling out wheat, too.

Mr. Schultz lived with Newton Thompson on the farm south west of us. They did their own cooking.

"If you are not feeling better tomorrow morning", mother said, spreading a blanket over his knees, "I'll keep you in bed. Hannah can look after the school for you very well and a day in bed will break your cold. Hannah

put the black pot full of coals upstairs in the boys' room
—it will take the chill off the air."

We had a wonderful evening under the hanging lamp
with its fringe of crystal beads.

After a hot dinner and a dose of mother's cough
syrup of honey, butter and vinegar, Mr. Schultz declared
himself to be on the highway of recovery. He said he
did not believe he would need the foot-bath of mustard
water and the reason for his reluctance came out later.
He had holes in his socks, and did not want to let that
be known. "Maggie would kill me if she knew I was
going around like this", he laughed. "Maggie", was
Mrs. Schultz who lived on their homestead near Pelican
Lake.

Then mother decided that he must have a new pair of
socks and she would finish a pair she had on the needles.
"This is the last of my yarn", she said wistfully, "my own
carding and spinning and I will be glad to have you take
them."

"I will be proud to own them", he said as he thanked
her warmly. "Proud indeed, but I will not let them be
worn out, for they are a symbol of an era in our history
that is passing. Hand work is being superseded by machinery, and the fine creative household arts will be
forgotten."

She tossed him the finished one, as she set to work to
take off the toe of its mate and he examined it admiringly.
"Women are very resourceful", he said, as he watched
her bringing the other one to completion. "They have
seized all the resources at their hands and fashioned
them to human needs, with great cleverness. Can you
knit?" he asked me suddenly.

"Not very well", I confessed—"I am afraid I do not
like it."

"Learn all you can from your mother, Nellie," he said.
"You'll be proud of her skill when you grow up, you'll be
glad to boast of it. Just think of what these socks mean.
Wool on a sheep's back, converted into socks on a man's

feet, and all done by one pair of skillful hands. And you didn't bring your spinning wheel or loom, Mrs. Mooney? Too bad, they would be great treasures in forty years or less. You would be asked to loan them for art exhibits and it would be a great source of interest for the young women to see how you made cloth, and set the patterns. Why didn't you bring them?" he asked, after a pause.

Mother hesitated—it was a tender subject. "I wanted to", she said, "for I loved doing these things, and never was happier than when I set the shuttle in the loom, but Will was against it—he said we were getting away from all this. I know how the young people feel too, though it hurts me to see it. They are a little bit ashamed of home-made stuff. They want machine-made clothes. They are dressier and more the style. Hand-made cloth will wear ten times as long, but that's not what they want. . . . It was a kindness too, on Willie's part—he knew I had plenty to do without weaving, but weaving was not work—it was my pleasure—because. . . ."

"Because you were creating something", Mr. Schultz finished for her, "something beautiful as well as useful."

She nodded her head, and went on with her knitting in silence.

The conversation turned to the trouble in the North West, but fortunately mother was busy counting stitches as she finished the sock, and so said nothing.

"It was too bad the half-breeds sent for Riel," Mr. Schultz said, "he was safely away in Montana, teaching school and doing very well, for he's well fitted for teaching. But in their distress they turned to him, and asked him, coaxed him to come. He can talk well, and write well, and they knew he is sincere. If the Government had had the good sense to send out a man who would explain away their troubles, they would have never thought of Riel. I've heard him speak many times, and talked to him and I believe he is sincere, but he is flighty, and emotional, and fanatical. Sincerity may be a curse to

people, when there is not good judgment to guide it.
Look at Bloody Mary, she was certainly sincere, but that
sincerity took the form of killing Protestants. She believed she was doing them a good turn, killing their
bodies, and thus saving their souls from heresy."

He told us about the first Rebellion in 1870. He had
heard it discussed in Kildonan, where he had taught
before he came to us. Kildonan being near to Winnipeg
was in the affected area, and the events of 1870 were
fresh in the minds of the people there.

"The trouble was stirred up largely because of the
overbearing ways of some of the government's agents,"
he said. "They belittled the half-breeds, sneered at them,
they were "dirty half-breeds." Letters were written back
to the papers in Toronto making fun of the natives, by
some members of the Snow Commission, who had been
sent out to investigate conditions. Insulting letters,
smart-aleck letters, the writers of which did not think
the half-breeds would ever see them, but the printed page
has wings. Good manners would have saved the whole
situation, just as good manners will hold a home together and bad manners can destroy a home.

The ill-feeling between England and Scotland was
kept alive the same way. . . . Words, words—the tongue
is an unruly member. You know what the Bible says
'about a soft answer turning away wrath'. . . . It does."

He turned to my father.

"Strange isn't it, Mr. Mooney," he said, "that after
more than eighteen hundred years of Christian teaching, there is so little of real Christianity in the world.
Governments still think a bullet is the best argument."

"It will come," father said slowly, "but we all have to
work for it—line upon line, precept upon precept, here a
little and there a little, and you are doing something
yourself, I can see. Get the minds of children set in the
right mould and in one generation the world could be
changed."

I remember the glamorous happiness of that evening. My burden was gone. I was no longer afraid.

Father liked a bowl of gruel before going to bed— it warmed the marrow in his bones he said. That night, the black pot of oatmeal porridge was put on early, and simmered on the back of the stove, while we talked, and at ten o'clock we all had a bowl of gruel, flavored with nutmeg, and piping hot.

Mr. Schultz declared he was going to institute this fine custom at once, "but you'll have to show me how you do it," he said to mother. "There's a trick in this, I never tasted gruel like this. The kind of gruel the boys in Squeers' School got was described by Dickens as 'diluted pincushions', and I always thought that was about what it was everywhere. I've learned something tonight. This is delicious."

The evening ended on a high note. I was very proud of my family which is surely one of the most satisfying emotions a child can have. That night I noticed for the first time, that nutmeg is a sweet, significant, honest, homely flavor, and to this day, it brings back soothing memories. It is the incense that rises from the happy hearths of contented people, and has in it the solidity of the soil, the blessing of the hour of rest, the essence of goodwill and neighborliness, Nutmeg! I rank it with lilacs after rain, and wild rose leaves pressed in the pages of an old school book!

I went to school the next day feeling as well as I ever did in my life.

After Mr. Schultz goodwill visit, life settled into a pleasant round. Nap had quite recovered and grown to be a bigger dog than he had been before, and now, almost the size of his Newfoundland ancestor, he was the finest sleigh-dog in the neighborhood.

John Rae, a neighbor, for whom Mother baked bread, had made me a little hand sleigh with steel-shod runners, and painted a dazzling red, with my initials in black paint, on the middle of the top, and I had an elaborate harness for Nap, made by myself from straps and snaps taken from old horse harness. Harness making occupied a large place in my life at this time, and I was quite handy with a canvas needle, linen thread, bees wax and binding twine; and when some one gave me a string of shining bells to buckle around Nap's ample chest, I felt I had a very creditable turn-out. I have always felt that a real good harness-maker was lost to the world when I began to do other things.

With this fine equipment, I carried on a very nice freighting business from Millford each Saturday morning.

I rode going to Millford, with my moccasined feet stuck under the cross bar of the sleigh to hold me on, as Nap galloped over the drifts. But coming home, with a load of groceries tightly roped on the sleigh I walked behind and carried the mail in my leather book-bag slung over my shoulder. Always there was the *Family Herald*, with its great wealth of reading, from Family Remedies and the Etiquette Department to the continued story and the Irish News for father.

Remembering his delight and interest in the pathetically bare little colums, given each week, a sorrow comes over me, as I write these words. Why didn't we subscribe for an Irish newspaper for him? It would have pleased him like nothing else. This business of remembering is heavy work at times, so many things come back out of the past to stab me. I know my father was bitterly homesick for his Irish glens, after we came to Manitoba. It was not the stony soil of the Garafraxa he remembered with longing, it was the misty bogs of Tipperary with the little hummocks standing up like islands in a silver sea; he often told me there was music in the very air of Ireland, crickets in the grass, the whirring of wings at nightfall, and more than that, a gentle soft piping that is both merry and sad, and can turn the very heart in you. I asked him is this was the music of the little people who dance on the leaves and he said he was not rightly sure, but he had heard it many a time.

I do not know why we did not persuade him to go back to see the old home. Of course, the expense was a barrier at first, but good years came later, and money was no longer the question that decided everything. But we thought of Ireland as a poverty-stricken country, mouldy with rain, a country of tumble-down cabins, tragic old people, rebellious young people, waiting for a boat to take them to America, and we thought he was well away from it. But I know now that to the end of his life he was under the spell of the mystic beauty of his native land, and in his dreams he saw again the blue hills of Tipperary and smelled the turf fires burning in the bog.

But I was telling about our enjoyment of the weekly newspaper. The continued story was really the high point of interest for we had a whole week to speculate on the development of the plot. There was one story that shook our neighborhood to its foundation. It was called *Saved, or the Bride's Sacrifice,* and concerned two beautiful girls,—Jessie, fair as a lily, and Helen with blue black hair and lustrous eyes as deep as night. They each loved Herbert, and Herbert, being an obliging young fellow, not wishing to hurt anyone's feelings, married one secretly and hurriedly by the light of a guttering candle, in a peasant's hut, (Jessie), and one openly with peal of organ and general high jinks, at her father's baronial castle, (Helen).

This naturally brought on complications. There were storms and shipwrecks, and secret meetings in caves, with the tide rising over the rocks and curlews screaming in the blast, there were plottings and whisperings; a woman with second sight and one with the evil eye. And did we love it?

I can remember staggering along through the snow, behind the sleigh reading the story as I walked and when I drew near home, members of the family would come out to shout at me to hurry.

CHAPTER XXII

TROUBLE IN THE NORTH WEST

AS the winter wore away, and signs of spring began to
come in the honey combed snowdrifts that lowered and
blackened in the soft March winds, we became more and
more agitated by the news that came through from the
North West.

Two women, Mrs. Delaney and Mrs. Gavanlock were
taken prisoners by the Indians and raids had been made
on the settlers' horses and cattle. The fate of the women
was a shivery subject for conversation. Up to that time
the "trouble" was a vague and abstract state, far away
and impersonal, but now the menace had come out into
the open, and the evil had assumed shape and image;
painted savages, brandishing tomahawks and uttering
blood-curdling cries had swarmed around the lonely and
defenceless farm houses, and overpowered these two women and carried them away to the Indian teepees somewhere in the wood, holding them as hostages.

The newspapers flared with the news; and every inch
of print was read and re-read by us. The Naismiths
took the Arnprior *Chronicle,* the Ingrams, the Woodstock
Sentinel, and we had the Owen Sound *Advertiser* and the
Family Herald. But the news was old when we got it
and that worried us too. Under the strain of anxiety
the neighbors came together more, and there were many
gatherings at our house. When the boys came home
from Brandon, they brought more newspapers and much
oral news. Sometimes they saw the troops going through
on the train, with the cheering crowds at the station.

On the occasion of these gatherings, every wild
scheme was advocated. We should build a fort in Millford, using the mill for the main room, boring port holes
in the walls for the rifles and putting in flour and bacon

and potatoes, in case of a siege. There were four rifles in the neighborhood and two shot guns. There were persistent rumors of a "rising" at Swan Lake and Marieapolis on the Indian reserves there.

My mother stood firmly by her belief that the Indians would not hurt the women. "Women are safer with Indians than they would be with some white men," she said, but she was talked down by the others, who had terrible tales to tell of atrocities in Minnesota and it seems that most of them had relatives who survived that terrible time.

At that stage in the conversation I was always sent to bed.

"Hannah take Nellie to bed—see that she stays there."

Now Hannah was a stern and conscientious jailer but a very pleasant one too.

"Your business and mine is to get on with our school work, and not be turned aside even by Indians," she explained to me one night above the sound of excited voices in the room below.

"But if the Indians should come, what would we do?" I begged her to tell me.

"Nothing that we can arrange now," she said. "You can't get ready for Indians, but I'm not afraid of Indians; especially our own Indians who come selling baskets. They're friendly and they don't know anything about the trouble in Saskatchewan. They can't read and the trouble is three hundred miles away. Anyway, it's in Saskatchewan and this is Manitoba: now I'll hear you your spellings and don't try to listen to that clatter. They're having a good time. It's as exciting as the First of July picnic or a barn raising. Jack Naismith and our Jack are killing Indians by the dozen in their minds and piling them up like cordwood and it's not hurting anyone. I wish Lizzie didn't have to stay down there for she hates all this awful talk. But she has to stay to feed the crowd. You and I are well out of it."

At night when I wakened in fear, dreaming of shrieking savages with burning brands in their hands, I was comforted and reassured by Hannah's regular breathing. No terrifying dream disturbed her rest and I kept telling myself if the Indians did come to kill us in a red rage of anger, Hannah would talk them out of it, and mother would make tea for them and feed them currant buns and get them persuaded to go back, and make their baskets and behave themselves.

One day in the early spring the cry arose at Northfield school that the Indians were coming! Coming in their carts in a procession a mile long, Billy Day said. Someone had seen them winding around Pelican Lake like a jointed snake, as far as the eye could see. They were all in war paint and feathers and their carts were creaking like ten thousand wolves howling and they were coming this way.

Billy had been staying home to seed, but no one could stay at home after hearing news like this, so he came riding on horseback; and rushed into the school, breathless with haste, and so pale the freckles stood out like bran on his face.

Consternation sat on every face as Bill's excitement spread.

"Sit down, Bill," Mr. Schultz said quietly, "school is in."

Bill shouted his message again.

"Yes, I know," said the teached unmoved, "they come every spring, on their way to Brandon. I've been expecting them. These Indians are no relation to the Indians in Saskatchewan. They are Crees, and ours are Sioux and they are not friends. They won't hurt anyone, certainly they wouldn't fight for the Crees. Indians have their friends just like white people."

"Dad said to tell everyone to get their guns loaded and shoot to kill," Bill cried. Things weren't breaking as well as he thought.

"Now listen, Bill, and all of you," Mr. Schultz' eyes

glowed now; and pink spots came out on his cheeks, "a shot fired would be fatal. These Indians are friendly. I know Indians. They are peaceful people until they get frightened and you know how even a quiet dog will bite when taken by surprise. They are like that. The Custer massacre happened because some white fool shot at three Indians, who came to a house to ask for something to eat; and the Indians got frightened and shot back. My wife and the two little boys are alone, in a house right beside the trail, where the Indians pass and I know they are safe. I think I will let you all go home and tell your people not to be afraid, just buy their baskets the same as ever, and give them tea or whatever they want; and don't let on you know there is any trouble."

We rushed for our things and came out into the sunshine. Bill was in a rage at the turn of affairs. "The teacher is yellow," he said, "he's afraid, that's what he is. My dad ain't, you bet, and he'll take a shot at the redskins; he says, there's only one good Indian and he's a dead one."

It was one of those breathing days in spring, when mist comes from the soil, and the sun draws the young plants out of the ground. There was a palpitation in the air, a sense of movement and growth. Every sound was magnified in the still air, The hens' cackle and the rooster's crowing in Davy Dick's farm yard a mile from us, sounded clearly on the air. Tommy Kennedy put his ear to the ground and motioned to us to keep quiet. He sprang up hastily.

"Gol, they're comin'," he shouted, "I hear carts squealin' in the hills, but they're only a few, and they're not comin' this way."

Mr. Schultz came out bare-headed and spoke to us again. "Now don't get excited," he said, "remember this country all belonged to the Indians once and they see us as usurpers. We took their land and drove out their best friend, the buffalo. Use your imaginations now, and think what you would feel like, if you saw another

race living on the land that had been yours; another
color; other ways of living; feeling themselves superior.
I'll stay here and talk to them—they will have to come
this way and don't let a gun be seen; go now, young
messengers of good will, you have a real duty to
perform."

We went; we raced like the wind, watching the Tiger
Hills, south of us, for some sign of the long caravan of
creaking carts, that Bill had said was on its way.

We were tingling with excitement and thrilling with
a sense of adventure. Now we knew how the heroes of
the Fiery Cross could run so far. Our feet were shod
with speed, that ate up the miles.

Nap met me at the usual place, and even he was
bristled up and barked at us. He had something on his
mind too; but we hadn't time to bother with him, beyond
yelling at him to shut up.

We were half way from Will's house to ours before
we noticed strange objects in our yard, Indian carts—
Indian ponies hitched to carts and strange dogs.

Nap barked out again a "didn't I tell you" bark.

What would we do? Hide down by the creek in the
bushes? Run back to the school? We paused for a
moment, irresolute. No, there was only one thing to do,
we must go on. We saw there were three carts
and the ponies had wandered over to the oat stack and
were pulling out the straws. Nap bristled up to twice
his size and stepped like a hackney at the sight of two
Indian dogs with curled tails, under the carts, as
peacefully withdrawn from public affairs as dogs could
very well be, but Nap resented their presence, on his
territory and began a preliminary growl in the back of
his throat.

"There can't be anything wrong," Hannah said, but I
could feel my heart beating in my throat. All the stories
I ever heard of Indans and their evil ways came to my
mind. I thought of the Donnelly murder in Bedolph and
of how young Jim Donnelly escaped by being at a neigh-

bor's house that night, the only one of the family to survive.

But nothing could be more peaceful than the farm yard that moment. Hens and chickens circled the space in front of the horse stables, the hens scratching and calling, and the little balls of feathers coming in like the spokes of a wheel, a rooster crowed from the top of a manure pile that steamed in the warm air, cows lay at ease beside the straw stack, for there was no green grass yet to tempt them away from the oat straw.

On the three sides of the group of buildings, the creek ran full between its low banks, with a brown glint in its swift current. White clouds loitered above us in the blue sky; every aspect of the day and the place spoke of peace.

Hannah did not falter in her gait, and I followed her. When we opened the kitchen door the room seemed to be full of Indians; at least the floor was covered by them, for with their blankets and shawls, one squaw, with a papoose can cover much space; the acrid smell of burned willow roots and tanned hide filled the air.

On the other side of the stove, with the oven open open, Mother sat in a rocking chair, with a flannel on her knee on which lay an Indian baby, a poor little wrinkled thing with a face like an old man, whimpering softly like a sick puppy. She was rubbing its chest with goose-grease. The mother, a young squaw, was on her knees watching with impassive face.

The table was full of their baskets and the kettle on the stove was beginning to steam. Lizzie was in the pantry buttering bread.

"Shut the door, girls," Mother said, "and come in, and see what I have. Yes, he's been sick, poor little fellow, but I think he'll be better now. He has had a heavy cold on his chest, and needs to be more warmly dressed. Now look, Mary Paul, roll him up this way, so his feet won't come out, keep his feet warm and his head cool. Yes, keep the flannel on him and rub him each night with this; giving him two or three drops like this, see, no more than this—it will loosen his cough."

She handed the baby back to his mother and a succession of appreciative grunts came from the circle. The young mother said something we did not understand but her face lost its mask of indifference. She actually smiled as she took the baby in her arms.

Another squaw came over to where mother sat and showed a sore ear, moaning as she touched it with her grimy hand. After the ear had been washed with soap and water, a few drops of laudanum were put in, and an onion was put in the ashes to roast, and when it was well heated through, it was cautiously put on the sore ear and bandaged with a white rag.

Before the visit was over, it appeared that all of the squaws were birds with broken pinions. The last one, a big woman who smoked a short clay pipe, complained of a pain in her stomach and received a generous draught of baking soda. The two men were evidently sound or at least did not reveal their ailments. But they drank cups of tea with every sign of delight and ate heartily.

It was well on to the middle of the afternoon when they left—mother bought two baskets from them and just as they were leaving the sick baby's mother went out to her cart and brought in a mat of sweet grass in which was woven a pattern of porcupine quills, and gave it to mother.

They went the rounds of the neighborhood, and were so well fed and showered with gifts of flour, potatoes, eggs and butter that they must have wondered, if Indians do wonder, at the sudden warming of hearts that had taken place. Houses that had been closed and locked to them, on former visits, while the owners had looked out from behind the edge of factory cotton blinds, now were opened hospitably and kettles were boiled and meat was fried for the visiting delegates. So it came about that the misdeeds of their brethren in the North West brought gifts and friendliness to the Indians at

Pelican Lake, and they, very wisely, took the tide, as it served.

The "risin'" that Bill's friend had seen coming round the end of the lake, like a jointed snake, must have been lost in the labyrinthine hills, for the three carts were the only Indian visitors until the following autumn, when the trouble was over.

The day that the sick Indian baby got his rubbing of goose grease, was April 24th, the day that guns roared at Fish Creek.

The *Family Herald* were advertising a cheap rate in their daily paper—three months for $2.00, and I determined to get it. I had a feeling that daily news was what we needed, in this time of great import. So I sold my best white duck to Mrs. Kennedy who paid me $1.50 and I had the other fifty cents (won from Jack on a bet. He bet I could not finish the stockings I was knitting in a week, and I did, though it nearly killed me, for I was a slow knitter). I sent away for the paper and I think I expected to get one each day, for when five of them arrived on mail day at Millford, not one date any later than the *Weekly Star*, I felt a bit cheated, but I carried one to school each day, still unwrapped, and so the prestige I hoped to win, was not all lost.

We had a map on the board and followed the troops, under General Middleton, as well as we could; and talked long and loud, and earnestly over the daily reports, before and after school and at noon hour. Piapot, Poundmaker, Big Bear, and Louis David Riel and Gabriel Dumont's pictures were stuck on the wall with molasses, furnished by Thos. James Kennedy's lunch. We dwelt in the midst of alarms, but no one ever enjoyed it more.

At noon, we played one game and one only. Indians and soldiers. I was an Indian Chief (Poundmaker) and had a red and yellow lap-robe for my blanket. Billy Day led the Free Lances, a force of young bloods who fired on the Indians at all times, even when we—the Indians—were holding a parley with the Government forces led by Bert Ingram who was General Middleton. We had to expect the odd death-tipped arrow from Billy's forces, who did not believe in any other means of communication. No talk, no conferences, no truce, just extermination. "If I don't get him—he gits me" was Billy's slogan, and so in this way we had all the excitement of a three-cornered conflict.

I made a good Poundmaker, for I had the two long braids of hair, with moccasin laces braided in, and tied at the ends; and as chief I had many opportunities for making speeches.

Bert's forces were very active and spent much time in throwing up breast work, which meant moving the wood pile and arranging for port holes for their rifles.

My forces had bows and arrows of home manufacture, decorated with tufts of red and blue yarn, and we beat the tom-toms as we advanced on the Fort and ki-yied. The tin lids of dinner pails make very good tom-toms.

While we circled and ambushed and surrendered and fought and died outside, Hannah sat at her desk, taking no time for play but improving every dull or shining minute, as she poured over Lord's big blue History or "factored" great long phrases of x's and y's and z's with a springling of a's, b's and c's.

I felt a bit guilty about the time I was spending as Poundmaker, but it was too much fun to forego, and I loved making up his speeches about waving grass and running streams, waning moons and setting suns, with plenty of references to the White Queen across the shoreless waters.

CHAPTER XXIII

THE TRAGIC ENDING

WHEN in July the news came that the North West rebellion was over and Riel captured a great wave of thanksgiving swept over Western Canada, not entirely free from a bit of disappointment that our excitement would now die down. However, there was still the fertile field of speculation as to the final outcome.

The die-hards cried out for blood. The death of Thomas Scott in the first Rebellion, fifteen years before, must be avenged; no mercy had been shown to him. But the moderate party, of which Mr. Schultz was the leader, believed that no good end could be served by Riel's death, for he would thereby become a martyr in the eyes of the Metis, his followers, and great bitterness would result, and surely if there had been wrong-doing on the part of the half-breeds, they were now broken, scattered and utterly defeated. They were our own people after all and it was always the part of wisdom to show mercy in the hour of triumph.

Mr. Schultz did not think that the Government had any desire for further retaliation, and thought they would have been relieved if Riel had escaped after the final rout at Batoche. It was rumoured that he might easily have done so, and made his way unmolested back to his home across the border in Montana. But he did not want to escape, for it was his desire to defend the half-breeds in an open court where he would have the ear of the whole country.

Each week we read the *Family Herald* and the Brandon *Times* for the last word on the situation and waited anxiously for the trial which was going to be held in Regina where Riel was imprisoned.

Riel wanted to make his own defence and refused the offer of counsel. But in spite of this the Government sent two famous lawyers from Montreal to defend him, and they without consulting him, decided to enter the plea of insanity as the surest way of saving his life, and there is but little doubt that they would have succeeded but for Riel himself, who, stung by their arguments, forgot his intention of presenting the case for the half-breeds and spent all his time trying to establish the fact that he was perfectly sane.

He could have saved himself, we thought, if he had carried out his original plan, but, as it was, he made a poor impression upon the court and alienated public sympathy. The whole trial was a tragedy of cross purposes, and the verdict of the court was that he was guilty of treason. The date of his execution was set for October but on appeal to the Judge twenty-nine days more of life were granted to the condemned man to allow him to finish the Memoirs he was writing. He wrote a letter to the Judge thanking him for this favor and praying that one year for each day would be added to his life for this act of clemency.

We did not believe he would be hanged. A reprieve would surely come. We had read about reprieves and a very thrilling business it was with a dishevelled rider, on a foaming horse galloping up to the foot of the gallows waving a document and shouting "The pardon of the King."

As the seventh of November drew near we talked of nothing else as we walked the two miles night and morning to school in the crisp autumn weather. We had convinced ourselves that Riel would be pardoned basing our hopes on the fact that a Commission had been sent out to the half-breeds and all the difficulties had been settled so we argued that Riel and his followers had not asked anything unreasonable, and we knew that the French people were asking for his pardon. A reprieve would surely come and we loved to picture the scene though

Hannah said there would not be a galloping horse, that was all out of date. The pardon would come by telegraph if it came at all.

But we set that aside. Perhaps the wires would be down. We were so sure that a reprieve, or a pardon, would come that we arranged the scene and if we could have been free from the restraining presence of the teacher for one noon hour we would have acted it. Joe Rothwell had his pony and he would have ridden in with a clatter of hooves from a mile down the road, rising in his stirrups, and shouting. He had the best part of all. We painted the scene with a broad brush.

Dawn in the cold grey jail-yard of the Mounted Police barracks in Regina, on the morning of November the seventh. The melancholy procession from the death cell. The guards pale and wretched, hating their job, hands trembling, teeth chattering. Louis David Riel pale but calm with head erect walks to the scaffold and mounts the steps, without a quiver, disdaining the hand of the guard who would have helped him. . . . He stands aloft, a gallant figure of a man against the flushing sky. . . . When asked if he desires to speak, he shakes his head and cries "God is my judge and to Him I commit my soul." When the bandage is put over his eyes he politely thanks the hangman and holds it away from his eyes for one moment while he looks around the landscape and up at the clouds flecked with sunrise. . . . Then pulls it down and gives his hands to be pinned behind his back and waits. . . . The priest begins the prayer for the passing soul and the noose is placed over his head. . . .

A shout goes up from the guard at the Barracks gate and the hangman stops with his foot on the trap. There is a thunder of hooves on the frozen ground, and a foaming horse is reined back on his haunches and the rider flings himself out of the saddle srying one word that runs from lip to lip, 'The pardon has come.'

It was a great scene and we were not the only people who thought and hoped and prayed for this ending but it was decreed otherwise. The distracted Cabinet at Ottawa had argued and reasoned and disputed up to midnight the night before uncertain of what course they should take— weighing every political advantage, and disadvantage. When we heard that the sentence had been carried out we were shocked into silence and we stopped talking about it.

We read in the *Family Herald* that there were riots in the streets of Montreal when the news of the hanging broke and that the effigy of Sir John A. Macdonald had been burned on a public square. One of the leaders of a hostile demonstration was a young Frenchman who said that he too would have shouldered his rifle if he had been a half-breed on the banks of the Saskatchewan, and when the House of Commons assembled he defended the rebels in a fiery speech that had never been surpassed in eloquence. In it he taunted the Government that they had granted everything the half-breeds had asked for but not until all the harm had been done and the blood spilled and the bitter wedge put between the two races in Canada.

His name was Wilfrid Laurier.

CHAPTER XXIV

THE DRAMATEURS

OUR next venture in dramatization was made a year afterwards in the safe realm of fiction. We decided to do something for Millford School, five miles away, for their closing exercises.

Millford School had paid us a visit on several occasions, and on May 24th had beaten us in a spelling match, (who would have thought that "skilful" would have only one "l") ; and by way of return we set about to produce a scene from "Ten Nights in a Bar-room" to give at their closing concert on the last day in June.

We had worked more than a month on it, and rehearsed it in the shade of the sun-baked woodpile every day at noon. We made our own properties, had written our own lines, and now, in our best clothes, carrying our shoes to save them from the dust of the prairie trail, we were on our way to fame and glory.

The hot moist air of June was heavily freighted with the sweetness of wolf willow blossoms, as our little band of bare-footed pilgrims took their way over the North trail. Bob, who played the part of Simon Slade, the fat and prosperous proprietor of the "Sheaf and Sickle", carried his own bar, a high bench painted barn-red. The bottles, of which we carried a generous supply, were distributed among all the members of the caste, and stuck out of pockets and dinner pails, giving our band a rakish and sinister appearance which must have been offset somewhat by our serious young faces.

I, being poor Fanny Morgan, the drunkard's wife, carried, carefully wrapped in a big newspaper, my mother's shawl, which had come from Dundee. It was a green shawl, with red, yellow, and black lines, making an elaborate pattern, and it had belonged to my grand-mother. . . . I had not asked my mother for it. I knew I could not convince her of how badly I needed it, and I couldn't ask any of the other women for a shawl when there was one in my own family. So I took it—and that lay heavily on my conscience . . . but what could I do? I had to carry the baby in a shawl, when I went to Simon Slade's barroom to look for Henry.

We had come straight from school, and walked the five miles, carrying the remains of our dinner in the tin pails, and we had our last rehearsal when we stopped to eat, at the junction of Spring Brook and Oak Creek. But first we washed our feet, put on our shoes, and the ladies of the party released their hair from its many tight braids; then we set up our red bar on the gravelly shore, and put on our act, glad to get one chance to present it undis-turbed by the young dissenters, who, with no appreci-ation of the classics had mocked us, and hindered us, with their interruptions at our other rehearsals behind the woodpile.

The "baby" should have been a little girl called Mary, according to Mr. T. S. Arthur's text, but we had no little girl with fair curls, and I was determined to have fair curls showing at one end of the green shawl and bare feet at the other, so we had a little boy of seven, who had a mop of yellow hair. We had to have a fair-sized child who could walk the five miles there and back, and Benny was able for that and more. The part was a minor one, but important. He had to say, "Father, won't you come home?" but he had to say it in a "low pleading voice, full of sorrowful love, too deep for the heart of a child." I am quoting Mr. Arthur's own words, and as director of the play I had put a lot of time on Benny,—and had promised him a beautiful glass alley, if he said his words nicely.

The final rehearsal was entirely satisfactory, and with light hearts and high hopes, we continued our journey, walking well up on the grass to keep the dust from our

shining shoes. We crossed the bridge, skirted the high
bank of Oak Creek, and climbed the hill to the level field
where Millford School stood, surrounded now by horses
and rigs, and a swarm of people.

Our teacher had not been able to come with us, so
Bob, (Simon Slade) who was sixteen, and the eldest of
the company, made our presence known to the Millford
teacher; and we were warmly welcomed, and invited to
come over to the long table where the women were
clearing up the remains of the supper. We were given
salmon sandwiches and tea, and everyone was glad to
see us. After that we inspected the stage and the curtain,
and found all in order. The stage was small, but well
lighted with bracket lamps, and we put up our bar and
the bottles, and wished that we might begin. We knew
our parts, and were fearful of delay. The sun was still
several yards high, and did not seem to give an inch, and
we knew a play would hardly seem right without artificial
lights.

The baby had been left at the table, with his brother
Joe (the bartender), while Bob, Bert, Lena, and I inspected the stage. He had given us a little trouble in the
dress rehearsal, and seemed to be holding out for another
alley, but we were entirely unprepared for the blow that
fell on us, when Joe came running in to tell us that he
couldn't find Benny anywhere, and was afraid he had
gone home. We dashed out and called. Everyone looked
and shouted. Then a little girl said she had seen a little
boy go over the hill, barefooted and travelling fast. It
was Benny! He had deserted us! The baby had gone
home over the sandhills—curls, and barefeet, and the
low pleading voice full of sorrowful love—and what could
we do?

A search began for a substitute. I canvassed the
crowd, now filing into the school. I coaxed and bribed.
"You won't need to speak—just cry a little, and I will
pinch you when the time comes." There were no bid-
ders. At last I got a big eight-year-old girl, a heavy

child, who lay like a bag of wheat in my arms. She had no curls, and she wouldn't take off her boots; they were new ones. And she wriggled. But we put on our act. With that squirming sand-bag in my arms I made my speech. I told Simon Slade he would have been a happier man, if he had remained an honest miller, grinding wheat into flour to feed and nourish his neighbors. I warned him that the ruin he was bringing to others would fall upon him and his. Then I pleaded with Henry, my Henry, to come home. The fat one cried at the right place, but spoiled the effect by tapering it off with a giggle.

The barroom loafers jeered at me, and asked Henry why he didn't keep me at home. Then Henry seemed to sober up a little and said he was not going to have his wife insulted, and would never put his foot in this cursed place again. So Henry and I and the baby go out, and the fun goes on. Mrs. Slade comes in just in time to see her boy, who is minding the bar, take a drink on the sly, and foresees his ruin. She cries and wrings her hands.

Henry, who evidently has given me the slip comes back and lines up at the bar. Simon Slade applauds him. Then the curtain falls, and three years pass.

When the curtain was drawn back on Act II we were all there, except little Mary, who had died, and I stood there bereaved (but relieved too), draped in my shawl. I am older and grayer and still looking for Henry. Simon Slade had grown coarse, dishevelled and stout (Bob had roughened his hair, and stuffed a towel under his vest, and the effect was wonderful.) Old Judge Hammond, the Mayor of Cedarville, stood, a trembling old man, leaning on his cane. But we weren't sorry for him— he had thought a barroom was a good thing for Cedarville. Willie Hammond, his son, lies dead on the floor. Someone had thrown a bottle and killed him. Mrs. Slade comes in, sees what has happened and screams. Frank Slade, the proprietor's son, is asleep in his chair, too drunk to notice. Simon Slade turns to fly, but the

sheriff appears with a warrant for his arrest, and an
order to close the "Sheaf and Sickle."

And it is all over!

We walked home in the starlit night, travelling together about half the distance. Then our roads divided.
An old moon hung low in the southwest, and the sky
was clear with millions of stars. Little warm breezes
came curling up from the hollows, fragrant and friendly.
About a mile from the home the old dog met me, and although I was not afraid, I was glad to have him. And
suddenly I felt tired. But it's nothing to be tired when
you are happy. Our act had gone well. The people said
it was "wonderful". I did not lose the shawl, and when
the sun rose the next day, it would be the First of July!

The first novel I read, was *Meadow Brook* by Mary
Jane Holmes, a worn and battered copy of which fell into
my hands somehow. It was a lovely story written in the
first person, and the heroine was the youngest of her
family, who was misunderstood by them and criticized
by them for talking too much. All these circumstances
helped me to see myself in its glamorous pages.
I read it eagerly and with rapture, and when this wonderful little girl, with a heart of gold, was so bitterly misunderstood that she decided to lie on the dewy grass,
catch cold and die, to spite her unfeeling family, I
thought it a fine idea, and served them right.

Indeed, there were many times, when I, sitting out
minding the cows from the crop, spent a happy hour
planning by own funeral. I marched my whole family
past my coffin, and let them look at my poor pale,
withered face, beautiful even in death, and I listened to
their belated penitence with keen satisfaction. Especially
Jack; I certainly let him repent, in a big way. Tears
streamed down his cheeks and his voice was choked with
sobs as he bitterly cried "She was too good to live!"

Having all the arrangements for the funeral in my

own hands, I spared neither trouble nor expense. The flowers were beautiful, and their perfume loaded the air. And there was music—Lizzie sang. Lizzie had nothing to repent of, so I let her sing and hoped the words of her song fell heavily on the hearts of those who listened. I hoped they fell like clods on a coffin;

> "If we knew the baby fingers
>   Pressed against the window pane
> Would be cold and stiff tomorrow
>   Never trouble us again.
> Would the bright eyes of our darling
>   Catch the frown upon our brow
> Would the print of baby fingers
>   Vex us then, as they do now."

The young heroine in the book did catch cold on the dewy grass, and did get pneumonia. But I did not go that far, I knew what I would get if I got a cold. It would not be anything as romantic as pneumonia. I would have a mustard plaster on my chest and get goose-oil, in large, and regular doses.

When my delightful little heroine grew up she had many lovers, who wooed her on bended knee, but coldly she turned away from their gaze, for once she had seen a face in a crowd, a dark, but beautiful face, chiselled in lines of surpassing loveliness, with burning glowing eyes, and to this dark unknown she gave her love.

She had a friend who had married a drunkard, and was having a hard time, and often my little friend had wondered how her friend could endure her life of trial. Certainly she would never let Herbert (the drunkard) away with such rough stuff. But then she thought "If it were the dark man of my dreams, with the radiant glowing, burning eyes . . . . would I endure it then? . . . . And the answer welled up from her faithful, loving heart. Ah, yes, with gladness!

I do not know why this appealed to me, but it did. I loved every page in the battered old volume.

CHAPTER XXV

THE PARTY

MY brother Will's new house before the partitions were put in, was used for a dance, a community affair, to which the invitation was the usual flat one of "Come Everybody." Social occasions were so few that no one must be left out, and the settlement was still too new for quarrels. So if you knew of a dance you went to it and were sure of a welcome. The word was passed around by various means, drivers of grain sleighs going to Brandon, men cutting wood along the river banks, people getting their mail at Millford carried the news, and the few worshippers at the Monthly Service in the school spoke of it too.

Real old-fashioned shouting Methodists spoke of it, but did not come. They shook their heads, and said no good ever came of a dance, especially round dances. My father objected to them too. Reels and quadrills had symmetry and beauty, he said, but round dances were nothing but "hand-dragging", and an offense to the eye. Usually I followed my father in everything, being proud of his dignified speech; but on this subject, I was at variance with him and quite ashamed of his attack, and particularly of this coarse expression; though Mr. Alfred Noyes, in his poem "The Victory Dance", many years later used an equally offensive one when he spoke of "a fat wet hand, on a fat wet back."

I could not see any objection to round dances. At School, we spent many happy noon-hours, when Mr. Schultz went to his boarding house for lunch, circling around the stove to the strained notes of Billy Day's jews-harp, breathing forth the "Jenny Lind" Polka and the "Arkansas Traveller".

There would be round dances at Will's party, and at first father said he wouldn't go, and at that a gulf of despair opened under my young feet, for if he stayed home I would not have a chance of going. My only hope of ever getting to a dance was that I could not stay at home alone. I put that to him when we were tying in the cows one cold evening. He stood leaning on his pitch-fork, behind the cows, and did not reply for a few minutes. I knew I had to approach the subject in a more subtle way.

"I saw a picture of a dancer, with her hands on her hips, twirling around," I said, "I wish you'd show me those steps."

"Step dancing," he said, "is a fine art and if it were not for my rheumatism I'd be glad to show you—then, when it comes to 'balance-all', you could let your feet twinkle and cavort."

I saw my advantage, and pressed him to show me, and in the warmth of the stable I took off my coat and prepared to imitate every movement. He lilted the "Fisher's Hornpipe", and showed me two pretty steps, and when I got them he was pleased with me, and I knew I could go to the party; or at least he would not bar my way. "Strike into this one," he said, "tap with your left and whirl on your right and you'll have them all watching you! It's a graceful movement!"

I had another reason for wanting to go, one which I now discreetly kept to myself. Jimmy Sloan, who in addition to his many attractions, was a fiddler, had called out to me when we met on the road that he was going to have a dance with me at Will's party.

The night of the party came at last, a clear moonlight night, with a great sky full of stars, and a glistening world of snow. As early as seven o'clock sleigh bells chimed their cheerful notes through the frosty air as the sleighs came crunching along the heavy trails.

Our long table had been taken over to Will's house and was piled with cakes and sandwiches covered with a red and white table cloth. Rolled jelly cakes with apple-jelly filling, cinnamon buns, and apple pies, fruit cake, doughnuts, and cookies were there in abundance. Mrs. Naismith would bring cakes, too, and Mrs. William Johnston gem-jars of cream for the coffee; they were the only people in the neighborhood who had fresh cows. The coffee would be made in two preserving kettles on Will's big new stove. Cups would be brought too, with red and blue or grey yarn tied around their handles; to distinguish them, for they were all plain white iron-stone.

"We'll have the full of the house tonight," Mother said, "for the night is so fine. There will be no room to dance but they'll be glad to get together anyway and maybe they can play games; but remember Will don't let anyone start the kissing game; I'd rather have dancing any day." She was wearing her brown poplin, which Lizzie had made over with a cream lace jabot.

"We'll be able to dance all right," Will said. "We have three fiddlers coming and can't waste all that good music, and Tom Clyde will call off. I've been at plenty of dances where we hadn't half as much room.' '

Will had grown a moustache and looked very hand-some in a navy blue striped suit. He and Lily, the girl he was to marry, would be the finest couple on the floor. Mother's criticism of Will's choice was that they were too much alike, hair and eyes the same color and both had small hands and feet. Mother had not forgotten the beautiful blonde he had left behind him in Grey county; the blue-eyed Anne with her fine capable hands.

At the dance Lily was dressed in a gray blue silk dress with flounces on the skirt, and her slippers had silver buckles. She was a little bird-like thing with a childish voice, and graceful movements, who looked no more than seventeen, and being the youngest of her family was still considered a child by her elders. When Mother spoke of her she always shook her head but we knew it was because of her loyalty to the Grey county

girl. I felt sorry for Annie too for to lose my brother
Will must be desolation, indeed. Still Will had his own
life to live and must make his own choice.

What an evening that was, lasting until the saffron
light of morning stained the east!

Fortunately for me there was a dearth of ladies, so
I was asked for the first quadrille by Dan Thorne. He
was one of our neighbors and his wife, who was much
younger than he was, was dancing with Jimmy Sloan,
who lived on the next farm to theirs. Mrs. Thorne should
have danced with her husband, for this was the first dance
of the evening, but everyone knew she didn't care anything about poor old Dan. The sympathy of the neighborhood was with Dan. The women said he was too
good to her and she did not know enough to appreciate
him. He even brought her breakfast to bed on the lid
of the boiler. At any rate Mrs. Thorne was the neighborhood mystery, with her city clothes. Then there was
the ruby necklace, which she always wore even around
the house. She was never seen without it. It may have
been glass or it may not, opinions differed. Certainly it
glowed like fire. She had been a waitress in a hotel
when Dan met her and it was more charitable to believe
the necklace was an imitation, for how could a hotel
waitress have a real ruby necklace set in gold?

I was dancing with Dan Thorne at the third figure
when the fiddlers began the Fisher's Hornpipe and I got
my chance. When the caller-off gave the command "dance
to your partner, and corner the same;" I did my steps,
and so well, that I did receive applause, and plenty of it
and the caller-off gave me the floor.

But there is a law that never ceases to operate in
human affairs, and I fell under its operation in this
intoxicating moment. . . . It is called the law of diminish-
ing returns. Being able to dance had brought me to this
place of delight, but being able to dance well caused me
to be banished from it. My Mother was horrified to see
me whirl and bend with my hands on my hips; while the

company watched and cheered, and when the dance was over she called me aside.

"It's more your father's fault than yours," she said "but you're too young a girl to carry on like this, whirling your legs like a play-actor; with everyone looking at you. Now I want you to go upstairs and quiet yourself. You looked like a wild thing there and I couldn't bear to look at you. Don't think the people applauded you because your performance was pretty; people are always willing for someone else to play the fool for their entertainment. Now, you can stay upstairs until the refreshments are served and then you can come down. There's three babies on the bed and you can look after them. They might cry and nobody would hear them. I can't watch you when I have so many things to look after, and I won't be worried about you, if you are there."

I wanted a word with father before I went or even a look. I wanted to know what he thought. If I had pleased him, and I was pretty sure I had, I wouldn't care for anything. I had had my fling! He was standing near the stairs when I passed. I pulled his coat sleeve to let him know that I was there, "Well done, Sparrow-Shins!" he said with a smile and patted my shoulder. I could have gone cheerfully to the Black Hole of Calcutta after that. I went upstairs humming the Fisher's Hornpipe. A light burned low on the homemade dresser, and the heat from the stairway augmented by a black pot of live coals made the big room comfortable. I looked at my three small charges sound asleep on the bed. There were two beds in the room; the other one held the wraps of the women.

The babies slept soundly in spite of the noise that came from below; the music of the fiddlers, the scraping of feet, the voice of the caller-off, rising above the waves of conversation that had a rhythm of its own. It was strange that they could sleep so well. I stole back to the stairway to hear what I could but the fragments of conversation that came up did not interest me, it was all of horses, and harness, and grain prices and heavy roads. But I was still glowing with the sense of elation that came when I danced, a glorious feeling that swept me out of myself. I could understand why girls climbed down from upstairs windows to go to dances. I could do it too; probably would some time. There was nothing wrong in dancing. How could there be? Dead leaves whirled and circled and soared in the wind, so light and lithe, and graceful. I wanted to dance like them, just by myself, with music lifting my feet as if by magic. There was something in my blood that answered the rhythm. . . . But I must be quiet, or I would disturb the babies. I was not lonely in my temporary exile for I had the best part of the party in the music that cut through all the sounds and came up to me in a crimson tide of melody. . . . .

I thought of the prairie chickens in the spring, just before they settle down to hatch out their young. I had seen them dancing in circles, bobbing and bowing, nodding and hopping with their feet tight together, like a man's in a sack race. And so carried away by excitement were they, that anyone could creep up on them. . . . Many a bird came to an inglorious end that way, struck down by some unscrupulous person.

I knew very well that Mother was more afraid for me than for either Hannah or Lizzie. And there were times when I shared her fears. There was the time when I met the Kennedy family who settled on Section 22, just east of us, and I went away with them, forgetting that I had the cattle to herd; forgetting that I had on the one pair of boots that Hannah and I used to protect our feet from the hard grass. Boots and all I went and stayed half the day. I had a glorious time while Hannah in her bare feet had had to mind the cows. It was a mean thing I had done and what frightened me was that I had entirely forgotten Hannah and the cows. I had been another person in another world.

I tried to be fair to Mother, I could see her side of it.

She was afraid I would fall into bad company and be so
fascinated with dancing I would not know what I was
doing; but she was wrong in thinking I wanted to dance
only to be seen.   There was more than that in my dancing.   It was the elation of it, the joy, the freedom. . . .

One little one coughed, and I turned it over.   It was
Mrs. Thorne's baby, and seemed to have a heavy cold.
Its little forehead was dewy with perspiration and I could
see she had laid it down with its heavy wraps on and it
was too hot.   I loosened its shawls as well a I could.   The
other little ones were in their night clothes, and slept
comfortably.   Mrs. Thorne had no sense about the baby,
everyone knew that.   She hadn't had a stitch of clothes
ready for little June when she was born for she said she
had a feeling the child would not live.   That showed what
sort of woman she was.   June Thorne, poor little soul,
was a sour baby, never quite clean.

I was not very deft in handling a baby, for I had
never had any experience but I wriggled the little thing
out of her smothering clothes some way.   There was
another smell on her, too, a sickly sweet smell new to me.
I noticed it when I was loosening her shawls and I had
wondered about it.   I knew that there was something that
women gave their babies to make them sleep at times.
I had heard it mentioned as another evidence of the
wickedness of dances.   Maybe this was what smelled on
little June's breath and made her seem so heavy and
lifeless and her breathing so deep. . . . It made children
stupid when they grew up, I knew that too.   June was a
pretty little thing, who seldom smiled and always had
bumps on her forehead, where she had fallen.

I lay down across the bed, watching the light from
below stairs flickering on the new rafters and thought of
Mrs. Thorne.   It must be terrible to have a baby you
didn't want. . . . I was quite determined I would never
have any—though I hoped there would be plenty in our
family for I liked minding a baby and washing its fat
little hands. . . . But I might be wild to go to a dance some

time, and be mean enough to give the baby a dose . . . . if there was no other way. Mother was right. Maybe she saw I had it in me to be mean like that! Well I'd never get married so there would be no danger. I remembered the picnic I was at the summer before at Stockton and how draggled and tired Kate Simpson was. She had just been married a year, and had a baby a month old, lying on the seat of the buggy. She couldn't come over to see the baseball game or anything and wasn't a bit like herself. The fun had all gone out of her. Babies were all right for older women who didn't care for sports or dances, but it was tough to have one when you were young. . . .

I was awakened by voices quite near me and lifted my head and saw two people sitting at the head of the stairs, a man and a woman. Her head was on his shoulder and his arms were around her.

This was all very thrilling to me. Here was Romance just as it had been pictured in the *Family Herald*, but the scene should have been in the conservatory or on a bench in the garden over which the trees obligingly spread their branches. But here it was and near enough for me to hear the conversation. I could not help hearing.

"Take me away Jimmy," she was saying, "I hate everything and everybody here. I can't stand it any longer. This country is too hard on women, with its hard water and awful cold. I have to get away and can be happy anywhere with you. I would starve with you Jimmy and be happy but I will go crazy if I have to go on this way. I'll be an old woman before I am twenty-five."

"Don't cry Fay," he said soothingly, "you have had it tough and I will do anything for you that I can. I'll never go back on you."

Fay——Jimmy! It was Jimmy Sloan and Mrs. Thorne! The talk about them was true! And here she was asking him to run away with her and her a married woman with a little girl depending on her. This was terrible and what could I do? I knew an eavesdropper was the lowest thing made. And yet I could not let Jimmy Sloan go like this. He was too fine a boy to have his whole life ruined. She probably wanted to get away so badly she did not care who took her. ... I could not lie still and let this go on. It was too much like watching the mink robbing the hen-house.

I did not catch all that Jimmy said. He was on the other side of her and his voice did not carry so well.

Then I heard her say, "I have money, Jimmy. Six hundred dollars. Dan gave it to me to keep when he sold his wheat. That will give us a start."

I could feel the change in Jimmy's voice and I knew he drew away from her.

"You took Dan's money," he said. "You did that! Say what do you think I am? I would not take you now for anything on earth. I am a good bit of a fool but I am not a thief. If I took you away now knowing that you had stolen this money I would never be able to look any decent person in the face as long as I lived. No, Fay, I will not go with you. I am done."

"But Jimmy," she coaxed, "don't get so mad about it. I did this for you more than for myself, because I love you. Any woman will steal for the one she loves. We will be able to find good jobs and we can pay it back if we want to. I can go back to where I was in the hotel and I know lots of people there and they will get you into a dance orchestra Jimmy and you can study music. And Jimmy, Dan will never tell a soul that I took this money. He would not let anyone know that for June's sake and he will not follow us or make any sort of a row. I know Dan."

"I know him too and he is the squarest and best friend I ever had. Neither you or I are good enough to blacken his boots. So it is all off, Fay. Let us forget everything. No one knows about this and no one ever need know. I was crazy and so were you but there is no harm done."

In her rage she forgot to whisper. "Do you think you can ditch me like this," she cried, "I tell you I am desperate and I am going out of here if I have to shoot myself. . . . And what is there to stop me from telling Dan that it was your ida to take the money—he will believe my word before anybody's. . . . I despise you anyway for being so mealy-mouthed about the money. You would steal a man's wife but not his money—that is a fine code of morals."

Jimmy was unmoved by her fury.

"Don't be a fool, Fay," he said, "there is a difference. But I am not taking either. I am sorry for all this but I can see how it would end. I could never get along with you. We would be fighting before we got half way to Brandon."

Someone was coming up the stairs then and they began to talk about something else.

"I just ran up to see how June was," Mrs. Thorne said, "and Jimmy and I have been sitting here waiting for her to wake up. She has done well to sleep all this time. It is not often she sleeps so long."

Mrs. Gray had come up to see her baby, and as she stooped over the bed she discovered me.

"Why Nellie," she said, "sound asleep and missing all the fun. I did that once too when I was about your age and slept until daylight when the people came up to get their things. And I certainly felt cheated. Your Mother did not mean for you to stay here all the time. Go down now and have your cake and sandwiches."

Jimmy and Mrs. Thorne had gone down before me. I washed my face at the wash-stand and went down stairs yawning.

The party was about to break up for a blue dawn was showing through the windows and dulling the glow of the lamps. The women looked tired too with the curl coming out of their hair. In an armchair one man was asleep. I could see by Mother's face that she thought the people should have gone home some time ago, and I wondered why she had not sent them. But she explained afterwards that this was Will's party and she did not like to step in. They were not children and should know themselves when it was time to go.

I looked around for Jimmy Sloan. He was putting his fiddle in its case and looked worried. He saw me too and called out to me that we had not had our dance, but I shook my head. There was no fun in dancing now. The glamour had gone from everything. Dirty dishes stood on the tables, plates with a few sandwiches, and cups half-full of coffee, with broken bits of cake on the saucers.

Upstairs the babies cried and someone was calling loudly, hunting for one overshoe. Dan Thorne went up and brought June down in a bundle of shawls. Mrs. Thorne said goodnight to Mother and tried to smile when she said she had had a good time but her mouth seemed to have stiffened.

"You have gone to a lot of trouble, Mrs. Mooney, and it has all been so pleasant. It gives us a chance to get acquainted. I always feel like a different woman when I have been to a party." Her face had the look of a withered white lily. But the ruby necklace glowed and gleamed. I was glad she had it.

The gray dawn was full of shivers and I wanted to go home. Father and Hannah had gone an hour ago Mother said, and I had better go off too and get to bed. Out in the fresh air of the winter's morning I soon ran the quarter mile. A cheerful column of smoke arose from our chimney with its assurance of warmth and comfort. It was just like Hannah to leave the party at exactly the right time and I wished again that I could be like her. She was always right. I would forget all about Jimmy Sloan and Mrs. Thorne and get back to the safe complications of King John and the barons and the peaceful atmosphere of the Wars of the Roses.

It was in the spring of that year that little June Thorne died and on the day of the funeral there was a cold snow storm. I remember the smothering smell of wet fur in the front room of the little house where the neighbors gathered, when in the heat of the big black stove the snow began to melt on the buffalo and coon coats. The small white coffin stood on the table surrounded by pots of blooming geraniums which the women had brought when they came in to clean up the house. Everyone knew that Mrs. Thorne was no housekeeper. So the women had scrubbed the floor and made newspaper curtains for the shelves; and hung clean muslin curtains at the two front windows, put a white spread on the bed and pillow-shams over the pillows. Poor Mrs. Thorne had no knack for housework and could not make a home if she had all "the wealth of the Indies." So I had often heard.

I was glad I had not told anyone what I had heard on the night of Will's party. That was all I could do for her and I had done it with a stupendous effort, for that story would certainy have been a scoop in our quiet neighborhood, if I had released it and I would have gained a certain importance too. But something held me back from speech. I think I held my tongue as a wholesome spiritual exercise but I did wish that my Mother could know. It would be an eye-opener to her to see how noble I could be. And she would surely be sorry then for the time she upheld my brother Jack when he said that my tongue was hung in the middle and worked both ways.

Little June's funeral was one of unrelieved sadness. Her father, weather-beaten, gray-haired Dan Throne, sat beside the little coffin and wept uncomforted. Mrs. Thorne's grief was terrible. She rocked herself in the rocking-chair crying out that she was a wicked woman and had never loved little June until now and now it was too late; that she was not fit to live but was afraid to die.

When Mr. Adams, the minister, came Mother got her to come with her into the bedroom and the service began. I knew Mother would comfort Mrs. Thorne if anyone could for she had a wonderful way with people who were sick or in trouble. Just before the coffin was closed Mrs. Thorne came out of the bedroom quite composed and tearless, and looked her last on the little white face. . . . Then suddenly she reached over and put something on the two little folded hands. It was her ruby necklace.

CHAPTER XXVI

THE FAMILY IS EXTENDED

THE night my brother Will was married, everyone went to the wedding but Father and me. I think Father would have liked to go, but he stayed with me, and we had a great evening together. He told me of fairies that dance on the bogs in their little brown and gold velvet dresses, and of banshees that come to windows combing their hair, and crying, before a death in the family, and of his friend Ned Miney who worked with him in the lumber camp at Bytown, a devout Catholic, who came back to Bytown every three months for confession and told his beads every night and morning, and how all the men respected him, and hushed their talk, when Ned knelt by his bunk. And of the time he went with Ned to church, in Bytown, and enjoyed the music, so soft and impressive and the flickering candles on the altar.

"But remember," he said, when he had finished with his description of the church service, "it was among the Methodists that I learned the way of life. Religion is more than an emotion or an impulse, it is a way of living, and I saw the lives of the Methodists, there in Bytown, simple, sincere and godly people, and so I threw in my lot with them. I've wandered from the path, but I've always come back.

"I went to the Episcopalian church first, when I came out, for I had been confirmed in the Established Church at home, but I felt strange with them. I got never a handshake, or a kind word, nor even a look, and me just a lonesome lad of eighteen. The pews were high, and had names on them, so I felt like an interloper among them, and there they sat, each one, keeping up his or her dignity.

214

"At home in Ireland, there was always a lot of friendly talk before we went in, and around the headstones when we came out, and Mr. Jordan himself, after he took off his cassock, would come down to the door. But the clergyman in Bytown did not seem like a man at all, but just a high and hollow voice; cantering through the service and cutting in on the heels of the stragglers, if they gave the responses a little more slowly than he thought they should. It was just one rigmarole to me with no worship in it. So when one of the boys took me out to the Methodist chapel, I stayed, and found them friendly, simple-hearted people and I loved their hymns." And in a few months after that he joined the Methodist church. The services were held in a home, for they had no building. And once he heard the Rev. Edgerton Ryerson there, explaining the trouble about the clergy reserves and the way the Anglicans were trying to keep all other denominations from having a share in the great grant of land set apart for all churchs in Canada. He could see, he said, the Anglican tradition of apostolic succession and special privilege was out of place in a new country where friendliness and neighborliness were the great needs.

We sat up as late as we liked, there being no one to hurry us off to bed, and I made him his gruel the way he liked it, with a flavoring of nutmeg, and ate a mug of it myself. Then I brought him the drawing-knife, and a piece of board to make the shavings for the morning and I stood on a chair and wound the clock, and brought in the dog, and took the two cats down to the stable, where they would sit on the cows' back all night, very warm and welcome. About twelve o'clock I brought in the bootjack and he removed his boots, leaning on my shoulder to steady himself. Then he sat down in his carpet slippers, and asked me to read the ninety-first psalm, and after I read it, he sat a long time thinking, and the clock's tick seemed to grow louder, until it filled the house.

I knew he was thinking of Will, and wishing him well.

He got up and fixed the fire for the night, putting in some green wood to hold back the dry from too rapid a burning and filling the oven, to have plenty of dry wood for the morning, then he told me we had better "be for our beds", for tomorrow was another day.

The next morning, when I was on my way to school, Hannah and I went in to see our new sister-in-law. She and Will were sitting at breakfast, and she kissed us both, and poured us cups of coffee, "I have a big pot," she said, "so there will always be plenty for the two girls on their way to school." She had on a plaid dress, green and black, and a white apron, and she had brought her cat, a lovely yellow one, who lay asleep in the rocking chair.

It was a sweet bright spring morning and a patch of warm sunshine stretched across the bare floor. This was the fifth of March.

Hannah of course, knew what to say, "We hope you will like us, Lily," she said, "we know we are going to like you!"

We went on our way, feeling very happy and much richer. We had two houses now in our family, instead of one, and another cat, yellow as amber. Soon after Will's marriage, George went to live on his own farm a mile and a half north of our house, on the bank of a wooded ravine which ran down to the Souris. Lizzie was married in 1887 to Tom Rae who had built a frame house across the ravine from George's and nearer the river. These changes saddened mother. She would have been glad to keep her family under her own roof, all their lives. The women of that day, seeing their family leave them, foresaw the desolation of an empty old age. My father was more philosophical.

"It's the way of the world," he would say to comfort her. "People must expect to see their children branch out and do for themselves. We should be thankful to see them able to make their own way, and Lizzie is not far away, and you can still bake and wash for George."

My new brother-in-law was a Scotch Canadian whose people lived in Paisley, Ontario, and I think his fine Scotch accent did as much as any other quality to win mother's heart.

To George's little house, Mother and I went each Saturday afternoon, to do a little cleaning, and "tidying". We emptied the tea-leaves, made the bed, scrubbed the floor, and brought his clean clothes; George's house, and his experience with housekeepers formed the background of a story I wrote years afterwards called *The Runaway Grandmother*.

CHAPTER XXVII

Hands Across the Sea

THERE was no unemployment in the West in the eighties. Indeed, the problem of help in the harvest fields began to trouble the farmer, and through the railway company, arrangements were made to bring out men from England and Scotland.

The procedure of getting a man was simple. You went to the railway office and put down your name, and agreed to pay to the newcomer, five dollars a month for the first year, and endeavour to teach him the rudiments of farming, and the railway, in turn, brought the men and gave notification of their arrival.

Our farm now had a hundred and fifty acres under cultivation and an extra man could be put to plowing, after the seeding was done. There was still another hundred acres to be broken. Will put down his name for a man, too, and the Northfield District had an allotment of nine men.

The day the men came to Brandon, the farmers went there to pick their men. Will got a slim, fair-haired, good-looking man, named Edwin Guest, but Jack brought home one of the queerest looking Englishman we had ever seen.

It was impossible to tell his age; he might be nineteen or thirty-nine, awkward and big, with a broad face, thick lips, and an oily shine on his skin.

Jack's explanation was that no one was willing to take him, because of his looks, and he couldn't bear to see the poor fellow's feelings hurt; and he might be a good man at that; a hired man did not have to have looks. Mother supported Jack warmly, and from the first glimpse of William, liked him. To her, homeliness always made an appeal. There was something steadfast and de-

pendable about homely people removed as they were from
one zone of temptation and William justified all her
hopes; for he combined the strength of Louis St. Cyr, the
French-Canadian hero, with the gentleness of a sheep
dog. He was never tired and never out of humor, and
after a few weeks we saw we had the best man of the
nine. And besides, William was a Wesleyan, from Yorkshire, from the valley of the Ribble, and among his books
were sermons and lectures by the great Yorkshire
preachers.

The nine Englishmen were quickly assimilated into
the life of the neighborhood and brought many con-
tributions to our quiet life. They brought us books of all
kinds which we would not have had, Kingsley's *West-
ward Ho, Evilena* and Captain Marryat's *Phantom Ship*
which I read until I was afraid to go to bed, loving every
word of it.

They introduced us to peaked caps made of tweed in
large checks, and they gave us our first sight of yellow
tin trunks. Edwin Guest brought an accordian, and
grafted on the sturdy stalk of our musical education, from
the music halls of Manchester, such frivolous blossoms
as *McGee's Backyard* and *It's a Great Big Shame.* But
Edwin had a Sunday repertoire too, and introduced into
our Sunday School, *Master the Tempest is Raging,* with
fine effect and bewildering variations, greatly appreciated
by his audience.

So it happened in the eighties that the old land and
ours met and profited by their association.

We had another element in our neighborhood, too,
from over the water. There came, a few years after our
coming a doctor with his family who took up land across
the river, and started his sons in farming. The estab-
lishment, he set up there, belonged not in our times, but
to the shadowy period we call the middle ages. He ruled
his small domain with a heavy hand and brooked no opposition. His wife, a slender little dark-eyed woman,
with a skin as fine as a faded rose leaf, fluttered about

him, in a frenzy of patient solicitude. The sons whe were
grown men came in from the fields to receive his direc-
tions, and when he did come forth to personally inspect
their operations, the family followed, at a respectful distance, in silence.

He had not intended to practice medicine; but some
one discovered that he was a medical doctor, and so the
needs of the neighborhood pressed him into service. He
had come to Canada to get away from sick people, most
of whom he said would be better dead anyway. Why
did they hang on to life, if they believed in heaven? He
had some interest, (although a scornful one) in the land
of his adoption, for on occasions he took his pèn in hand,
and bitterly denounced the governments of Canada in
letters to the newspapers. I remember one letter of his
which appeared in the Brandon *Sun* under the caption
of "What the ignorant farmer pays for his stupidity".

No one resented this, and the old man was regarded
with a feeling of tolerance in the neighborhood, mingled
with not a little awe; for he was an impressive figure
when he went abroad, wearing a wide-brimmed black
hat, and a long cape and a flowing Tolstoi beard.

There was another Englishman, who came to our
neighborhood, as a farm hand, too, who must be
chronicled by me for I owe him a tribute of affection and
gratitude.

He came in a later assignment of farm laborers, and
went to the farm of our nearest neighbor, the Ingrams.
He was a thin young man called "Alf", with a sharp nose,
large dark eyes and bushy hair. The family were all
away one day to a picnic leaving Alf at home. When
they returned they heard strange sounds in the house,
some one was playing the piano! They came in on
tiptoe, and listened. They knew they were listening to a
great musician. In blue overalls and long boots with his
bushy hair standing straight up, Alf was playing, making
his work-worn hands do his bidding once more. No one
spoke or moved. When he was done he arose and took

the applause of an imaginary audience. Then he saw
the family and with an apology went out to do the evening
chores. "I thought I was through with it," he told Mrs.
Ingram, "but it got me again." She urged him to play
whenever he felt like it but it was six months before he
did.

When his year was completed, he began to teach music
in the neighborhood. He made his journeys on foot, and
in all weathers: coming regularly on his rounds, a genial,
pleasant man, always the same and always a mystery.
He became Professor Grainger at once and was a
privileged person from that day, welcome at every table
and fireside. He wrote no letters and recived none. No
one ever knew where he came from though he taught
music there for twenty years. But he gave us a love and
understanding of music, and added greatly to the happiness of our lives. He was always ready to play; and
made an imposing figure at church anniversaries or wed-
dings, when he came forth in a Prince Albert coat, and
top hat. He told me once his life was divided in periods
of twenty years and at the end of twenty years he would
go on. He thought he would go to California, he said.
Then having broken all records in that burst of confidence he lapsed into silence again. He went as silently
as he came, like the sparrow that came into the lighted
banquet hall by one window and out by another. He said
goodbye to no one, and has not been heard of since by
anyone of the friends who knew him then.

From William's books we read of the great William
Dawson, the Yorkshire preacher, whose eloquence had
swept many a sinner into the ways of peace and righteousness. Born on a farm, William Dawson had done all sorts
of hard work, even worked in coal mines, below the sea,
but the hand of God was laid on him when he was
eighteen, and wherever he preached the spirit of God
fell on the congregation. We read his sermons aloud,
and I always heard a voice like a rushing wind in his
words. I remember one sentence because I wrote it in

one of my school books. "The gospel of humanity, like the gospel of the silent earth, must begin with the raw material." I did not understand it, but it thrilled me.

Another supply of reading matter which came to us from the Old Land was addressed to our farm, "Section 20, Township 7, Range 16" but without a name. Periodicals, papers and books came every three months for years and as there was no trace of the sender, we could make no acknowledgment. The service went on for ten years. One day there came a letter from her secretary telling us of the death of Miss M. E. Breasted at whose request the papers had been sent. She was an invalid lady of some means, who had used her income to send reading matter to the settlers of Western Canada, choosing one family in each township. We wrote back, telling of our gratitude, and of how we had passed the books and papers around to the neighbors, but it has always been a matter of regret that we had not known of Miss Breasted while she was living.

CHAPTER XXVIII

The First Sorrow

My sister Lizzie's first baby died.

She had been out gathering the eggs, and slipped on a loose plank in the granary, and because of her fall the baby came prematurely, and lived only five days.

The doctor from Glenboro, sixteen miles away, had been brought; and Mother was there, but nothing could be done.

The loss of the baby was a great grief to Lizzie for she had been very happy about its coming even though she had not been well all summer. But she had scalloped white flannel barricoats and embroidered little dresses, sewed and knitted and told me that she would soon forget all her ailments when the baby came. I was not so sure. . . . I felt sorry that she had to be tied in with a baby. She seemed too young to have to take up life's burdens when she was only twenty-two and have to stay at home from all the parties and picnics. When a woman had a baby her good times were over!

But, when I saw the baby's sweet little wrinkled face; and heard his protesting cry, I would have given my heart's blood, if it could have saved him. I stayed at home from school and helped with the house-work and all day long, as I worked in the kitchen that little hurt wail, like a spring wind mourning in a chimney, cut through me. Sometimes he slept, but even then I heard it through my ears, laying my heart wide open. It was such a little helpless cry, a complaint against a world which he had not wanted to enter.

One afternoon, when Mrs. Ingram had come to relieve Mother, I went out to the bank of the ravine behind the house, where no one could see me cry, and laid my face on the earth's cold breast, and tried to make a bargain with God. I would renounce every ambition I had ever known if He would let the baby live. I would burn my books, and turn to household work—which I hated; I would carry the baby in my arms night and day. I would shelter and care for him, and find all the joy of my life in him if God would let him live.

But the clouds sailed on, wild geese flying south keened above me, a cold wind shook down dead leaves around me and the hard grass of the hillside hurt my face. . . .

When I came back to the house, the stillness of it struck me like a blow. I knew without any one telling me that the little flame of life had gone out.

Tom went to Glenboro, and brought back a little coffin, covered with white brocaded velvet; and Mr. Adams, the Methodist minister, came and read the burial service in the house. In the Millford cemetery there is still the little green mound, marked with a small white stone, on which "Baby Rae" is carved. He was the first of our family to be laid there.

After Lizzie had recovered, life settled down, and I was back at school again, sobered somewhat by what had happened; I was not quite so sure of myself, and not a little afraid. Life might take a snap at me any time. I thought of the prairie chickens off their guard, when they danced their mating dance; easy victims in their one mad delicious hour. Women were the same and for them life was as treacherous as ice. I had thought I was strong like Queen Elizabeth who kept clear of sex complications, but now I could see I was wavering. I knew that I would like to have a baby of my own some time. I had resisted dolls all my life, not without a struggle. I had been scornful of the great trunk full of pillow shams and splashers and hem-stitched sheets that Lily Dewart had all ready. Marriage to me had a terrible finality about it. It seemed like the end of all ambition, and hope and aspiration. And yet I knew now since the baby had come that a child is greater than all books and all learning and that little first cry is mightier than the cheers of ten thousand people.

I wished very bitterly that I was either one thing or the other; hard as nails, and able to do without all family connections or as simple and contented as little Mrs. Billings who had just come to Millford. She said she had never read a book in her life for after all "they only take a woman's mind off her work and maybe make her discontented," but she did like having a newspaper coming in each week because there were cooking recipes in it and besides "scalloped newspapers looked nice on the pantry shelves."

Life was a direct and simple thing for the people who knew what they wanted, I thought, reasoning from the lives of the people I knew. There was the old man Ferguson who took delight in his potatoes. Mat Moggy had trotting horses. Billy Henderson of Brandon was the wit of the community and played practical jokes which were told and retold by his friends. Many of the men I knew had the lust for more and more land and got their thrills out of mere possession. Women had not so diverse a program. Well, anyway, it seemed that the way to be happy was to have enough of some one thing. Even crazy people could be gloriously happy if they were very crazy! But not those who have only a slight derangement. I was fearful of being the sort of person who had a little of many things and not much of any thing. I tried to get some light and leading from Milton whose "Il Penseroso", "Lycidas", and "L'Allegro" were a part of the prescribed literature that year. I had committed many lines to memory as I walked the two miles, night and morning, and turned them over in my mind looking for some plan of life. Best of all I liked the Ode to Mirth with its rollicking metre, so easy to remember:

> "Where the plowman near at hand
> Whistles o'er the furrowed land,

And the milkmaid singeth blithe
And the mower whets his scythe,
And every shepherd tells his tale
Under the hawthorn in the vale,
Straight mine eyes have caught new treasures
While the landscape round it measures."

I loved that. But there were times when I wondered
how happy the mower and the milkmaid and the plow-
man really were, interesting and romantic as they were
to the poet, when he was out for his walk and knew he
was going home to a warm fire and an easy chair and a
good meal which some one had cooked for him. What
did he know about them any way? Quite likely the
milkmaid had chapped hands and the shepherd chillblains
and stonebruises according to the season. And all of
them were probably underpaid and overworked and lived
lives of chill stagnation.

When I wrote I would write of the people who do the
work of the world and I would write it from their side of
the fence, and not from the external angle of the casual
visitor who likes to believe that the poor are always
happy.

CHAPTER XXIX

WHEN THE DOOR OPENED

WE were getting on. There was a new carpet in the front room, full of scrolls, and flowers of great beauty, but of no known family, bulbous lilies with spotted leaves like serpents' tongues; and chintz curtains on the windows, and real blinds, green with a roller and brass ring to pull them down instead of the crotcheted cord; and the kitchen had been given another layer of boards, so it could be used all winter; and Mother had a silk eiderdown on her bed, old gold on one side and flowered with red geraniums on the other.

Even in the face of an abundant crop, the acid little economies of the household went on, little restrictions which burned into me. Coal-oil cost money, and was not to be lightly consumed by night-reading after lessons were done. This was to me the most irritaing of all. Lack of shoe-blacking was another sore point. Lard and lamp-black was just as good, and even if it was more trouble, what of it? We had more time than money. Better people than we had used it all their lives!

How I hated all this! But in my fiercest moods of rebellion I was glad of these irritations; they kept alive my ambition. I would make my escape; I would gain my independence, and every day brought me nearer. I thought of John Wesley, who, being my father's idol, was mine too. He had a nagging, uncomfortable wife, who gave him no peace at home, and perhaps that was one reason he give himself so freely to the world. A soft chair, comfort and domestic calm might have held him to his own fireside. . . .

I had another grievance too, the last year I was at school. In getting winter clothes for me, this year, my bloomers were made from mother's old dressing gown, and because mats were indicated, the gown was dyed before it was made over. So I found myself clad in scarlet bloomers, and although held in by elastic at the knee, inclined to droop when I ran.

I raised a mighty storm of opposition for I felt utterly disgraced. How could I play "shinny" with these flaring outrages showing under my skirts. Mother said I did not need to play "shinny." That wasn't what I went to school for! I should be glad to have nice heavy comfortable clothes to keep me warm! No, I didn't need the exercise, two miles night and morning was enough exercise for anyone.

I wore them. I had to. But I tightened the elastic until it cut into my legs and left a red mark, each night, above my knees. And I played no shinny that winter, thereby losing my seniority on the team. I had been third "pick." I sat in the school, nursing this secret scarlet sorrow. But I got on with my history and literature. So perhaps, as in the case of John Wesley, the wrath of man was again made to contribute to the glory of God.

Looking back, I can see how unfair I was to Mother. She was as ambitious for me as I was for myself, and never begrudged me money for books or necessary clothing. She would gladly deny herself to this end; and she knew how slowly money came, with eggs ten cents a dozen and butter eighteen. But, with the intolerance of youth, I only knew that I was being held down with bit and bridle.

My sister Hannah enriched the stream of our family life in many ways and gave us all many reasons for being proud of her. When she attended the Normal in Winnipeg she did such good work in her teaching that the Department of Education raised her certificate from grade "B" to grade "A". She brought back with her the Toronto College Song Book with its mirthful airs.

I remember exactly how she looked when she sat on the organ stool in her red henrietta cloth dress, made with a peplin which hung down over the stool, for she was careful not to sit on it. She had profited from Professor Grainger's music lessons, and now played the organ for the church services when Mrs. Merrill was not there. From her, the songs learned at the Normal spread to Northfield school and we were now singing the "March of the Men of Harlech," "Into a Tent Where a Gypsy Boy Lay," and "Hail Smiling Moon."

After the Normal she got a school at Indian Head, west of Brandon, where she took the train; it was I who drove her the thirty miles and very proud I was to be trusted with the horse and buggy. I wanted to stay the night in Brandon where I could perhaps go to a concert or a theatre but mother forestalled that by telling me I must drive back five miles on my homeward way and stay at Mrs. Spicer's Stopping House which was a "much nicer and safer place for a fourteen year old girl than a city hotel."

So I did this and still felt very grown-up and happy to be travelling on my own and paying my way like a seasoned traveller. Mrs. Spicer's unpainted and weather-beaten house was a landmark in this part of the country with its high pitched roof and long windows, and a welcome sight to the teamsters drawing wheat into the city for Mrs. Spicer "set a good table." She was a tiny little woman with snow-white hair framing her rosy face, and looked smaller still with her tall children around her, not one of whom was less than her six feet. But "Ma" was the head of the house and directed all the outside activities as well. The morning that I was there sitting at the family table I noticed one of the sons who came up behind his mother's chair and politely waited until she had finished what she was saying and then he asked in a subdued voice, "Ma, where is the ox-harness?" She told him and returned to the story she was telling me about the neighbor across the ravine, who suffered from tooth-ache, when she came to the country ten years before, when there were no dentists or doctors to pull a tooth, and at last in desperation she heated a knitting needle red-hot, and with it killed the nerve in her tooth! . . . .

"Oh, but she was a caution!" Mrs. Spicer went on. "Nothing could stop her; she got so lonesome once to see a neighbor, she set out one day carrying the year-old baby and leading her cow, determined to get over to see Mrs. McVicar, who lived at Grand Valley, and when she came to the river, what did she do but take off her clothes and tie them on the cow's horns and go through the river that was pretty nearly too deep to wade, and then on the other side, dressed up again and went on. . . . She stayed a week with Mrs. McVicar, and I've often heard them laugh about it. . . . People now do not know anything about the hardships of pioneering, and it's fine to see the country advance. . . . But I like to tell young people what courage it took to come in here and get a foothold. . . . Everything is soft now for women to what it used to be. Now you can even buy your bread if you want to. I hear the bakers in Brandon are going to run a waggon out this way. . . . You wouldn't think it would be worth the trouble, for surely no woman minds baking a batch of bread, though, of course, it would be a convenience in threshing time. Baker's bread is flimsy stuff though, all whitened and fluffed up with alum, and there's no nourishment in it. I'd be afraid to eat my fill of it."

In July, 1889, I wrote for my second class certificate in Brandon, in the old school on Tenth Street.

If Hannah had been at home to help me I would have gone more confidently to this ordeal. The algebra was the worst, and with Hannah away teaching, I was fearful of the result.

I had two new dresses and that helped me meet the waves of this troublesome world. One was a brown cashmere, with velvet collar, and lapels, made with a basque and skirt, and the other one was a white barred muslin with a pink sash. Mrs. Ingram had helped Mother to make it. I had pink bows for my hair, too, which I braided in two braids, and my white straw hat had a pink ribbon that came down at the back with fish-tail ends. I had two new sets of underwear with gordon braid trimmings, and a flounced petticoat of all over embroidery.

Jack and I drove to Brandon in the buggy, and we took a Miss Freeman with us. Miss Freeman was a Nova Scotian school teacher from the Oak Creek neighborhood, with dark eyes, and that lovely Halifax way of speaking which I secretly admired. She seemed to be quite a woman of the world to me, being as much as twenty-one years old.

Miss Freeman and I shared a room on the top floor of Mrs. Brock's boarding-house on Eighth Street, a tall narrow slice of new unpainted lumber which seemed to have been built to fill in the vacant space between the two business blocks. The lady proprietor refused to make any reduction to us for sharing a room. "Oh, no," she said, "the wear and tear is just the same, any anyways I like to charge my boarders plenty then I won't be begrudgin' them."

The first week of July in that year was as hot as an oven. I had felt intense heat before, of course, but it was wide-open country heat, windy heat that dried the sloughs and cracked the ground, but the air was always fresh and sweet with honest earthy odors. This was worse; for the air here seemed polluted with perspiring human beings. I had never seen so many people in my life, and I couldn't understand the presence on the streets of idle men, of all ages. Why did they not go home when they had done their buying? They surely did not all belong to the city.

The nights were very uncomfortable, for our room up under the roof grew hotter and hotter, and each morning I seemed to be more fatigued than when I went to bed.

John D. Hunt, now of Edmonton, Alberta, was the

presiding examiner, and on Tuesday morning he glad-
dened us by telling us we had all passed our geography
examination, written the day before, for he had set the
questions and had read the papers. I believed I would
make a pass on everything but algebra, and it did not
come until Friday morning.

On Thursday night I tried to study, but there seemed
nothing I could do. Then I tried to resign myself to my
fate, thinking of Mary Queen of Scots, and Anne Boleyn
and other beautiful ladies who had gone to the block
"every inch a queen". I took off my clothes, put on my
white cotton night dress (long sleeved and high necked),
and knelt at the window with my head on the sill, and
prayed for deliverance.

Down below on the street came the Salvation Army
with their fife and drum and cymbals. A woman began
to sing in a thin clear voice, piercing through the noises
or the street:

"Do not fear the gathering clouds of sorrow,
    Tell it to Jesus, tell it to Jesus,
Are you anxious what will be to-morrow,
    Tell it to Jesus alone!"

Then the chorus joined her with all their instruments.
Was I anxious? I was. I was more than anxious, I was
desperate, but as they sang on I was conscious of a stream
of comfort and assurance coming to me. I grew calmer
and, strange to say, cooler. I would do my best. . . . I had
done my best. . . . I had wrestled with my algebra as
Jacob with the angel, and now if I perished, I perished!
I fell asleep with my head on the sill.

The next day came the algebra test, and I spent
the three hours on it. It was terrible. So many questions contained words I had never heard. But I
worked on and on, and did not turn in my paper until I
heard the sound of the bell.

There were nine of us writing and we met on the
steps when all was over, and held a post-mortem on the

paper. John R. Gregg, now a lawyer in Winnipeg, had the only smiling face at the meeting. John R. had written exams before and could look any problem in algebra in the face. He had the answers written on his paper and he passed it around. I saw I had three right—but I handed the paper back to him before looking at any more. There were ten questions and forty per cent. was a pass. I did not want to cut the last string of hope. . . . I wanted to be able to think I had passed.

Bob Naismith was in the other room writing, and when I came down the steps and met him coming out I could see he was feeling low in his mind too. He had been writing his literature test. Neither of us felt like eating so we walked around to the Trotters' livery stable and got his horse and buggy, and we drove out in the country a few miles. We had only one more exam, "Writing", at three o'clock that afternoon.

The air was a little cooler, and the country was beautiful with wild roses and tiger lilies, while the air carried the scent of mown hay and sweet grass and wild clover. The cattle on the meadows looked peaceful and secure, untouched by fear or failure. I had never seen much in a cow's life before, but that day, still stinging from the blows of the algebra paper, I envied them with a deep and earnest envy.

I told Bob about the Salvation Army the night before, and how sure I was that the hosts of heaven would be with me, just as they were round about Elisha and his young man at Dothan; and how I had slept without fear, and gone into the room to write like a conqueror.

But that paper! with its unknown terms; God had nothing to do with setting that paper—and the killing part of it was that these problems would be simple enough if I had known what they meant. Mr. Schultz had worked so hard to get me through, too. . . . and I had perished for lack of some little insignificant bits of knowledge.

Bob contended that he could not believe that I had failed. Even if I had gone low in algebra, I would have such good marks in the other subjects that they would not hold me back.

"Anyway", he said, waving his hand to indicate the countryside, "examinations are not everything. Look out there. Look at that field of wheat rising and bending before the wind. You don't have to pass an examination to enjoy that. . . . If I fail, and I think the literature to-day finished me, I am going to raise the best horses in the country, big bays with three white feet and a star on the forehead.

"I know," I said. "You'll do it too, Bob. You'll get married and have a happy home, and be the secretary of the school district and go on just like your father, with everyone coming to you for advice, and depending on you. Your life is cut out for you, Bib, it lies straight ahead, but mine isn't. I will never get married. I'm going to be like Queen Elizabeth and keep clear of entanglements because I have work to do that I can't refuse. Life is easy for you, Bob—you will be all right even if you do fail. You wouldn't teach long anyway, for your heart is in the farm. But I want to get a toehold on the ladder of literature. This exam is the first step, if I get this I can go on. If I have failed, what will I do? I could come to Brandon and work for my board and go to the Collegiate, but I am not smart around the house. No one would keep me: I'm not like Hannah or Lizzie who can do two things at once. They can work and go on thinking, but I stop working. . . . No one would keep me. But I have something in me that will not let me rest. I want to give people release from their drab lives! This is not all of the life—this sowing and reaping, cooking and washing dishes. There is an inner life that can be deepened and widened. Frank Kinley has it. So has Mrs. Kinley, it keeps that little flickering smile on her face when her body is ground with pain. Milton had it, and so overcame his blindness. I caught glimpses of it in his poems and I want to pass it on. Listen to this, Bob, and see if it does not make you shiver with its beauty. I wish you had been taking "Lycidas" with me all year; that literature you had is dull stuff. Lycidas had been drowned and Milton is mourning for him, but not without hope, for he knows Lycidas will live again, but see how he says it:

Weep no more, woeful shepherds, weep no more,
For Lycidas your sorrow is not dead.
Sunk tho' he be beneath the watery floor
So sinks the day-star in his ocean bad
And yet anon, repairs his drooping head
And bricks his beams, and with new-spangled ore
Flames in the forehead of the morning sky.

There's comfort in that, and healing. That last line, 'Flames in the forehead of the morning sky', changed something in me. . . . I want to know more and more, and so be able to lift the burden from people. We can't change the facts of life. There's sorrow and sickness and death, binders break and horses get cut in barbed wire, but these things can be softened and brightened and lifted if we have a wide enough outlook. . . .

"I like you, Bob," I said, "because I can always talk to you and tell you things which lots of people would think were crazy. Wheat farmers are so intent on raising wheat they have no time to watch the sunset or raise flowers, plant trees, or do anything to make their homes beautiful. Beauty has a power to heal and comfort people and help them over the rough places in life. Mrs. Spicer told me she had a bed of pansies in the first year she was in the country, and they kept up her spirits. But so many people have nothing to look forward to, or take delight in.

You know how the McFaddens live—they haven't spoken for ten years—quarrelled over something, and froze; and take a pride in their silence . . . . narrow, single-track minds, with no outlet—prisoners of silence and temper; and the poor little boys are living in that atmosphere, which is about as healthy as a dark cellar. . . .

"I think about these things and I want to help. . . .

But I have no confidence in myself. I couldn't talk to most people, even if they would listen. . . . I would freeze over, too . . . . and all my bright vision would fade. So I think if I can get through now, go to the Normal, get away and teach, learning all the time and getting older, maybe people will listen to me, especially strangers. I am afraid I shall always be an upstart to my own people, though. . . . They can't forget how I ran away with the boots, and left Hannah to mind the cows. Then they lost faith in me over my story of seeing a green wolf on the school section."

"Never mind, Nellie," Bob said soothingly. "I believe you saw a green wolf. There are no green wolves, but if you say you saw one, I'll swear you did."

I felt better after this, and when we drove back to the city and went into a confectionery and had two dishes of ice-cream with fruit biscuits the world had grown in brightness. That was my first taste of ice-cream, and it came at a time when not only my throat was dry, but my heart had been scalded by that terrible algebra paper.

The next day, Saturday, I drove home with Bob. I remember what a lovely day it was, and how I wished the road were twice as long. The country side was lush and green, with fields of grain in the shot blade; cattle on the meadows, wild ducks on the ponds, haymakers cutting around the sloughs, groves of poplar trees turning over their coin-like leaves, and all the brilliant flowers of July, gaillardia, golden rod and wild columbine in full bloom.

It was a sublime world through which we travelled that day, a world of abundance and sunshine, beauty and hope. I liked to remember it.

We talked about ex-premier Norquay who had just died, and we hoped his enemies were sorry for what they had done accusing him of playing fast and loose with the Manitoba Central Railroad. He had tried to get it for us, and done his best with the Government at Ottawa, but his own followers had turned on him and broken his heart. Oh well, God would know how it was; and wipe out all his bitterness. He was an old man anyway—he would be glad to have a rest. So we thought of him. He was forty-seven, but between fifteen and forty-seven there is a great gulf of years.

We would not hear the results of the examination until August. When I announced that I was afraid I had gone down in algebra, Mother was very philosophical about it. "Maybe it will be a good thing for you if you have failed," she said. "You're younger for your years than Hannah, and it will be just as well for you to be at home another year. You can go on studying here, and it maybe will do you no harm to have a little of the conceit taken out of you."

I protested at that. I was not conceited, I said. Did she really think I was conceited? She was shaping loaves of bread for the oven, and stopped for a moment to settle this fine psychological question.

"No, I don't think you are", she said at last, "but you are very impulsive and talk too much for a young girl. But the world will smooth you down, Nellie. It's a great teacher. The winds of the world shape us all. We're like the pebbles in the ocean that the waves move and turn and buffet until they are smooth. It's not always pleasant, but we have to take it and it's good for us."

Hannah came home that summer from Kenlis and the summer was delightful in spite of my anxiety. The crop was coming along with a promise of being the best we had ever had. My father believed money could be made on fifty cent wheat, and it would be that much any way.

Life for me now had resolved itself into one question: had I passed? If I had, I could go to the Normal. Mother would buy me a new coat and cardigans, and I had three dresses. Hannah's books would do for me. If I failed I would have to get to Brandon for a few months at the end of the term, and try again. I hated the thought of working for my board! not that I minded the work, but I had no confidence in my ability.

I alternated between the two moods. When I thought

I had passed I radiated goodwill to all the world; washed dishes with great heartiness, singing as I worked; looked affectionately on the house and farmyard, even sentimentally; now that I was about to leave it. . . .

But in my moments of discouragement, how I hated the work in its endless circle; carrying water in and out; pulling lambs-quarters for the pigs; feeding the hens, peeling potatoes, weeding the garden. Not one part of the work had any permanence; it all had to be done over and over.

It was drawing near the fatal day. I would soon know. I had gone to Millford alone that Saturday for the mail and groceries, driving our gray pony in the buggy. The examination reports might be out.

My heart was beating into my throat when I went into Mr. Errett's store, which was also the post-office; and I did my buying first, the nails, sugar, tobacco for the men, tea and pepper, before asking for the mail. If I had failed I would know soon enough. I saw Mr. Errett going in behind the rack where the mail was kept.

"Nothing for your people to-day, Nellie, but a postcard." I took it from him and caught the address, Miss Nellie L. Mooney. Then I read the sweetest words I had ever seen on paper: "Having passed the recent Second Class Teachers' Examination, you are eligible to attend the September to February session of the Normal School at Winnipeg, etc. . . .

The road was paved with gold and every clump of silver willow burned with fire as I drove up from Millford. God had heard my prayer. The Salvation Army was right. I had cleared the first hurdle and was out in the open. Let the winds of the world blow now, let the hurricane roar. I would meet them with my head up!

The countryside that day as I came home, is etched on my memory. Now that I was about to leave it, it became very precious to me. When I had climbed the long grade of Oak Creek's bank, and came up to the open country, rich now with the burning colors of harvest,

James Duffields's house lay on my right, a tall bare house sitting on the edge of the hill, with a drop to the river below; a sad looking house, with drawn blinds. Then when I turned south I passed Arthur Rinder's scattered buildings; poor Arthur who loved his horses so, and even then saw their final defeat by machinery, and mourned it bitterly.

Beyond, to the west, were Tom Ailsby's house, my brother George's, and still farther, now a tiny speck against the horizon, was my sister Lizzie's little new house, the pinkness of its raw lumber dulled a bit by its two years of wind and weather. The houses all looked very small in the great expanse of prairie, brave little outposts, fortifications against winter's cold and summer's heat. I loved them all, and all the people who lived in them, with their sore problems, their disappointments and strivings. In my new expansiveness I vowed I would not forget them when I came into my kingdom. The grand mood was on me and I wanted to do something for my people here.

Everything about these farms had a demanding look, a clamorous, imperative voice. Cows coming up to the bars to be milked, pigs squealing in their pens, hens stepping up to the door to see what was causing the delay in their feeding time, men working in the fields, getting hungrier every minute. And it was the women who were responsible for everything. They must bake bread and peel potatoes for the men, pull pig-weed for the pigs, boil wheat for the hens, and save the crusts and the peelings for them, milk the cows, keep everything clean, and raise a family in their spare time.

I drove in to see Lizzie; I must tell her the great news.

"I am so glad, Nellie," she said in her generous way, "but you deserve to succeed. . . . It will be bare without you, you have always meant a lot to me. . . . There is something tragic about a family scattering, one is taken and the other is left. You and Hannah are away now, we shall see you only in the holidays."

She looked pathetically young as she stood in her little house with its bare scrubbed floor. Lizzie was always an immaculate house-keeper and loved pretty things. That little square front room with its three windows hung with white muslin curtains; the black cookstove set on a square of galvanized zinc, the rocking chair with its log cabin cushion, the bedroom beyond, with a chintz covered box-seat, the little footstool made of seven tomato cans, the home-made dresser with a mirror hung above, the home-made mat. . . . I wondered if it satisfied her. Of course all farm houses are built on the hope that some day beautiful houses of many rooms will be built and life will be easier. Every woman has that hope at the very core of her heart.

I wondered if this little house felt like a prison to Lizzie as it would to me. I knew she would miss me but I would write often and send her books and magazines when I began to earn money.

When I reached home I found the peaceful waters of our domestic life stirred to its depth by the loss of a monkey wrench, and I had been the last person seen with it. My return had been eagerly awaited; the delay in my return commented on. It seems the whole family activity was held up by the absence of the monkey wrench. I got out of the buggy feeling my exaltation leaving me. I was deflating like a punctured balloon.

I had been using the monkey wrench to tighten the nuts on the buggy before I left and had carelessly left it in the buggy and so took it with me. I was in wrong with everyone. It was almost as bad as the time I had absconded with the boots. There were uncomplimentary prophecies made concerning my future, the shortness of my term at any school.

Knowing what I did, I made no reply to anything, no defence. The hour of my deliverance was at hand. I could afford to be silent. And besides I was sorry about taking the wrench with me.

I unhitched the pony and put away the buggy without a word, and I could see my silence was disconcerting, I had both Mother and Jack wondering.

I took the pails and went out to milk, still wrapped in this mantle of silence. No, I had not eaten at Lizzie's, but I was not hungry. I would get something after the work was done.

It was pleasant to be out in the pasture with the cows. My people would be sorry for the things they had said when I was gone. At the moment I was pretty sure I would never come back. I would send a box of monkey wrenches instead. Mother and Jack were going to make it very easy for me to leave. And I would tell them so, I would tell them. Now that I was independent of them. The years of bondage were coming to an end, and not a minute too soon. I would have my liberty. Even if I had to go out and work for the money to take me to Normal. Liberty! Now I longed in that stormy hour for liberty. I wanted out.

> " 'Tis liberty alone that gives the flower of fleeting
>   life its lustre and perfume,
> And we are weeds without it."

I remembered that from Cowper's "Task."

When I finished milking the last cow and was walking into the milk house, Jack came out of the kitchen. I hoped I looked pale and wan. I tried to wear a sad proud look. He sat on the step of the milk house door as I strained the milk. Neither of us spoke. Then he burst out, "Say, kid, did you fail?" I worked on for a few seconds without speaking. If I could give him a few bad moments, I would.

My silence frightened him, he thought I was crying. "Never mind, Nellie," he said, in a voice that was new to me, "don't take it so hard. You're young, and remember this, you have the education. No one can take that from you; you're better off than I am. . . . I was always too ready to work and pretended I did not care about going to school. I wanted to be a man, drive horses, team out the grain, but I did care. At least I care now. I've been a big fool in some ways."

I went over to him and sat down on the step beside him. In that moment every bit of resentment I had ever felt against him passed away, never to return.

"Jack," I said, "I was just acting mad about the monkey wrench and I'm sorry I took it, and I'm sorry I've been so 'lippy' with you." I couldn't think of any other word. "You and I will get on better now. I always thought you were picking on me. . . . You're only twenty, Jack, and lots of people who knew nothing at all have educated themselves after that. You're smart too, and there is not a boy in the country who can hold a candle to you for good looks."

He shook his head sadly. "There is always something to do on a farm if you're willing to do it. I've been too willing. You were blessed by having a saving streak of laziness. You wouldn't piece quilts or crotchet, or knit, and you raised a row when you had to stay at home from school, but I hopped in and did a man's work since I was fourteen. I wanted to be a big fellow. I wanted to be praised for my strength and hardiness. I wanted to face the wind and show that I did not care if my ears did freeze. Going to school was too tame for me after teaming wheat to Brandon. I'm not blaming anyone. I was stubborn and wanted my own way, and, unfortunately, got it."

We talked on and on. I never knew Jack until that night. I should have finished straining the milk for it was cooling in the pails, and the cream was risng, but neither of us thought about it. Something more precious than cream was rising in our hearts, a mutual respect, friendship and understanding that has travelled with us down the years.

The frost came early that year and crushed the crop beneath its iron heel. There would be cattle-feed in plenty but not much grain that could be sold, and there would be very little money after the bills were paid. I could not expect to go to Normal now, and my heart was heavy; a year is so long at fifteen.

But Hannah had money and came forward with an offer to finance me; and Lizzie, too, came to my aid in the matter of clothes, and by September the first I was away.

The train from Glenboro left at five o'clock in the morning, having a long one hundred and thirty miles to travel before night to reach Winnipeg. In order to be on the station platform in time, I went to Glenboro the night before and, stayed with Emily Bell, at the home of Mr. and Mrs. R. S. Thompson. Emily who now lives in San Francisco, had gone to Northfield School for two years and had been my blithe companion on the two-mile walk night and morning; and I knew she would share her bed with me. Emily was a lovely blonde with braids of golden hair, white even teeth, and a lilting laugh.

I don't know whether Emily and the Thompson family were informed of the fact that they were going to have a visitor or not. But I can remember their friendly welcome, and that Emily and I talked until the roosters began to crow.

Mr. Thompson had been the Liberal member of the local legislature for years, not from any help given by the voting members of our family, and from that fact came my first conviction that women should vote.

Opposing Mr. Thompson seven years before was a young lawyer from Winnipeg, whom we had not seen until he came out electioneering. My brother Will, who was an ardent Conservative, drove him around to the meetings and spoke for him too. But my mother was against the young city man and openly hoped for Mr. Thompson's election. This led to much stormy argument and one day when the conversation was heated and loud, I tried to find a basis of agreement by telling my mother that she and Lizzie could vote for Mr. Thompson anyway. It was then I heard the bad news that women could not note at all. No woman anywhere; and I knew there was something wrong about that, and said so until I was compelled to hush my talk.

At five in the morning I began my all day journey to the city; a glorious day for me. I was dressed in a green cloth dress with brass buttons and bound with black military braid; I had money (carefully sewed into my chemise) to pay a month's board bill and buy books; fine new goatskin buttoned boots on my feet, black cashmere stockings, a crotcheted petticoat blue and yellow in a V-pattern, with a white one over it and kid gloves on my hands. I had a coat of dark grey heavy cloth with a high storm collar and lapels that would button over, lined with red flannel, and a home-made red and black "cloud" to wear in the cold weather. When I found that most of the girls at the Normal had fur collars on their coats I grew very much ashamed of my "cloud" and did not wear it until both ears had been frozen.

The long day on the train was a delightful experience, full of new scenes; little towns of bright new lumber and once in a while a great red water-tank running over; long stops at each of the towns when the conductor went into the station to see the agent. We could see them through the window. The train carried the freight too, being of the kind known as "Mixed." So there were pigs to be loaded and cattle, and the length of the train grew as the day went on.

It was strange to see how many idle men there were around the stations, the platform swarmed with them. I did not know that I was looking at the solid citizens of the little towns, who had come over to see the train come in, and who counted this time well spent. The postmaster walked apart with his canvas bag of mail, and sometimes someone brought a letter down and handed it to the mail clerk, and I wondered what the postmaster thought of that.

At Elm Creek we went back on the spur line to Carman, and after picking up the exports from Carman, came back to the main line. The country we journeyed through had low-lying marshes and monotonous levels. Not one part of this country seemed to me as interesting as our grove-dotted prairie with its encircling hills, and again I thought of my brother Will's good judgment when he made the choice.

I think it was dark when we reached the city, but I was again in an exalted mood. The brakeman had talked to me. Came right over and sat opposite me; a handsome man with a black moustache and beautiful eyes. He said I was young to be going to Normal and that I would be homesick. I thought of the "dark man" in "Meadow Brook," whose clear-cut, noble yet sad face seen on a train changed the whole life of the heroine. Suitors came and went, but her heart remained steadfast to her ideal. I wondered if he looked like Mr. Thompson, the brakeman.

Of course I was not looking for a handsome face in the crowd or anywhere, nor was I ever going to fall in love. I was pursuing knwledge and believed I could do this only with a single mind.

I went to board with a family from Owen Sound, consisting of the father and mother and two boys younger than I. There was a grown-up daughter but she had gone to Vancouver and I had her room. It was with some misgiving on the part of the mother that I was let into this sanctuary where everything had a drape or a bow of ribbon.

"You know Margery is so feminine," she said, when she conducted me upstairs, "and so beautiful, really Nellie such beauty is an embarrassment to a girl. Men fall in love with Margery at first sight; she can't go out but some man follows her."

I expressed my wonder and sympathy.

"Oh, but she will make a brilliant match, I know. It's her eyes, they shine like stars; you will be careful of her things; nearly everything here is a present. One young boy in a bank got wrong in his accounts just because he would buy her a necklace—wasn't it a pity, the foolish, foolish lad."

"Is he in jail?" I asked, much more interested in the boy than in the irresistible Margery.

"His father came to his assistance," she replied somewhat stiffly. I knew she did not like the direction of our conversation. "My, but you are like your Mother, Nellie," she said somewhat brusquely, "in manner more than in face.

"I hope I am like her in some ways," I said. I suddenly realized that mother would never rave over a daughter's beauty or her conquests, even if one of us had been a raging beauty, carrying scalps at her belt, and I was grateful to her for her good hard sense. I thought about the deluded boy in the bank, and again saw what a curse love was. Men could suffer too; that was another aspect of the prairie chicken dance.

When we went out together my landlady often pointed out to me Margery's disappointed suitors.

"Do you see that man in the buggy there Nellie, yes, with the beard. He wanted Margery to elope with him. He told her he would give up everything for her. He is a great surgeon here. He begged her, on bended knee, to fly with him. Yes, he's married and has a family. It is terrible. My heart aches for him. . . . Don't look at him now, he might see us. . . . I'm afraid sometimes he may do something desperate."

The bearded gentleman, driving by, did not look to me like a broken-hearted swain but I soon learned that these thrilling romances of Margery's conquests were Mrs. C——'s golden stairs to paradise. I did not know anything about the psychology of release but I knew that the glamorous Margery, and the prospect that she might make a brilliant marriage which would lift the family fortunes, tided her mother over the bleak places in her own life, and they were many.

So I am glad to remember that I took the stories without asking upsetting questions. I knew there was a pathetic background in her vain imaginings, as there was in Mrs. Burnett's little song to her children of "Grandpa will come with the wo-wo."

CHAPTER XXX

WINNIPEG IN 1889

THE Normal was held in the Stobart Block on Portage Avenue, one flight up. We made our way through an unheated warehouse where furniture was stored, lovely chairs, couches, and a whole library bearing the nameplate of "Brydges."

I was the youngest person at Normal except a bright-eyed, red-cheeked Icelandic girl, named Buarg Buargson, who knew but little English. She had been in Canada only six months but made such rapid progress that before the Normal term was over, prepared and read a paper on Iceland, that held our close attention for an hour.

The Normal had two rooms; I was in the larger room where the second class students received instruction from Mr. W. A. McIntyre, though the Principal, Mr. Goggin gave us logic and talks on deportment. The days I spent there, five months was the term, were days of pure delight. New books on psychology, history of education, school management and other aspects of the profession of teaching, all smelling delightfully of new paper and ink, were carried by me back and forth in a new leather bag, and studied with rapture.

We would not be sent to the schools for two months, but classes came in and we saw model lessons taught; and the days went by so quickly I dreaded the end. I was learning, I could see my horizon widening. I was learning how to think. We had debates every week and memory gems every day, and these we wrote in a book in our best writing. (This book is still one of my treasures.)

When we were sent to the schools, Margaret Neilson

and I were paired off, and we stood against the wall for
two weeks observing and going from school to school.
I remember the dull acrid smell of these rooms, chalk,
carbonic acid, onions, and unwashed humanity; but I
did not mind it then. It was part of this new life that
I had been permitted to enter.

Miss Nimmons, who taught Grade Two in the Carleton became my ideal, with her lovely gray eyes, soft
brown hair and beautiful dresses. She must have read
the dog-like devotion in my eyes, for she invited me to
dinner one night to the big stone house on the river-bank.

Agnes Laut had gone to the Normal the year before
and was teaching in the Carleton School, too, and one of
the first lessons I taught was in her room. Such perfect
discipline I had not seen. I think her pupils adored her.
And when near the end of a term, I was sent to substitute
in her room, I had three happy days. The sickness of a
teacher became the opportunity of a Normal student;
and three dollars a day was wealth to us. I got many
days in this way. I suppose Mr. Goggin gave me the
work because I was one of the few students who were
boarding. The others lived at home.

My greatest humiliation at this time was my lack
of knowledge. I had read so little and the others seemed
to have read everything. When they talked of D'Artigan,
Charlemagne, Ivanhoe and Sairy Gamp, I had to sit silent
and ashamed.

At lunch time they all went home except Ellen Walker
and myself. Ellen, who was one of the First-Class
Students, and the daughter of an alderman, did what
she could for me, pitying my dark estate. Ellen also
shared her lunch with me and gave me my first sight and
taste of celery. I knew about it, but just as a word. It
was in the list of Vegetables in the Spelling book. The
taste of celery still brings back that upstairs room and
my sense of having entered a new world of bewildering
fascination.

Main Street in Winnipeg was a gay and exciting spect-

acle on Saturday nights in the winter, with the clip-clop
of the horse's feet, the passing street cars, horse-drawn,
their windows all alight and the radiance of the shop
windows lighted by great coal-oil hanging lamps. The
drug store windows with their showbottles, green and
gold and red, always drew my astonished gaze; I liked to
believe they were costly jewels and not just glass bottles
filled with colored water.

Then there were barber poles like great candy sticks,
turning and winding their red and white stripes. Best
of all was the thrill of seeing the aristocracy driving by,
brown buffalo robes with red flannel scalloped edges
thrown over the backs of their cutters, and a driver on
a high seat with a round cap of fur, his fur coat fastened
with snaps and straps like a bit of harness, the silver
sleigh bells jingling melodiously as they passed. We
sometimes saw the passengers alight, and got glimpses
of party dresses held up daintily, showing fur boots on
little feet.

We often went into Richardson's book store to get
warm at the big heater, where a good fire glowed behind
the sheets of mica, and there was always plenty to feast
our eyes on there; the sheet music strung across on a
wire, riding horizontally but showing, when we held our
heads sideways, lovely ladies at pianos with young men
in tail coats bending gracefully over them, and yellow
moons rising over snowy mountains, and summer scenes
where boats glided under bending willows and ladies with
great flower-laden hats, trailing white hands through the
blue water. Then the books! tables full of them, shelves
bursting with them; Pansy and Elsie books, and the
Leather Stocking tales, and sets of Dickens and Scott and
Balzac and Ouida.

My only comfort in looking at such wealth was that
some day I would be able to buy them all.

Just before Christmas I did buy "The Traits and
Stories of the Irish Peasantry," by Will Carleton, and
brought it home for my father, who loved every page of

it. I had had a day's substituting and so was in funds. I was not wishing any harm to the Winnipeg School Staff, but, if the Lord, in His wisdom, should see fit to lay one of them on a bed of languishing, and Mr. Goggin would send me to teach in her place, I would return to this house of enchantment and buy more. By the laying low of Miss Hill, with mumps, I was able to add Edward Bellamy's "Looking Backward" and "Twenty Leagues under the Sea" together with Longfellow's poems to my small store. I was hoping Miss Hill would have her mumps first in one jaw and then in the other, but she took a short turn on me and got it all over at once, and so I got only two days out of it.

We had a picture taken one night coming home from the Normal, Helen B. Bishop, Belle Poole, Helen Cawston and myself, a tin type. We carried our books to show that we belonged to the literati.

Some of the older girls had beaux and talked about them to each other with much high-pitched laughter, which sounded very foolish and undignified to me; I believed that all affairs of the heart should be embalmed in decent silence. One of the girls had an unrequitted passion for Mr. McIntyre, our teacher, and wrote verses to him in school hours. I sat near her, and she often showed them to me. Some of the girls laughed about her; but it was all terrible to me. She told me she would gladly die if she thought he would come and drop one tear on her dead face. . . . Years afterwards, I met her at the Winnipeg Exhibition, a portly young matron standing beside the merry-go-round on which three of her children were riding. I took it for granted that she had recovered. We did not speak of it; we discussed the relative merits of Steedman's and Steadman's teething powders.

Mr. Goggin's talks to us on Friday afternoons must have been miracles of tact and truth. I can't remember how he did it, but I know he inspired us with a love for the English language, pure and undefiled, a desire to walk with dignity and grace; to love righteousness and eschew evil, even the appearance of evil, and to dignify our profession. He glorified soap and water, and impressed on us that toothbrushes were better than face-powder. Only in one instance do I recall his words. At parting, he said, "Demand decent salaries, and wear clean linen."

At the Normal and in our section, there was a Miss Dale, who boarded on Jemima Street (now Elgin Avenue) and who began to have her lunch with Ellen and me when the weather grew colder. We often walked home together. There was a horse-car on Notre Dame and one on William, but walking was cheaper. I decided to go to board with her in December. My room at the Kate Street house was too cold to study in now that the real winter had come.

Then I began to go with Miss Dale to the First Baptist Church, where the Rev. Alex Grant was the preacher, and where the great friendliness of the people amounted to a rollicking joviality which I enjoyed.

One night Mr. Grant spoke from the text, "Be sure your sin will find you out," a wonderful sermon, dramatic and rather awful. He was the athletic type of preacher who wiped his glistening face, threw his arms about, took off his coat, kicked a chair out of his way, made faces, gesticulated, but never forgot what he was putting over to his people.

His wild ways fascinated me though I did not like that sort of preaching, and wondered why my quiet and dignified Miss Dale should be so keen on it, "He's a mighty man of God," she often said in her meekly positive way.

Suddenly as I listened to him that night, I had all the sensation of a lost soul. I did not see it coming. I had no bitter sins to account for, though I did run off with the boots and I forgot the monkey wrench in the bottom of the buggy, and I lied to save Nap, but I always felt that debt had been paid in full. But that night in the Baptist church I became conscious of sin, not isolated sins. It was Sin, black, heavy and cold that clutched my heart. I had all the loneliness and isolation of the damned; and when Mr. Grant asked all who felt the need of prayer to stand up, I stood. I think there were others, but I am not sure. I knew I needed anything I could get. There was an after meeting and some noisy conversions. I had every sensation of spiritual sea-sickness. My heart was as heavy as lead.

We walked home without a word, but I knew Miss Dale understood how I felt. When we went upstairs she began to talk to me in her sweetly persuasive way. She said we were all sinners until we came under the sacrifice of Christ, and then we became free and that there was no other way to find peace. "Lord I believe, help thou my unbelief," she said had been the text that floated her to shore, when she found herself just where I was, lost and alone. I am always grateful that I found so wise and gentle in interpreter. She did not make any emotional appeal to me, but simply explained to me the plan of salvation. Perhaps it was my knowledge of her unselfish life, her kindly spirit, that made me want to be like her. I told her so and we shook hands solemnly. Then she told me we had better pray about it.

That night I slept a new sleep of great refreshing; psychologists may say it had a touch of hypnotism. But I know I awakened in a new world, and to a new vision of being in harmony with God.

The first change I noticed was that I was no longer afraid of the dark or of the lightning or sudden death. I was emancipated from all fear, and with that came a buoyancy of spirit. Mr. Grant's shouting and gesticulations still bothered me, and I told this to Miss Dale. "He is a revivalist," she said, "and a great man in his own way. He has a vision of a lost world. He sees the stream of humanity drifting to the cataract and rushes out to warn them. So he shouts and swings his arms. . . . If you knew your neighbor's house was burning, you would rush over and scream the news; your voice might be very un-

pleasant but you would not think of that. But this is
only one aspect of religion. It's the beginning. Life is
progress and growth. People must choose their own.
Religion is largely a matter of temperament. The Bap-
tists think that Baptism is important as an act of obed-
ience, you might not interpret it as such. It is the spirit
that counts, not the form."

I went back to Grace Methodst Church but I have
always been grateful to the Reverend Alexander Grant
and to dear Annie Dale.

The term closed the end of Fabruary but I went home
for Christmas thrilled at the prospect. Jack met me at
Glenboro, and we talked all the way home. I seemed
to have been away for years.

It was a glorious night of stars, but no moon, and in
the dim light the horses trotted along the road they
knew so well, their bells chiming cheerfully. "Mother
made be put the bells on," Jack said, "She said there
could not be a real Christmas without sleighbells, but I
think that's a sort of down-east notion."

"I like them, Jack," I said, "bells are like voices, and
you can imagine how glad she has often been to hear
these bells, through the dark and through the storms,
telling her her men were coming home. . . . It's the law
anyway for teams to have bells or lanterns."

"Yes," he replied, "but half the teams on the road
have no bells. Billy Hawkins was stopped by a policeman
in Brandon and told he had to have sleigh bells attached
to some part of the harness, and so he got one bell and
put it on the end of his lines; so he is obeying the law, all
right."

"That's the difference," I said, "between the letter
and the spirit. I wonder why people think it is smart
to evade the laws, that have good sence back of them
and are made for the protection of the public."

I have had many occasions since for the same wonder.

Lizzie had made me a new dress, the prettiest one I

had ever had, fawn ladies cloth, and Jack had bought me a new pair of kid shoes with clear glass buttons.

We had a party one night while I was home, and Bob and Jack Naismith came and a visitor, Turie Kinley, from North Dakota, Bert Ingram and some others.

"I guess you've pretty nearly forgotten us, Nellie," Bob said when we shook hands. The gulf of years divided us now. It was all of four months since I had seen him. Bob was still my first choice among all the boys I knew. I would have been glad to have him in Winnipeg to show the girls for he was a handsome boy with his fine blue eyes and straight shoulders. He had a new suit too, and a blue tie with a horse's head set with ruby eyes for a tie-pin, and from the upper pocket of his coat protruded the hemstitched corners of a white silk handkerchief.

The Doherty organ with a lamp on one side and a blue vase filled with dried grasses and rose haws on the other, standing diagonally across one corner of the room; the new carpet with the spotted lilies and all the best sofa cushions on the home-made lounge, and the long white lace curtains at the windows freshly done; the bright fire burning behind the mica windows in the round stove; and the smell of coffee coming in from the kitchen, showing that this was a real party, all combined to make me well satisfied and quite proud of my home folks. Most of all I was proud of the flow of conversation. At our house we always had good talk.

Hannah and Jack had been at a wedding the week before and Hannah had played the Wedding March; and then been asked by the bride to sing, "When Gathering Roses Look Out For the Thorns," which some of the company who knew the bridegroom thought was a most appropriate selection.

We played charades and the guessing game, and it must have been half-past eleven when the party broke up. I remember the songs we sang, "Clementine," "The Dying Nun," "Nellie Gray" and "Lily Dale" and other touching melodies. The mortality rate among the song heroines of that day was high indeed. They snuffed out very easily .... one breath of cold air and then crape on the door and a new mound on the hillside!

> "She sat at the door
> One cold afternoon
> To watch the wind blow
> And see the new Moon."

That was enough. She was gone before the spring flowers carpeted the fields or the robins had nested again. The Dying Nun, too, was a sad story but we loved it:

> "Let the air blow in upon me,
> Let me see the midnight sky,
> Stand back sisters from around me,
> God! it is so hard to die."

Then there was another about a young woman of great beauty and promise cut off in her prime, who answered to the name of Maybelle:

> "Maybelle, Maybelle, my beautiful pale proud wife,
> You are sleeping alone 'neath the cold gray stone
> While I lead a darkened life."

And the recitations at that time were a bit on the sombre side, too. The Dismal Swamp told the story of a young man who had become crazed by the loss of his young love and believed that she had gone to the Dismal Swamp and that he was on his way to join her:

> "Her firefly lamp I soon shall see,
> Her paddle I soon shall hear;
> Long and loving our life will be,
> And I'll hide the maid in a cypress tree
> When the footsteps of death drawns near."

Then, of course, we had "The Curfew Shall Not Ring To-night" and the "Last Hymn" with its tale of heroism on the high seas; and a fiercely dramatized one I had been taught by Mrs. Schultz, called "The Burning Prairie." American influence was shown in "Barbara Fritchie," which was one of Hannah's offerings.

> "Shoot if you must, this old gray head,
> But spare your country's flag," she said.

(As I write this a forgotten radio at the other end of the room is crooning away under its breath something about smothered kisses and ladies gone in the dawn. I turn it up to give it a chance to compete with the sad old songs of long ago; and the words I get are these:

> "I would give anything under the sun to get you
> under the moon."

I shut it off hastily and return to the melodies of other days.)

CHAPTER XXXI

My First School

THE Normal closed at the end of January, and I had now a Professional Certificate which would give a license to teach during the pleasure of the Board; but I did not avail myself of this privilege until August of that year.

Annie Dale had gone to teach near Manitou when the Normal was over, and at the end of the first term was offered the home school at High Bluff. To fill her contract, she would need to find another teacher for her school at Manitou, and so wrote to me. I put in my application and was accepted.

I had stayed at home after the Normal closed, partly to help around the house. Mother was determined that I should do this for she thought I was too young to teach. The time had gone quickly; Jack and I had been asked to the parties in the neighborhood, and I had gone to one public dance in the new town of Wawanesa, on the bank of the Souris, five miles west of our farm, where the railroad crossed the river.

Mother had been quite willing that I should go to the ball for Jack wanted me to go. That was sufficient reason for her; and I have no doubt she was glad to see that Jack and I had stopped quarrelling. Mother had the Old-world reverence for men, and attributed to her sons qualities of wisdom and foresight which, no doubt, surprised them. She had no faith in my discretion at all, and if I were out after sundown, she had visions of disaster, especially train disaster. I was warned of the train every time I went to Wawanesa. But if Jack were with me, I could even go to a public dance-hall, which I know she regarded as a wicked place, not so much because of the dancing, but because, in a room adjoining there were games, "with the devil's books."

"You should be proud to go out with your brother," she often said, "and it is very good of him to want to take you." I resented this, and after Jack grew up, he did too; but we knew she couldn't help it. It was part of her day, and was partly caused by the fact that she had never known the companionship of a brother; and had never ceased to mourn for her two little brothers, who had died in infancy, and whom she could not even remember.

On August 16th I left from the new station at Wawanesa to ride the seventy-five miles to Somerset, where I would be met by one of the trustees of Hazel School, and driven the seventeen miles to his home, where I was to board. My new tin trunk was in the baggage car, and I had a check for it pinned into my alligator purse. It was not more than half full—the trunk, I mean—although it contained all my earthly possessions, and it was securely roped as well as locked.

Hannah and Mother and Jack came to the station with me and shook hands solemnly when we said good-bye; Mother did not believe that kissing belonged to a public farewell.

"Now Nellie", she said, when we heard the high windy whistle of the train on the other side of the river, "You're getting to be a big girl, and you are out in the world. At the Normal you had teachers, but now you are a teacher yourself, and you must keep that in mind. Don't talk, but listen, and don't believe all you hear, and don't be afraid to admit you do not know. And remember, no matter what happens to you, you can always come home, and be welcome."

We could see the train coming down the long grade, on the other side of the river, its shrill whistle echoing through the hills. It tore through me with a new and rather terrifying significance. I was leaving home! It was too late to turn back now!

But when I was in the train, which wound its way through the wooded valley up to the plain again, and looked across the long sweep of prairie flowing into the sandhills of the Assiniboine to the east and north, and picked out our home, and all the neighbors' houses, seen for the first time in this perspective, some of the exaltation of the occasion came to me. I had longed for freedom, and now I had it!

It was a blue misted morning, heavy with the fragrance of ripening grain, and harvest flowers that the dew had mellowed, golden rod, wild sage and gaillardia. I stood out on the back platform holding to the rail, for the road bed was still rough, and the train seemed to fly. Its long plume of smoke was thrown from side to side as the track twisted, obscuring at last the whole neighborhood. At the other side of the train lay the rough country we called the Tiger Hills, with sloughs and hay meadows and a few scattered farm houses. Soon it was all new to me; and I was off and away in a strange world.

In many of the little places there was not even a station, just a store and perhaps a lumber yard. I told the conductor I had not been over the road before, and he would have to see that I was put off at Somerset, for I wouldn't know it. He assured me he would see to this.

"No one would know Somerset," he said, "it's just a stop; no more. There may be a horse and a haystack and maybe not. But I'll see that you get off. You're sure someone will meet you?' '

I thought of what Mother had said, that I always could come home, and I wished she had not said it. It worried me, for it suggested a possibility I might fail, and have to come home because I couldn't manage the school. Then I thought of poor Louie Smith, whom no one had seen for months, and no one could ask for. She had been working in Brandon, and got into trouble and come home, and there was great sympathy for her family.

For a few moments I had a panicky feeling of dread,

the world seemed full of unseen dangers; what did I know of this place I was going to? Of course Annie Dale would be safe any place, safe as an angel; all the hosts of heaven were around her.

I went out on the back platform again and sought comfort from the open air, and the harvest sunshine that lay on the fields. Horses in a pasture galloped away from the train, snorting and full of terror. They needn't be so terrified. The train stayed on its track and pursued no one. Life was like that too, I argued.

Then I remembered that I had three oranges given to me when I said good-bye to Mr. Storey who kept the store in Wawanesa. No one who had three oranges could be entirely fearful or cast down.

I was put off at Somerset, in the bush, and was surprised to see so many trees. There was no horse in sight, but the haystack was there, and a new unpainted platform, bare except for my trunk, which seemed to have shrunk since I had seen it. I stood beside it and watched the train as it pulled away in the distance; the conductor standing on the platform waved back to me.

There was a house about a mile away which I could see through an opening in the trees; and it gave me reassurance. I was sure I would be met by some one. The rounded and slated top of my trunk wasn't a comfortable seat, so I got off and sat on the edge of the platform; and time went on; a few mosquitoes came out of the bush and circled around me, and I wondered if there were timber wolves in this wild region. I could still see the train for the track runs straight east from Somerset for several miles. Its whistle came back lonesomely and soon it dipped out of sight, though I could still hear its rhythmic beat on the rails.

Having lived with people all my life, being one of a family of six, this was my first time to be alone in a strange place; and a new feeling not entirely unpleasant, came with it. Time seemed to have suddenly stopped here in this quiet spot, with its two parallel lines of steel leading in and leading out. This empty space, this silence marked the end of an era. The curtain had fallen on the first act, and even if the audience grew restless, there was nothing it could do but wait. The play would go on. It was the first time in my life that I became conscious of the film of time that comes in, and goes out; the future at one end, and the past at the other, with only that split-second, ours to use, that changing line as thin as paper, which we call the present. . . . The drop curtain ahead of me with its lines of steel leading straight into the unknown . . . . and at last the turn of the road. Life had picked me up and was carrying me along. I was on my way . . . . into a new world.

I had no way of telling the time, and though it seemed that I sat there for days, it may not have been more than an hour. Then I heard the sound of wheels coming in from the south, and a horse and buckboard came in view. I stood up and waited.

"Did anyone get off the train here this morning?" the driver shouted to me before he had reached the platform, nather needlessly I thought.

"Yes," I shouted back, "I did."

"I expected to meet the teacher for our school, she was coming from Wawanesa, but by golly I'll bet she missed it, and I've had my trip for nothing, and in harvest time and all."

I looked at him closely. I wondered if he were doing what the English call chaffing. But his solemn German face expressed only deep concern. He was a big man with a hardy sunburnt face, and closely clipped moustache.

He was full of recriminations. "By golly, it's no fun being a trustee, I'll tell you, and dealing with teachers. They never know their own mind five minutes. We had a dandy teacher, a real lady; but I knew she was too good to last. She just stayed the six months and then got the school at her home. And now we're sure in a fix, and all the children will be there Monday. I'm going to get out of the hull thing, this is my last year, and they'll never get me in a box like this again."

"Too bad," I said, "but maybe you can give me a ride. You came in from the south, didn't you? Well, I've had a disappointment too, I expected one of the trustees of my school to meet me. Probably he did not read my letter right, or forgot to come. I suppose he'll get here some time, but I can't sit here another day."

He got out of the buggy, and stepped up on the platform. We looked at each other critically. Then I put out my hand, "How are you, Mr. Hornsberg," I said, as pleasantly as I could, "fine day isn't it?" He broke into a laugh. "By golly," he said, "I was wondering how I was going to square myself for being late. I saw the smoke of the train soon after I left St. Leon, and I've been makin' up my speech all the way. But you don't mean to tell me you can teach. You don't look any more than fifteen.

He put my trunk in the back of the buckboard and we set out; reaching a good prairie trail at last. Our road lay through the French village of St. Leon, where a Catholic church school and convent stood on the shore of a small lake. The white-washed houses with bright blue doors and windows, swarmed with children, and dogs ran after us barking. The houses stood close together on the one little street, each with a square fenced garden with sunflowers and corn, and the cabbage in neat rows. A few poppies brightened the potato patches.

Flushes of garden scents, mignonette and healing herbs came to us on the breeze; the leaves of the trees made a gentle whispering, and stood like guardian angels with their branches outspread above the little houses. I sensed a peace of mind and tranquility; a vague heart-healing that comes in churchyards and holy places, and I would have been glad to sit beside the road and let this dappled sunlight fall on me. I would go back some day I thought, and refresh my soul in this sheltered, peaceful concordant place; with its untroubled faith, its ordered resignations. Even the children standing inside the fences looked at us with quiet eyes.

The wells interested me, one at each end of the street, each with a high windlass and a heavy stone in a canvas bag on the end of the rope to help pull up the bucket.

Years afterwards, I saw many such villages in France, with the same contrivance built over the well; the same white-washed houses, blue trimmings and the same evidences of thrift.

"Fine people, these French," said Mr. Hornsberg, as we drove slowly through the little street and around the end of the lake, "and a grand religion they have. I think I'll turn Catholic this fall when the work's done. Their God seems to do more for them. Of course they got to pay; up early, beads, prayers, early mass and confession, but they get results. See their fields and gardens, now take a look at them, for they are the last crops you'll see. All our stuff is flattened to the ground, hailed out—I forgot to tell you, we won't be able to pay you, we're broke. But as I was saying it beats all how the Catholics are favored, and I think I'll put in with them. . . . The hail has made a clean sweep across our district, and the gardens are flattened and black. There will be cattle feed from the crops, and that is all. But we'll keep you, even if you are not what we expected, and you'll get your board anyway. So you'd better eat hearty, for the more you eat the more you're getting."

I think my driver got quite a thrill of pleasure when coming over a rise a new district lay before us with a magnificent sweep of country falling away to the south, and I asked in sincere admiration, "Who owns the fine house?"

"That's mine," he said, "I mean its ours. My wife works harder than I do."

Then he laughed to himself and said, "I shouldn't kick too hard about the hail, we've had good years here, and we should take one backset without howling. One failure every five years isn't going to kill anyone."

When we went in by the back door to the fine, big, clean kitchen where Mrs. Hornsberg welcomed me, I could see that he had good reason for his cheerfulness; and I knew I had come to a pleasant place. The windows were full, and not too full, of blooming geraniums, red and white;—the stove shone black as ebony on a yellow painted floor, a rocking chair with a bright chintz cushion stood beside a table on which lay a book and a knitting basket. The smell of Saturday's baking, spicy rich and moist, told me there were apple pies, and fruit cake somewhere near.

Beyond the kitchen lay the dining room, the living-room of the house, and here were more flowers, petunias, predominating, and a hanging fuschia in a basket in one window, and the white star of Bethlehem in another. There were strips of rag carpet on the yellow floor, and a fine big shining stove in the middle of the room. It was not in use as a stove in the summer, but served as a stand for a stone crock filled with yellow sunflowers. I did not notice these details in my first glance, but I did know that I had come into a pleasant hospitable house, where order and cleanliness prevailed.

Esther, who was a few months younger than I, took me to my room off the dining-room, and when I was hanging up my coat and hat on the hooks behind the door, she told me hurriedly: "This is my room, but the teacher has always had it. Do you mind having me sleep with you? I am very quiet and won't kick . . . . I can sleep upstairs, but I'd rather stay here . . . . we've never had as young a teacher as you."

I knew afterwards that was a long speech for Esther to make, for she did not exaggerate when she said she was quiet. Esther stayed.

It was a pleasant room we shared with a big wide oak bed, with a matress and feather tick, and two huge goose down pillows. In the daytime the bed had a blue and white patchwork quilt which Esther always took off at night and folding it neatly, put it way with the pillow-

shams which matched. I suspected that this elaborate
set had been put on for my arrival, so I suggested one
day that they be put away for very special occasions.
Esther gladly did this, and told me her mother had made
them when she was married, and had given them to her,
"Though," she said sadly, "I'll never need them for I'll
always be at home. No man will ever look at me. I am
too quiet." I tried to comfort her. I told her men liked
quiet women; it was a distinct advantage to be quiet, and
she was good-looking, and that was what counted with
men, I knew. I had three brothers, and I had heard them
talk.

She was interested but not convinced. "Mother was
married when she was fifteen," she went on, "wasn't it
awful? There's only sixteen years between us. Dad is
ten years older. . . .

Beyond the dining-room, across the square hall, was
the parlor, a square papered room with lace curtains on
its two long windows and a real carpet that covered the
entire floor. Here, between the windows and angling
across the corner stood the organ, another Doherty with
its music racks well filled with Czerny exercises and sheet
music, for Esther went every week into town for a lesson from Miss Clarke. Esther took her music lessons as
seriously as she did everything in life, and every morning
when the alarm clock began it clatter she reached out
for it, deadening its din into a throaty gurgle. Dressing
herself without a sound, she went out, and began her
hour's practice. And how luxuriously rich I felt in being
able to turn over for another good hour's sleep, all the
sweeter because of the five finger exercise, runs and
chords that mingled with my dreams.

There were book cases in the parlor filled with E. P.
Rowe's and Pansy's books, and an Elsie Dinsmore or two,
the Pilgrim's Progress, Fenimore Cooper's Leather Stocking Tales, and Alexander Dumas' sombre romances, and
years' numbers of the *Youth's Companion* and the *Farmers' Advocate*. I always enjoyed reading aloud, and

many a pleasant evening we spent in the big room with a warm fire in the round stove, after the two little boys, Tommy and Fred, had gone to bed. I remember especially how we enjoyed "He fell in love with his wife," by E. P. Rowe, in the reading of which Charley, fifteen years old, took turns with me, while Esther crocheted, and Mrs. Hornsberg knit, and Mr. Hornsberg stretched out on the long brown sofa and slept.

Our evenings always ended in the same way; with terrible regularity the head of the house wakened with a loud shout soon after ten. "My landsakes alive Jenny," he would roar at us, "what do you mean, do you never look at the clock? Here it is getting on to twelve o'clock, and you let these crazy kids sit and read, and the teacher has no more sense than the others. We'll never get them up to-morrow, its all we can do to get them started when they go to bed in good time. . . . I can't even fall asleep without something going wrong."

The first night this happened, I was frightened at his violence, but that soon passed. He loved to rage and roar and shout. When he kept it up too long, Mrs. Hornsberg quieted him with a word, "All right, William, we hear you." Not once did I hear him answer back. Like Esther's touch on the alarm clock a word from his wife stopped the uproar.

I learned something of German thrift and foresight in the Hornsberg family. There was enough home-canned vegetables in the dark cellar to last two years, and so the hail which had destroyed the garden made no difference to our meals. We went on eating green peas, squash and cauliflower. The straw stacks were not burned on this farm as they were by the neighbors, but kept until the following year. So there would be cattle feed, and there was hay stacks two years old. The outbuildings too, were neatly painted and every bit of machinery was housed when not in use. The cows were tied in the stable at night, with a chain that came from a collar around their necks and the end snapped into a ring above their heads, just long enough and no longer, so there was no danger of an animal becoming entangled in the tie chains. There were two good wells, each with a pump, and the farm yard was kept clean of straw or debris. The wood pile had the precision of a pile of cans in a store window.

Sunday was the outstanding day of the week, preparations for which began on Saturday. Mr. Hornsberg was not a member of the church but he was a zealous adherent, and saw that the whole family was present at the morning service. To usher them into the family seat, take his place at the end, glower at the two young boys, who sat next him, to dry up the least trace of frivolity, dispose of his hat on the wires below the seat, and then settle down to a quiet hour of close scrutiny, without once turning his head, was one of the pleasures of his life.

Coming home, we heard a report of the congregation; "Mrs. Sears has a new hat at last. I wonder how she ever got old Abe to open up; and a pretty one. Gosh, but she looks a lot better. . . . Still, I'm sorry you didn't see the old one. It was high at the back, and sloped down to the front; had the look of a cow getting up. Do you know a cow gets up different to a horse? Yes, I knew.

"Aaron Smith looked sour as vinegar to-day. He traded a horse yesterday with Bill Jeffrey. I'll bet he didn't hear a word of the sermon, every place he looked he'd see a spavin. Did you see the man two seats ahead of us, the one whose neck is cracked like an alkali bed? I'll tell you a funny thing about him. He's innocent in his ways, says queer things. A man from town went out to insure his life and told him that Charley Brown, who had just died had a three thousand dollar policy, and had only paid one premium; paid fifty-two dollars and got three thousand, but Elias Smiley said, 'Oh, well, I'd never be lucky like that!' . . . .

"Did you notice the family that whispered when the sermon was going on. That makes me mad. If the minister would check them for it, I'd give him two bags of oats. How did you like our choir? That big fellow can sing, can't he? It sounds like hollering into a rain barrel but I always liked to do that. Mrs. Peters has a kind of a zither to her singing, sounds like she has a fine tooth comb between her teeth."

The sermon was not included. Not being a member, he said he didn't set himself up to judge preaching, any minister was good enough for him, for he kept all his religion in his wife's name anyway.

Life took on a new interest that first Sunday afternoon when Esther, Charley, Fred and I went to Sunday School. Esther and I went to one of the class rooms behind the choir loft, to the Young Ladies' Bible Class. We lived three miles out of Manitou, and so we had to step lively to get home from church, and have dinner, and get back for the 3 o'clock Sunday School, but it was the thing to do.

Now, this was a very particular Sunday, the first Sunday for the new minister's wife to teach the class. The new minister had come from Port Arthur, Ontario, and the Young Ladies' Bible Class was waiting for her.

She was a beautiful woman, in her late forties, and dressed exquisitely in a brown cashmere dress with smocked yoke and cuffs, with a moonstone brooch to hold her linen collar in place. She wore a velvet bonnet trimmed with folds of silk that make me think of the rosy tints of a winter's dawn, opalescent in their changing sheen; and her eyes! when looking into her eyes, I saw the browns and greens and gold of the moss in the meadow brook at home when the sunshine fell into its clear stream.

The lesson I remember, was the story of the Prodigal Son, and the group of 1890 flappers with their hair in braids with the ends teased out, were not especially interested in the Prodigal Son coming or going. So I, being a teacher myself, and having sympathy for a fellow-sufferer, fell upon the lesson with fervor. I drew lessons, expanded thoughts, asked questions, repeated the golden text and was able to tell where it was found. Indeed, I can safely say without pride, I was the best girl in the class, and though I was probably detested by the others, I saw gratitude in the teacher's golden brown eyes, and came home in an exalted mood, quite determined to keep to this breakneck pace of proficiency.

The family at home were greatly interested when we told them that the minister's wife had taught our class. A new minister's wife is always "news." Esther did her best to describe her, but even though she described the brown dress, velvet bonnet and moonstone brooch, I felt her description lacked something, authority, or conviction, or enthusiasm or something.

"In fact," I said, "she is the only woman I have ever seen whom I should like to have for a mother-in-law."

Esther's mother checked my enthusiasm by telling me the minister's wife had only two quite young boys.

I enquired their ages.

"Fourteen and ten."

Then I pointed out that I was not quite seventeen, and what was three years' difference in ages anyway? It would never be noticed when he was fifty and I was fifty-three. Having put my hand to the plow, I was not going to be turned aside by three little insignificant years.

CHAPTER XXXII

Winds of the World

The first days at school filled me with dismay. Nothing came right, and all I had learned from Baldwin's "School Management", seemed to have turned to dust and ashes. I could not keep the forty children busy. I do not know what I would have done without Esther and Charley, who turned in generously and became my assistants. They gave out spellings, and work on the board, took care of disputes over pencils and books.

In a week I knew all the names, and had my time-table working. But I felt ashamed of the way my Normal Training had deserted me. I stayed after school each evening and arranged my work as well as I could, and having done all and hoping for the best walked home to my boarding place, across the coulee. There was a fine flat stone in the bottom of the coulee, and on it I sat each evening, and meditated in great humility of spirit. I was failing as a teacher. The Inspector would discover my weakness, and he might come any day. Hazel School had had good teachers. Miss Evilena Bell was the first, even yet I heard echoes of Miss Bell's good work. Then a Miss Baker from Ontario, and Annie Dale, all experienced and capable. . . . I would have to go home and admit my failure. . . .

It was hard to be sad on those warm bright September evenings with the comfortable homely sounds, and sights; cow-bells tingling, crickets chirping in the long grass, the drone of mowers cutting the green feed, the rich amber sunshine dulled with haze. These, and the prospects of the good supper waiting for me, and all the comforts of the white house, would have lifted my spirits, but for that awful dread that I might have to go skulking home—a teacher who could not hold a job—I saw no way of escape unless the school would burn. But nothing could look more permanent than Hazel School, No. 365, pale gray in color, with a black roof, standing on a little eminence, secure, remote from harm with the sinking sun kindling a flame on its three western windows, a flame that glowed and gleamed, but would never consume it. I knew there was no hope of deliverance by fire.

The school attendance had been helped by the hailed crop, and so I had the peak load of students from the first day. All the big boys and girls who in a good season would have been at home for the harvest were coming to school, and it seemed impossible to get time for all the classes in the whole eight grades.

My difficulties were increased by the fact that nearly all the families came from the same place in Ontario, and carried with them into the new life, all the sins and sorrows of the past. They knew each other too well; and some of the old grudges had their roots in the past generation. This led to fights on the school grounds, rather serious affairs, that worried me. In the heat of anger, the opposing factions went deeply into the past and dragged out old skeletons, flung out old taunts and innuendoes, horrible on the lips of children. After one of these bouts my senior classes were demoralized, and even the little ones suffered from the emotional upheaval.

An older teacher might have been able to suppress these outbreaks but I was afraid to take a high hand with boys and girls almost as old as myself. And I was disappointed to note that "Feuds" were not listed in "Baldwin's School Management."

I knew the root of the trouble was in the homes where these old sins were freely discussed. Drab lives crave excitement and these neighborhood fights were the outlet for suppressed emotions. I must find a healthier form of excitement, or the school was headed for ruin. I could not expect help from the trustees; they came from the same place in Ontario, too, and were not entirely friendly to each other.

I had brought with me a copy of Dr. Egerton Young's "My Dogs in the Northland," and I read it for ten minutes following the morning prayers to insure punctuality. This began the day pleasantly for us. With my first salary payment I bought a football, and presented it to the school, telling them that I was going to play with them, and we would see if we couldn't play with good humor. If a fight should break out, the ball would be locked in my desk for one day. I told them about the English school boys (I had read Tom Brown's School Days) and how the Englishman's sense of fair play and good humor had won the admiration of the world. I told them about the "Old Spites" in Ireland, and how the "Fairs" were often the scene of bloodshed though no one knew exactly what it was all about. I tried to make them laugh at such foolishness which belonged to the age of superstitions and ignorance, and had no place now in the lives of sensible young people.

We drew up rules for the football games and everyone had a voice in the making of these. Everyone played, and the school room was deserted at noon by all but little Libby Stiles, whose poor little white face looked wistfully out from the window. Libby had a weak heart.

So all went well for a couple of weeks, the football took up all the surplus energy, and I began to hope. One day, one of the girls came to me almost in tears, and told me her mother had been over at Jeffreys, and Mrs. Jeffreys and her sister, Mrs. Miller, had said I should not play football; it wasn't a ladies' game; and they were going to speak to the trustees about it, and they thought the football should be taken away for children were just crazy about it, and that's all they were going to school for.

The next day I wore my longest and best dress, and I went to see Mrs. Jeffreys. I had met her in Manitou one day, and she had asked me to come over for supper some night—one of these flat and wide invitations that mean nothing—"Come any time," she said. "I always have plenty cooked."

She seemed to be pleased to see me in a constrained sort of a way. She wore her wool challey dress and brought out her spiced pears and many kinds of cake.

Mrs. Jeffreys was the mother of one boy of fourteen, and step-mother to three others who were away from home. So, having no children to keep her at home, she went about more than the other women; and she had her own driving-horse, which added to the evil she could do. She was a positive woman, with a cut and dried opinion on every subject. Her knowledge of the neighborhood was profound, and the people were afraid of her. She had her own money too, and that gave her an added importance. I knew I had to have Mrs. Jeffreys with me, or my scheme would fail. She would go to the trustees and raise a row. The trustees were afraid of her too, and the old spites would all be revived in added bitterness; although I was sure now, that with the football and plenty of stories, I could handle the situation if I were left alone.

After supper, Mr. Jeffreys and Frank went out, and I helped her to clear the table and wash up. We were getting along very well I thought. I let her talk and listened attentively, knowing even then that a good listener is more sure of popularity than a good talker. I had no finesse, no adroitness of approach. All I could do was to put the case before her plainly and bluntly and in getting the case started, I was somewhat hampered by the fact that she wouldn't meet my eye. She looked over and around me with her darting black eyes.

At last I plunged in. I told her why I had bought the football, why I played with the pupils, my distress over their fights, and their slanderous charges. "It is horrible," I said, "to hear young boys and girls throw hints and sneers across a school ground. It's unnatural too; they shouldn't know these things. They hear too much at home, and it's all so useless and evil. These children cannot help what happened in Zorra, and should not be reminded of it. I think the best way to stamp out all this nastiness is to give them something fresh and clean and thrilling to think about. A game of football ought to be more interesting than the story of how one man's father opened a registered letter and lost his job twenty years ago."

"Who said that?" she cried, stopping her dish-washing in mid-air. Her tone was so sharp I nearly dropped the plate I was drying. "Who has been talking to you?"

"No one," I said hastily, "I merely used that as an illustration. The charges the boys and girls have been flinging at each other are more serious than that."

"That wasn't in Zorra," she said excitedly. "It never happened anyway . . . . that was a lie . . . . it was all a mistake." Her face had gone white and her eyes were full of fear. I covered her confusion as tactfully as I could by talking on, and leading away from the subject. I knew I had inadvertently stirred a bitter memory and I was sorry about it. No doubt she thought I had deliberately evoked the past to gain my point, and in that case I was no better than the young fighters I was trying to reform. I couldn't remember why I had mentioned a post-office scandal. There was no reason; I just happened to use it.

One good thing came out of my unpremeditated black-mailing; there was no more talk from her of going to the trustees, and our football games went on.

I think it was in October, Esther's mother brought back the news from town that the minister had also a big boy eighteen years old, who had stayed behind in the East to complete his teaching term.

"So you may have your mother-in-law yet," she said to me, as I helped to carry her parcels into the kitchen, "but," she added, "he has red hair."

"I like red hair," I said. I hadn't known it until that moment, but I knew then I had always liked it.

The next day when school was over, I went to town. I was dressed in my best dress, the dark green cloth trimmed with military braid and brass buttons, hair waved by the use of curling papers the night before;

shoes polished (lard and lamp black), my pale complexion toned up a little by a vigorous application of a hard towel (afterwards I used a leaf from a cotton rose on my hat). I had no business or errand that night. I went to see the boy with the red hair who was working in the drugstore. I had no excuse either, I remember. I made no pretence of being the Victorian maiden who sits on the shore waiting for a kindly tide to wash something up at her feet—not at all! Having seen something on the skyline rocking on the current, something that looked like a treasure, I plunged boldly in and swam out for it.

The red-headed boy was in the drug store, a tall, slim young fellow, with clear blue eyes, regular features and clear skin like his mother. I bought a fountain pen, taking quite a little while to decide, and being guided entirely by his superior knowledge, which wasn't too bad for a beginning considering that I was an unsophisticated country girl, seventeen years old, and had never heard of "Dorothy Dix." I paid three dollars for the pen, my last three, and I would not receive any part of my salary for a month. No matter, I paid over the money with a fine air of opulence, and came home well satisfied with the evening. But when Mrs. Hornsberg asked me about the young man with the red hair, I had very little to say.

Two days before Christmas, we had our Concert for which we had been practising since early Fall. There was an organ in the school, and Esther played it very well. So we had choruses and duets and solos. Esther and I sang "Whispering Hope," and eight of my little girls of assorted sizes sang "Every Little Wavelet," with white handkerchiefs on their heads for the white caps on the waves; and wore blue dresses of cheese cloth dyed with a quart of ink that had frozen in the school cupboard. When they swayed from side to side to the rhythm, it would be a dull person indeed, who could not see the blue waves curling and breaking into the white foam, and the whole wide circulation of the sea.

We were far from the sea, and these children had

never seen a wave, but they did not dull the picture as they sang:

> Once I got into a boat,
> Such a pretty, pretty boat,
> Just as day was dawning,
> And I took a little oar
> And I pushed out from the shore
> So very, very early in the morning.

> And every little wavelet had its nightcap on,
> Night cap, white cap, night cap on,
> Every little wavelet had its night cap on
> So very, very early in the morning.

Our last number was a dialogue, with three actors. I was a lady traveller intent upon taking the train to Morrow. Charles was my boy, and we were loaded with parcels from hat-box to a bird-cage, with a bird in it, yellow and green made of felt, but a good bird for all that, with large green eyes (beads loaned for the occasion by Mrs. Jeffreys). John R. McDonald was the station agent, and possessed of a sharp and cutting tongue. He was disposed to be scornful of my many questions regarding the train to Morrow, and could not quite make out whether I referred to time or place.

My son, Charles, absent-mindedly consumed the lunch reserved for the journey, while this verbal battle went on, and just when the confusion was at its height, and the station agent and I had almost come to blows, the whistle of the train tore through the air of the room (sound effect produced by willow whistles and one cowbell).

My son and I dashed for the door, dropping parcels as we went; my carpet bag flew open, and linen collars, hair brush, shoes and various garments fell out, including a wire bustle and a red flannel chest-protector; but we could not stay to retrieve them, and did not even look back. When we reached the outside door, we halted and listened to the applause, which was generous, and came back to take our bows. Then it was that Elias Smiley stole our show from us by rising at the back and calling out, "Oh, Teacher, did you get all your things!"

A boiler of coffee had been made at Mrs. McDonald's nearby, and when it was brought over and the thick white cups borrowed from Huston and Betts store in town, were passed, and two of the boys went down the aisles with blue enamel pitchers of coffee to which the cream and sugar had been added; and good thick ham and salmon sandwiches went around; followed by layer cake, spanish bun, marble cake and rolled jelly cake, and plates of home-made candy, the audience settled down into great good humor, and a truce was called on all old feuds, past and present, and east and west of the Great Lakes. Mrs. Jeffreys had arranged for the refreshments, and a vote of thanks was moved to her before we parted.

It was half-past twelve before we left the school, but what a night it had been! I couldn't sleep for thinking of it. Already I was planning what we would do next year to make the people laugh. Laughter was the cement that would heal the breaks in this neighborhood, laughter and something to talk of other than past sins and sorrows.

The next day Mr. Hornsberg drove me over to Somerset where I caught the west freight for Wawanesa. The passenger train came only twice a week, and the freight was my only hope to get home for Christmas, and Mr. Hornsberg said the conductor did not mind carrying a passenger.

The day was dull and threatening, with a woolly indistinctness that blotted out the horizon. Leaden clouds hung low, and although it was not cold, snow was indicated by the darkening skies. The roads were bare and hard as iron, and the seventeen-mile drive had been a rough one. I was fortunate in not having to wait for the freight. It came lumbering in soon after we reached Somerset, a long freight with the caboose at the end. Mr. Hornsberg spoke to the conductor, and he was quite willing to take me along.

I had a seat in the cupola of the caboose and enjoyed the wide view it gave me, but the windows soon misted over with spikes of ice as the weather grew colder.

"It looks like dirty weather," the conductor called to me, "but we'll try to get you home for Christmas. Snow is our biggest danger and may be fillin' in the cuts now."

He was filling up the round stove with coal; "We've lots of this anyway," he said, rasping his shovel into the coal-box, "and we've plenty of grub, so you might be in a worse place."

I assured him I was very happy to be allowed to ride on his train, and I thought it was a delightful way to travel home for Christmas.

About three o'clock we got into the snow-storm that was working down from the West; but the snow was dry, and the wind which whistled past us had kept the tracks clear. I could hear the brakeman and conductor below, gloomily discussing the chances of getting through.

When it began to get dark, and no more could be seen but a gray wall of whirling snow (even when I thawed a hole in the frost on the window) I came down to where the men were, and opened the fine box of sandwiches, cake and candy I had brought, and these served for dessert at our evening meal. I told them about the concert, and sang "Whispering Hope" and the school songs for them, and did all three parts in the "Train to Morrow." But the storm was worrying them, and they told me after we left Marieapolis that they were afraid we wouldn't get to Wawanesa until about noon the next day. And I might as well try to sleep. They made up a bed for me, and the conductor brought a clean towel to cover the pillow. So I climbed up and turned in, pretty tired after all the excitement of the last few days, and blissfully happy to be on my way home.

The road bed was rough and the freight ran heavily, creaking and groaning, but I slept although a bitter wind

was whistling past us, and one of the worst storms of
the season was raging. Snow sifted in through the windows and sizzled on the stove below, and I heard through
my dreams the anxious words of the train men, but nothing could disturb or dim the radiance that flooded my
heart. I was going home, I was re-engaged. I had
eighty dollars of my own earnings, and presents for
everybody.

At four o'clock in the morning we were stuck in the
snow and I was thrown up against the head of the berth
by the unsuccessful efforts of the engineer to buck the
drifts. The same jolt upset the stove and the red hot
coals were scattered on the floor. But the brakeman came
running in and righted the stove, and shovelled up the
coals before any harm was done, beyond a great smother
of coal smoke. Then I noticed that someone had spread a
fur coat over me, and I was glad of it in the deepening
cold of that wild Christmas morning.

We were stuck in the snow until about noon, when
the snow plow came from Brandon and released us. I
offered to cook breakfast for the men but they would not
hear of it. The brakeman, whose name was Joe, said
he was "terrible particular about his bacon, and couldn't
trust any one to get it just right." But they did let me
wash up the dishes for they were all working outside,
and when the train started to run, they came back to the
caboose and we all wished each other a Merry Christmas.

It was beginning to get dark when we pulled into
Wawanesa, but Jack was there to meet me and we were
soon home where the whole family had assembled for the
day. The big dinner was over, but the long table was
still set, and I was ready for a good fill of cold turkey,
mashed potatoes, turnips and apple-jelly tarts. I was
glad to see all the relatives looking so handsome in their
best clothes. I was especially thrilled with Addie, Fred
and Nellie, Will's children, who seemed so much bigger
than when I left.

Lizzie and Tom were there too, and they were all

anxious to hear about the delayed train. Mother raised a storm of protest when she found I had ridden on a freight, and slept in a caboose, but I stoutly defended my kind companions, and the hospitality they had extended to me. "Some girls could do it," mother said, "but that's not you, Nellie. You're not very good at keeping your distance. No doubt you talked to these men."

I confessed that I had. Not only talked with them but sang, and read aloud from a book called "Lucille", which one of the boys was taking to his girl in Brandon.

Mother shook her head. "I wish you had more reserve, Nellie, you make too free with people," she said, "I'm afraid you'll go too far with it some day. These men were strangers to you."

Tom, my brother-in-law, defended me, "You couldn't expect her to sit there like a bump on a log, Mrs. Mooney," he said, "Remember she was the guest of the train crew, and she did the right thing; you needn't worry about the trainmen, they are good company for anyone. I know the conductor, and I'll bet he enjoyed having her along." Will, too, added a word of approval, for which I was grateful, and my Father said he couldn't see that there was any harm in singing at any time; or in a bit of pleasant talk.

Our crops had been very good that fall, and that good fortune was reflected in the Christmas presents. The short winter days passed in a flash it seemed. But I did get my cherished trip to Brandon, and spent most of my eighty dollars.

I got a black cloth with a knotted stripe for an ulster, and black persian lamb storm collar, cap and gauntlets; and a checked "stuff" dress and brown velvet trim to it. Later I had my photograph taken in it, and I bought myself a copy of "Lucille," in white and silver binding (which I still possess).

CHAPTER XXXIII

RAW MATERIAL

WHEN I returned to my school I took back a set of
Dickens which Will gave me. They had been given as
a premium with the *Toronto Mail and Empire, Family
Herald* and some other publications. I felt immeasurably
rich in the possession of these long, paper-backed books,
tea-colored and closely printed.

I began with *Martin Chuzzlewit*, Charley, Esther
and I reading in turn at night. How we hated Pecksniff,
and sorrowed over Tom Pinch's disillusionment when he
discovered the arch-treachery of the man he had trusted.
That impassioned paragraph which described Tom's
feeling as he went out disgraced, beginning: "Something without a name; compassion, sorrow, old tender-
ness, mistaken gratitude, habit, none of these, and ye
all of them" never fell on more responsive hearts than
ours. Tom Pinch, with his homely face, his awkward
gait, became to me a sign, a symbol, a token of all the un-
attractive people of the world whose virtue and goodness
and beauty are not seen by our dull eyes. I thought of
William, the Englishman, so fine, so dependable, and yet
so likely to be underestimated because he was not good
to look at. As I read and thought and marvelled, a light
shone around me. I knew in that radiance what a writer
can be at his best, an interpreter, a revealer of secrets,
a heavenly surgeon, a sculptor who can bring an angel
out of a stone.

And I wanted to write; to do for the people around me
what Dickens had done for his people. I wanted to be a
voice for the voiceless as he had been a defender of the
weak, a flaming fire that would consume the dross that
encrusts human souls, a spring of sweet water beating up

through all this bitter world to refresh and nourish souls that were ready to faint.

I could not tell even Charley and Esther how I felt; I had no words to express the deep, poignant longing that swept my soul. I remembered the lines from Milton about fame being the spur that makes people scorn delights and live laborious days. Yet it was not fame that I craved. It was something infinitely greater. I wanted to reveal humanity; to make people understand each other; to make the commonplace things divine, and when I sat on the flat stone on my way home from school, I thought of these things until my head swam and my eyes ran with tears.

The depth of my ignorance appalled me. I was bound, fettered, gagged in ignorance. What did I know of the world's great literature? My words were but the ordinary workworn words of everyday happenings, and I knew nothing of life. . . . Moments of despair came to me when I wished I had never read a word of Dickens. I would be happier without this terrifying vision. Better to go on teaching a while, stultify my soul with frivolous things, attractive clothes and social life, settle down and marry, and forget this shining thorny path winding up the hill.

But I knew I couldn't do that. I must go on, even if I went barefooted, for I had seen a bright light and caught a glimpse of a heavenly country. I found comfort in knowing that Dickens had only a meagre education too. Life had taught him, and life would teach me. I had money now (forty dollars a month) and I could buy the books that I needed. I would hammer out my education on the hard anvil of life. I would mine for words as eagerly as any miner ever dug for gold. The stars in their courses would work for me. Years afterwards when I read Ralph Waldo Trine's "In Tune with the Infinite", I knew every word of it. It had come to me then when I sat on the stone at the bottom of the coulee; though I had no words to tell of it, or even think it with.

I had a copy of "Sesame and Lilies" and in its pages

I found much to comfort me, and I blessed John Ruskin because he gave me something I could get my teeth into. I did not like his general attitude to women, or his belief that they were made only to help, comfort, and inspire men, and that all their education must be to that end. But in the preface to "Sesame and Lilies" he said that girls should learn to know the life around them; and if they had time, "should go into the families of the poor and show them how to make the most of what they had, coaxing them into pretty and tidy ways, and pleading for well-folded tablecloths."

Esther and I had laughed about that, and wondered how we would be received if we went around our neighborhood to coax the women into pretty and tidy ways.

But one day, little Mary Wheeler asked very wistfully, when she brought her slate to my desk to have her work corrected, "Please teacher, can you sew?" I told her I could a little. "Would you make me a dress?" she asked. "Mother hasn't any time, and she's always sick."

I told Mary I would make her a dress, and asked her what kind she would like.

"We have the print," she said. "We've had it all summer, and I will bring it to school tomorrow."

I knew Mrs. Hornsberg would help me, and she had a sewing machine. We made the dress, a pretty little buff print with two pockets, pearl buttons, and an embroidered collar, and my fame was established as a dressmaker.

Then one day Jimmy Burns brought me a note and a pair of sharp scissors. "Dear Miss Mooney," the note said, "I wish you would cut Jimmy's hair. He looks like the colts do in spring, but I can't get it done, and I guess you won't mind; for you have more time than I have."

At noon I set Jimmy on my desk, tied my apron around his neck and did the best I could do to remove the winter crop from his hard, round head. Jimmy's sister, hovering near, asked a little anxiously, "Please teacher, do you think you could cut it curly? Pa said he just bet you would."

κ

As I cut Jimmy's hair I decided I'd give his head a long delayed washing, and put a basin of water on the stove to heat. I kept a good supply of towels and soap, and had a bottle of violet toilet water in my desk. So when Jimmy was well shampooed, dried, and scented, he enjoyed a brief bright hour of popularity, for all the children wanted to smell his head. There was a run on haircutting after that, and Charley had to turn in and do some of it.

Having made a dress for Mary Wheeler, we went on and made shirts for the little boys, and night dresses for Mrs. Wheeler. The annual baby was about to arrive. Poor Mrs. Wheeler, thin, hollow-eyed, with blue veins in her thin hands, and misery in her eyes, had too much trouble. The Wheelers lived on a rented farm, and John Wheeler was the neighborhood drunkard; that is, the most spectacular one; the one who drank out of season. Even in harvest time, with the grain shelling in the field, Johnny Wheeler could not refrain. I found that the people of this neighborhood drew a sharp line between summer and winter drinkers.

I had been over many times, and Mrs. Wheeler talked freely to me. "I know I shouldn't have married John," she said one Saturday when I had gone over to help her whitewash the house. We had pushed everything into the middle of the floor, and she sat in a rocker on the edge of the amassment, attending to the last year's baby. I stood on a chair that had lost its back and put the whitewash on the wall with a wide brush. "There was a fine man wanted me, and life would have been different with him for he was steady and thrifty, but he was the most homely man I had ever seen, and I wanted something to look at!"

I had heard that before. I had said that when Hannah put "moral worthiness" at the head of her list of qualifications for a husband. I remember the argument we had over it. I had stuck out for a fine face and carriage as qualification number one. Mrs. Wheeler rambled on, "Johnny Wheeler was the sort of man who would take any girl's eye. My! I wish you could have seen him then!"

She spoke in a monotone, her voice as colorless as her face, and as limp as a washed ribbon. It came to me now, punctuated by the loud slaps of the whitewash brush.

"You do not see him to any advantage now. He has grown careless and discouraged, what with the hail and the frost, so many children, and I have been sick a lot one way and another. Life is not what we hoped it would be, and it is hard on a man like Johnny. And he's a lot better than plenty of the men around here for he very seldom swears before the children, and you might say he never comes home drunk. He stays away and sleeps it off some place and then comes home with a shave and a hair-cut and a pleasant word for everybody. That's one thing about Johnny—he's always pleasant."

I did not see Mrs. Wheeler again until after the baby was born, and then she told me the story of Johnny's lapse from virtue at the time the baby came. "I never thought he'd be the worse at a time like this," she said, as she sat rocking the baby in the broken rocking chair, "and mind you, I am not blamin' him altogether. You see he thought I would be slower than I was, and he only intended to take one drink. But one led to another, and he said himself he took the first one just because he was feelin' so anxious about me, and he felt the need of a little bracin' up. He's very sympathetic, is Johnny, and can't bear to see anyone suffer. Well, anyway, he and the doctor had a bottle and I guess they were both feeling pretty light in the head when they left town, and as the afternoon went on and there was so sign of them on the road, Mrs. Drummond who was with me was so frightened I was sorry for her, and kept sayin' Johnny would come, I was sure he would.

But just when I was at the worst of my pains the minister's wife came in, not knowing anything was wrong, just came to see me, and she just took one look at me and peeled off her cuffs, rolled up her sleeves, and I'm tellin' you she was as good as any doctor, and it was all over when Johnny and the doctor came. Fancy her knowin' what to do. I always thought from what I had heard of her that she was more of a lady!"

"Wasn't it fine of her!" I exclaimed, "and what a fortunate thing for you that she happened to come at that time. What did Mr. Wheeler say!"

"Johnny felt terrible," she said, "after he wakened up. He lay down and slept as soon as he got in, and didn't realize that the baby was born for hours. He's awful fond of the children, you know, and thinks this little fellow is the best one yet. I suppose you think I should be pretty mad at Johnny," she went on, reading my face, "and maybe I should. Everyone says I'm too easy on him, but I'll tell you how that comes. My father was the exact opposite of Johnny. He worked hard, paid his debts, provided for my mother, and all of us, but never gave us a civil word; looked like a thundercloud all day long; never joked or even talked to us; and I was afraid of him and near-about hated him. . . . I was always afraid to come home. . . . I knew I was in for it. . . . Now. It's all different. . . . Johnny is always pleasant. Careless, easygoing, but pleasant—and a woman will stand a lot from a man if he's pleasant Now I know there are men who are both good and pleasant, but they're scarce. Maybe you'll get one. I hope you will, but get a pleasant one anyway, I say."

I pondered on what I had heard as I walked home across the fields.

Shortly after the Wheeler episode I went to the little town to spend a Saturday afternoon with a fellow teacher, and before the afternoon ended we went to a quilting bee at one of the big houses where I remember the wallpaper was red with green and silver dragons. There was a table in the hall with a rope cover fringed out at the corners like a yellow horse's tail, and on the table was a stuffed owl with yellow bead eyes. The quilt was being quilted by perhaps a dozen women and was going to be sent to the Manse for a Christmas present.

Soon after our arrival, one of the women gave out the news that the Methodist minister's wife and another woman were going around with a petition asking that women be allowed to vote, and a general discussion arose and surged and swelled above the quilt. I gathered that the ladies were opposed to the movement, and were bitterly scornful of the minister's wife and her friend for sponsoring it. One of the ladies, whom I knew afterwards (she was the wife of the town drunkard), said: "It's an insult to our husbands to even ask for the vote."

I wanted to speak; I wanted my friend the teacher to put them right. I knew it must be right if the minister's wife believed in it, it must be right. To my amazement, my friend was scornful, and just as the conversation became embarrassingly personal, a cry arose that the ladies were coming, and a knock sounded on the door. At once the quilters took flight upstairs, even my friend fled with the rest, and the hostess and I were left.

The ladies explained their errand, while the hostess sat stonily uninterested on the edge of her chair, and the house pulsed with strange rustlings.

"We thought we would meet with your guests, Mrs. Brown," the minister's wife said in her sweet way, "but it seems they have gone," at which the house seemed to fairly creak with suppressed emotions.

I signed the petiton, mine being the second name. The hostess repeated over and over, "I do not think I care to," and the ladies went on their way.

It was an embarrassing moment when the quilters came back, shrill with excitement and stormed at the petitioners, and I had to declare my allegiance to the Cause. My friend was ashamed of me I know. She felt she had harbored an anarchist.

I wanted to tell them about the minister's wife, how she had come into the Wheeler house and taken charge,

and brought the poor woman through when the doctor
and husband had failed. I wanted to tell them that they
should have stayed and listened to her for she was a
wonderful woman.

I knew these were good women, church women, were
they not quilting for the manse? I was surprised to see
how bitter they were.

I knew that women should help each other, and I
could see that the vote would bring an added importance
to women, but I could not put it in words. They had
me down.

So I came away and as I walked home the three miles,
I pondered with deep agitation on the world-old problem
of "Why are women so mean to each other?" I was glad
I had signed the petition. I would gladly sign anything
the minister's wife asked me to sign, and a fine frenzy of
high endeavor came to me whenever I thought of her.
I wanted to be like her with her quiet dignity and her
well-cut clothes. There was not a woman in that room
who could touch her in appearance, and how they did
attack her and her friends for "interfering Methodists".
That was the terrible thing about the whole experience.
How could these Christian women be so mean? I knew
vaguely that it was because there was a crowd of them.
Anyone of them would have stayed and listened and at
least have been polite. This was my first experience with
the mind of a mob.

There was a temperance chart in the school which
some clever salesman had sold the trustees for forty dollars. It folded up into a coffin-like box and stood upright
in the little cupboard behind my desk.

As the result of a temperance lesson in Sunday School
I began to study the handbook of lessons which accompanied the chart; and when a rainy day kept the children in at noon, I brought out the chart and taught them
from it the effect of alcohol on the human system. The
colors were bright and lurid, and I think the pictures of
inflamed membrane and hob-nailed livers fascinated

them. Anyway they liked to see the pictures, and I bought a bottle of alcohol for the experiments, and we showed them how alcohol eats up water, thereby rendering the blood unfit for its work of cleansing, we knew why a drunkard has a red nose, and why he loses his power of articulation. All went well until one day my new pupil, Robert John Ricker, challenged the whole theory in a few memorable words—but I must go back and introduce Robert John.

I was putting work on the board one day about a month before, when suddenly the busy hum of the school-room ceased. I turned quickly to see what had happened. Everyone was staring at the door.

On the doorstep stood a little boy of eight, with just the rim of a straw hat on his head; hair as yellow as fresh wheat stubble, dark beautiful eyes, cheerful freckles over his nose, and a new tin dinner pail in his hand.

"Hello kids," he called bravely, though I could see he was a little frightened. I brought him over to my desk, and found out his name and age, and learned that he had not been to school, and was not sure whether he was going to stay now.

"I'll come to-day, anyway," he told me quite honestly, "Pa said, 'Go on and give the damthing a whirl.'"

I could see that Robert John thought that "damthing" was one word. Robert John was the unspoiled child of nature. His parents were of German descent, had lived in the Middle West States, and had sold out there to come to Manitoba and homesteaded years before. There were three brothers of them, all with families, and the old grandfather, who was still the head of the clan. Robert John had never been to town, or to a picnic, or any gathering. Not one of the connection had ever been to church. Robert John swore as innocently as a bird sang; it was merely a form of expression.

He stayed that day, and I was careful to see that it was made pleasant for him. I allowed his profanity to pass unchecked, for I knew that one breath of criticism would blow him away. I gave him a new scribbler, and a bright red pencil, let him clean the boards, and began a story at four o'clock, promising to finish it the next morning.

He came back the next day, and I knew I had enlisted him. When he came to say goodnight to me, at four o'clock, waiting until the children were gone, and looking down at his feet, he said:

"If you like, Teacher, you can kiss me now." I looked at his downcast little face, and I knew there was something back of his words.

"Thank you," I said gravely, "but if I were to kiss you every night, I'd have to do it to all the others, and that would be quite a chore."

He looked up. A smile of relief lightened his cherubic face. Then a mighty oath broke from his, "Hell, wait till I get home. Pa said I'd have to kiss you night and mornin'. That's what kept me scared, the old——."

I wish I could record here that I was able to bring Robert John into the pleasant land of unsullied speech, but I can only say that he did try to lower the content of his profanity, but even that was a hard struggle.

"Hell, Teacher!" he said, when I approached the subject, "how can a word be bad? It's nothing. It's just a sound. It breaks no bones." One day when we were again in conference, he asked me, "What do you say when you're mad?"

The first day that Robert John saw the temperance chart and heard the lesson, he sat in front of me and listened intently. His face when I was teaching any class was a delight, in its expression of close concentration. But on this day, as I went on to show the effect of alcohol on the lining of the stomach, I could see he was growing rather restless, and I knew an interruption was coming. When the lesson was over, he stood up to speak.

"Teacher, did you make the pictures?"

"No," I answered, "these pictures were made in a big

city by doctors who have studied these things for years."

"Well, then, I'll tell you what they are—they're all lies. My father says a drink of licker is better than a meal; and he has been drinkin' since he was ten, and he was never sick in his life. Now, Teacher!"

The other children looked at the young heckler in horror.

For a moment I was nonplussed.

"There are some people, Robert," I said cautiously, "who seem to be able to do anything. I knew a man who declared he had never had a bath, and he was healthy, and strong; and I knew a family who never opened a window in their house, and they did not have any more colds than other people who did open their windows. I knew a little boy who could run through the snow in his bare feet, and he seemed none the worse. But one case does not prove anything. Anyway, your father is a young man yet; it is too soon to say that drinking does not hurt him."

This note of rebellion was well discussed in the neighborhood. The trustees who had paid the forty dollars under the spell of the good salesman, were resentful of his attack, and thought I should have rebuked him more severely. Some who were not trustees, took sides with Robert John.

Echoes of the conversations came to school, and the neighborhood seemed about evenly divided. I could see there was only one way to settling the matter. So, with the consent of the trustees, and Mrs. Jeffreys, who agreed to solicit refreshments, we had a public meeting one Sunday afternoon and everybody came. I showed the chart, and with the pupils help conducted the experiments.

Everything went off well and the audience listened closely. The crowning glory of the occasion was that Robert John's father came and made a speech when the lessons were over; a strange speech at a temperance meeting, but effective, too.

Putting his chew of tobacco in one cheek, "I guess I

started this, folks," he said, opening the window behind him and spitting at the woodpile, "by tellin' my kid that licker is better than grub for a man; and he shot it on the Teacher, and pretty soon everyone had a go at it. Well, I ain't sayin' I'm through, because I don't know, but I do say, a fellow is a damsight better without licker, and I think these pictures are————, good stuff, for kids to see."

I went home that night, walking on air. Right had triumphed. The victory was ours. I thought every man in the neighborhood was delivered, sobered and safe. The demon, Rum, had been excised, and cast out. There would be no more Saturday night sprees now that the real scientific facts were known.

But, the next Saturday night, through the quiet starlight, we were awakened by the thundering of horses galloping over the frozen ground, urged on by their tipsy riders, their voices just as raucous as before,— and a great disappointment was mine.

I lay awake a long time that night.

CHAPTER XXXIV

The Young Evangelists

ONE morning at church we heard an announcement that stirred us deeply. We were going to have a season of revival, and the evangelists were two young women, Miss Nettie and Miss Maud Judd from Ontario. They were coming fully authorized by the church, and would probably stay a month, holding meetings for five night in the week. And the time was set after seeding when the farmers would be able to attend.

These young women's labors in other fields, the minister said, had been blessed by God; brands had been plucked from the burning, and many young lives turned into the paths of righteousness before the enemy had time to sow the tares. And we were asked to pray earnestly that great good might come to us all.

Charley, Esther and I talked of it on the way home. We had seen a picture of the Judd sisters in the *Christian Guardian*, and thought they were beautiful. Mr. Hornsberg was opposed to the whole idea of women preachers. He said a man would have no chance. If the girls said "Come to the altar and we'll pray for you," it would be only common politeness to go. No, no, he wanted no pretty girls mixed up in his religion. He warned us there would be trouble in families, and he would not go near them.

Of course we knew he would. No one could hold him back. He had never missed a thing in his life.

I knew a little about women preachers. Mrs. Andrew Gordon had preached at Wawanesa and Treesbank, in her clear ringing voice, reasoning with us, patiently, as a mother with her erring children.

Mrs. Roy of St. George's Church in Winnipeg taught

a young ladies' Bible Class which I attended there, and I had loved to listen to her kindly messages.

I had read *Adam Bede*, and had been moved to my heart's core by the preaching of Dinah Morris. I had spent a whole afternoon in Mrs. McGregor's Boarding-house at Swan Lake, just a few weeks before, waiting for the mail man, Johnny Moorehouse, to pick me up and give me a ride to Manitou. The rain, which fell in torrents, delayed him, but what did I care. I had *Adam Bede*, and my house was thatched. The afternoon wore into evening and still the rain stroked the windows with its wet fingers, and I read on.

I sorrowed with poor Hetty Sorrell, and scorned the young squire who had brought such trouble to her, and laughed at Mrs. Poyser, but more than all these, I preached the gospel with Dinah Morris, up and down the lanes and greens of England. Every word she uttered fascinated me. Now we were going to hear two women preachers, young and beautiful like Dinah Morris. I wanted to be like her!

They did not disappoint me. Nettie, the elder sister, had a face like a cameo, delicate, sweet and martyrlike, and eyes that burned with a blue flame. She pleaded and she preached. I know she saw us all drifting toward the precipice, and she tried to snatch us in her little hands as we passed.

Maud, who was just eighteen, was more of this earth, and therefore, more attractive to the young generation. Her eyes were very dark brown, mistily purple like a pansy, and her hair, of the same shade, curled back from her face. She smiled too, when she talked, and her voice was a rich contralto. Maud's feet were firmly set on the common earth, and her appeal to us was not so much to save ourselves from destruction, as to come into harmony with God, because that was a good and pleasant thing to do.

When the Judd sisters sang, I thought the angels in heaven surely gathered around to listen. Nettie's sop-

rano voice, sweet and thin as a flute, ran up into the rafters of the church, and Maud's rolling contralto swept on
like an organ. I can hear them as I write:

> Softly and tenderly Jesus is calling,
> Calling for you and for me,
> See on the portals he's waiting and watching,
> Watching for you and for me.
> Come home! Come home!
> Ye that are weary come home.
> Softly and tenderly Jesus is calling,
> Calling, oh sinners, come home.

They preached and sang, and had altar calls, and
after-meetings; and Maud conducted the congregational
singing and set the men singing alone; then the women;
then the right side, then the left side, and managed to
loosen every voice, and give us all a feeling that we had
taken part.

Their greatest appeal was to the young men. The
young evangelists were beautiful, vital, and just a little
too well-dressed to escape the jealousy of the women.
They were so trim, neat, immaculate in their tailored
clothes. Maud had a reddish brown rough tweed, made
with a little ripple around the basque, and trimmed with
a fringed ruching on the neck and the sleeves, that was
so lovely that it made it hard for me to be "in the
spirit" when I looked at her.

The druggist, a big fellow who sang in the choir, was
their first notable conquest, and he came down from the
choir-loft one night, and in his testimony announced he
was going to live for the glory of God, hereafter; and
would burn all his pipes and tobacco in his store the next
day. This started a chorus of "Amens" and "Hallelu-
jahs."

Mr. Hornsberg leaned over and said to me in a loud
whisper, "You've lost your beau! Miss Mooney, the
preacher girls have cut you out!"

The druggist had come out on two occasions and taken me driving with a livery team; I did not know how to refuse when he came, and besides a drive was pleasant on a quiet Sunday afternoon. I wasn't worrying about him, the girls could have him. But when I went to town one evening after school intending to stay for the meeting, and passed Maud walking with the boy from the drug store, so deeply engrossed in each other, they did not even see me, I got a distinctly unpleasant feeling. Of course I knew their conversation was on a highly spiritual plane, but even so, she did not need to look up into his face so often; and I knew how shattering those brown eyes could be.

I felt very awkward all at once, and a bit shabby and gawky, and very much a country girl. What chance had I against these dangerous eyes with the purple depths, and those well-cut clothes. . . .?

Not that I cared, I told myself, loftily. It was nothing to me. . . . I was never going to marry anyway. I did not go to the drug store as I had intended. I went to W. D. Ruttan's store, and bought a new coat and hat, intending to wear them to the meeting, but changed my mind about that, too, and went home.

I had my own horse then, a sorrel saddle-horse, which I had bought from the mail-carrier, Johnny Moorehouse. I was never so glad to have a horse of my own as I was that night. Some way the independence I felt in this possession did much to restore me. If I had had to walk home that night, I might have mired down in a bog of self-pity.

As I rode home slowly, I reasoned with myself. It was all for the best. I must avoid all complications. I had work to do. I was going to write, I must travel alone—always alone. I told myself everything but the truth, which was that I was bitterly jealous of the dark-eyed, charming Maud.

The revival began with the burning of the pipes. Crowds came to the church every night, and dozens

came to the altar. Every Sunday morning people joined
the church, prayer-meetings were held in the afternoons;
even the country people were moved. I went back to the
meetings in a few days. I knew a great work was being
done. I wanted to help; I had a high exalted feeling now,
of bearing my cross, and a much less exalted, but infinitely happier feeling that Maud would soon be on her way,
and life would settle back into its pleasant ways.

The conservative element, Presbyterians and Anglicans, kept away from the meetings, and were outspoken
in their disapproval. They warned the people to stay
away. They foresaw disaster in the excitement of the
altar calls and conversions. They recounted cases of insanity that they had known of, and these criticisms were
answered by Nettie, in her gentle words, "We do well to
be excited," she said, "over the greatest thing in life.
Religion is greater than a horse-race, or a football game,
or an election. . . . Excitement and emotions which have
no outlet are dangerous, I know, but religion gives an
outlet. Christ said, 'Feed the hungry, clothe the naked,
preach the gospel to the poor.' Have you any hungry, or
naked, or poor, or erring, or discouraged, or lonely, or
sad, among you? If so, then don't worry about an outlet
for your emotion, pour out your new-found love on these.
Cry if you wish, over your sins! There is no water so
holy as the tear of a penitent sinner."

In spite of all opposition the meetings grew in numbers and interest, and the whole neighborhood was
shaken. Family quarrels were made up, old debts paid,
drunkards reformed. Churches were crowded, bar-rooms
emptied. We saw these miracles. I knew then why the
temperance chart had failed. It had shown certain facts,
as true as the multiplication tables, and given warnings;
but it had been powerless to supply the will-power to heed
these warnings. It showed the right way, but had no
power to make people choose the right way. It
appealed to the head alone, and because of this it failed.
This, then, was the secret of religion. It gave strength

to the weak, life to the dead; it made people want to do the right thing.

We started a Sunday School at our school, and old and young came. The Saturday night rides were over; and a new spirit came to our neighborhood.

I have spoken of the wife of the town drunkard, who did not want to vote because that wish would reflect on her husband. She, of course, being the saint of our community, attended the meetings, and early in them asked for the prayers of God's people for her husband. I was there the night she stood up and made this plea. A tall, pale husk of a woman, whose shabby clothes hung on her as they would on a clothes horse. I felt for her a sort of pity, that was mixed with contempt. She was such a door-mat; she even washed for the hotel-keeper's wife, to pay old Silas' liquor bills. And, needless to say, I lost no time in praying for Silas. I mean I did not pray for him; but Silas did very well without my prayers.

One night Silas was converted with all the emotion that went with a prodigal son's return. He was a fine looking man, and being something of a show-man, missed none of the fireworks. He confessed he had been a lazy bum, letting his wife support him—and she had been a long-suffering angel; and he said he was through with liquor forever; "so help me God."

I do not think many believed him, they knew him too well, or thought they did. But we can take the long view of Silas Brand's case now, for that was forty years ago, and all the returns are in; the books are closed and nothing can hurt his record now. He went to work the day after his conversion, in a lumber yard. He was received in the church the next Sunday morning on confession of faith. He became a new man; with a new countenance, and one of that district's best loved citizens.

Not long ago, one of his sons whom I had taught, sent me a paper in which his father's death was recorded, and in the obituary, written by the United Church minister of the little town, were these words:

"He was soundly converted many years ago, in revival meetings conducted by the Misses Judd, in Manitou, and his zeal for the work of God knew no languor. His memory in this neighborhood will ever be a happy one."

The conversions did not all last. All the grains, even of wheat, that most enduring and vital of seeds, do not grow.

Before the end of the month it became evident that Nettie Judd would have to take a rest. She was growing paler and thinner before our eyes; a cough often shook her frail little body. The minister's wife said Nettie did not take care of herself; did not wear warm clothing; did not sleep enough, did not seem to care whether she lived or died, belonged too much to the other world.

The girls went from Manitou to Pilot Mound and Crystal City, and conducted meetings with the same spectacular results. Then suddenly the flickering torch was blown out. Nettie died.

She was only twenty-six years old. It was not a long life, as we reckon time. But she influenced many. She burned the candle at both ends, but it certainly made a bright and beautiful light while it lasted, and lighted many a stumbling soul into the way of life everlasting.

Maud went back to Ontario with the little coffin. I remember how she looked standing on the back platform of the train, as it wound up the grade, dressed in a rough gray coat with capes, a little red cap on her curls, waving to us, a long good-bye.

We stood there, a sad little group, awed by the presence of death, and yet exalted too. We knew the Heavenly Portals had opened wide when Nettie went in, and it seemed that some of the glory was shining around us as we lingered. A spring snow was falling in big flakes, and the train was rapidly fading into the gray distance as it pulled up the grade past Luke Armstrong's. We watched it still, and did not move until it had gone from sight. Then, without speaking, we turned and crossed the tracks to go back.

I turned at the Ellis' house corner to go up Front Street, to Curistons' Livery Stable, where I had left my horse. I felt a gentle pressure on my arm, and you would never guess who was walking with me!

CHAPTER XXXV

I Saw E. Cora Hind

Miss Hind's visit to Manitou came during my second year in Hazel School.

The *Manitou Mercury* carried a news item which caused me to press my green dress, blacken my shoes, and iron out my black veil with the green dots.

"Miss E. Cora Hind of Winnipeg will arrive on Saturday's train to visit her friend, Mrs. W. D. Ruttan."

I knew about Miss Hind. She had been the first lady typist in Winnipeg, having come there as a very young girl from Flesherton, Ontario; and now she was on the staff of the *Free Press*. She wrote signed articles, interviews, spoke in public and I had seen her picture and knew she was a striking figure of a woman, well-dressed, and impressive.

I would see Miss Hind, maybe I would get a chance to speak to her for I knew Mrs. Ruttan. I would go to the station on Saturday. There were always many people at the station, for the trains crossed in Manitou, and that hour between twelve and one was the peak of the village life.

When I arrived at Curiston's Livery stable and put my horse away, I found I had plenty of time; the trains would not come for half an hour, but people were going down the sidewalk past John Woottons' store on one corner and the Ellis House on the other.

It was rather too bad that the trains came together. No one could watch both trains arriving; the East train from Winnipeg slipping easily down the grade, almost noiselessly, with its smoke blown back on its shoulders by the prevailing west wind; and the other bound for Winnipeg with its smoke standing high over the engine, laboring up the track. But it gave us a feeling that great events were breaking at our feet when the two great messengers of commerce stood for four minutes heavily breathing as they disgorged passengers, express parcels and mail. And how busy and important the station agent and his assistant were handing out orders to both conductors, while we could hear the telegraph instruments left alone in the office still talking to themselves in sudden rushes of clattering sounds.

Everyone who could, came to the station on that Saturday morning, even Mrs. Barnes from the section house came over with her apron turned behind her to show that though she came from her work and would return to her work, for the moment she had left all menial tasks behind her. The butcher, knowing that business paused for the trains to pass, came hastily down the sidewalk, bareheaded, with his suit coat on over his once-white apron; a farmer's boy drove rapidly down the street with his foot hanging out of the buckboard just to show that he was socially at ease and that coming to town was an old story to him; tied his horse in front of Duncan Gunn's store and came jauntily over the tracks with his hat on one side of his head.

Soon we saw the smoke of the East train. She was coming! Miss Hind, I mean. In a minute or two I would see her. Mrs. Ruttan was talking to a group of women, and I had not been able to catch a word with her. In my wildest dreams I had believed it possible she might ask me to come to see Miss Hind. I remembered that Mrs. Ruttan had once said that I should be in the choir, for she thought I had a good contralto voice.——— I wondered if I dared go over and speak to her now. The crowd gathered and swarmed across the platform.

I heard one woman say, "If the west train is late I declare I won't wait. Yesterday it was so late my potatoes got burned. I gave them plenty of water to-day but Tom likes them cooked with a bone in them. . . . I do wish the C.P.R. would give us a decent train time." The train came sliding in noiselessly and the passenger coach stopped in front of me. My chance of speaking to Mrs.

Ruttan was gone now but at least I would see Miss Hind.

There she was. No mistake, a young woman in a tan tweed suit with brown facings; a little hat to match with a saucy quill set at exactly the right angle; and a scarf with flaring ends. She looked over the heads of the people who were descending the steps, picked out Mrs. Ruttan and waved to her. Her face had a fresh and lovely color and her fine dark blue eyes beamed with health and friendliness—a break in the crowd gave me a full view of her as she stepped briskly down the steps, with her small square leather bag in her hand. Then it was I saw her little feet so trimly shod in russet leather shoes. I had never seen prettier shoes. The crowd drew back making an aisle for her, closing in behind as she passed.

I wanted to follow her. I wanted Mrs. Ruttan to speak to me. But a sudden shyness had fallen on me, the shyness of the country girl. I think it was those twinkling russet shoes of hers. Mine were black goat skin, peeled and a little bit dull; also buttoned and gaping a bit at the top—I should have moved the top buttons over but had never thought of it. I could not make a move, and quite miserably I watched Mrs. Ruttan and her guest crossing the track; Mrs. Ruttan insisting against Miss Hind's protest on carrying the little square brown bag. I heard her say she had checked her big valise. Tommy Coolidge, the drayman, would deliver it. I saw Mrs. Ruttan give him the check and I thought with longing of the treasures of attire it would hold. I watched them until they went in Mr. Ruttan's store.

I had seen her! I had seen what a newspaper woman could be at her shining best. Like the sad little girl of whom Katherine Mansfield wrote in the *Doll's Playhouse*, I could say, "I seen the lamp."

Before I went back to my boarding house I went to the post office and wrote to the Richardson Book Store in Winnipeg for a book on shorthand believing as so many people did then, that this was the key to success in newspaper work.

CHAPTER XXXVI

My First Political Meeting

WHEN I recall how little we knew or cared about public matters I cannot be critical of the young people of to-day.

I attended one political meeting in Manitou about this time and would not have been there but for the persuasion of Mrs. Brown, whom I met in Huston's store. Mrs. Brown, who was a widow, lived about four miles out of town and had come in to do her Saturday shopping, had heard of the meeting and decided to stay for it. She asked me to do the same and offered to drive me back to my boarding house when it was over. I had my own horse then and so could get home myself but her offer to drive me out impressed me, I wondered why she was so anxious to have me attend the meeting.

I knew about Mrs. Brown. The women admired her, but the men I had heard speak of her were critical of her and resented her independent ways. She was a tall, angular woman with a weather beaten face, criss-crossed with tiny lines, blue eyes and a pleasant crisp voice.

"The women here are asleep," she said to me, as we walked about waiting for eight o'clock. "Being all right themselves they care little for other women. The comfortably married woman is the most selfish person in the world. I've asked dozens of them to come with me to this meeting, I asked everyone I saw after I heard of it. You'd laugh to hear the excuses. They had to give Billy a bath, or they had to blacken the family boots, or their husband's wouldn't like it. They are afraid to make an independent move. Then I saw you and I had a sudden gleam of hope. I had heard something about you that sounded original. Is it true that you have two boys at your school who were always fighting, and you got tired of it and made them fight it out one day to get the matter settled?"

I admitted it, but hastened to explain it was not so bad as it sounded. There had been nothing more serious than nose-bleeds apiece, and one black-eye; and peace had settled down on the playground since and the boys were good friends.

"Well, I liked that," said Mrs. Brown. "It revealed an original cast of mind. And I'm glad you will come with me. I've tried very hard to rouse women and failed. Maybe I can get you interested and you'll do something. Who knows? Anyway I am going to risk the price of a dinner on you."

I protested that, but she insisted, and at a boarding house on the front street, facing the tracks, we ate at a little oilcloth covered table, in a dark corner; and Mrs. Brown explained to me why she wanted women to vote and be members of school boards and go to Parliament, and take their place in the community.

"I knew nothing of business until my husband died," she said in her even voice, "I was a nice girl equipped for life, my poor mother thought. I could bake, sew, play the organ, and recite the 'Evening Hymn,' and had made quilts, and a seed-wreath. But what good does that do me now, when I am the head of a house with five little children depending on me? I have to do a man's work, as well as a woman's, and in doing that I have found out a few things. Men are afraid of women, jealous of them, and unfair to them. They want women to be looking-glasses, howbeit false ones that make them look bigger than they are. Even my little boys want me to watch them when they are sleigh-riding down the hill.

"Especially strong in most men is their dislike of women, who know more than they do. I taught a hired man a new wrinkle about ploughing and he left me, he said he wasn't going to be bossed by a woman, and the neighbors thought he did exactly the right thing. . . . They would do more for me if I were a helpless, pretty, little thing who would burst into tears . . . . I cried plenty the first year I was left alone, and everyone was very kind to me then. Now, that I am really trying to run my farm and look after my family I met plenty of opposition. . . . But I can't keep on crying, even to get help. How I hate that song, 'Men must work and women must weep.' I can work like a man, I can plough, and run a binder . . . . and believe me, my girls will get a man's education. They won't be left helplessly floundering like I was. . . .

"We have to get the vote on account of the laws. In Ontario a woman has some claim on her husband's property, but none here. That was changed because of Indian wives. The poor Indian women were cut off from any claim on a man's property. They said they had to do away with the wife's claim too, on account of the boom in 1882 when property was changing hands so fast. But it won't be set right until women vote. You'll see.

"It's a man-made world, young lady, as you will find. Even nature works against women, by making them smaller and weaker, giving them all the human ailments, and a few of their own; and society has taken up the good work by laying heavier obligations on women and a higher standard of morality."

"But there are compensations," I protested. "Women lead a more sheltered life. . . ."

"Yes, on paper," she said sadly. "I did not know what life could do to a woman until I was left. I had a good home, and a good husband. But homes pass and husbands die. . . . Well, I shouldn't be so mournful with you and so discouraging. I am not so badly off as some. I would rather have a good husband dead than a bad one living! I am grateful for all my blessings, good children, and good health.

We went to the meeting in the Town Hall, where the Hon. Thomas Greenway was speaking. He commented on our appearance and said he was glad to see at least two women in the audience. Politics concerned women

as much as men, though he did not think women would
ever need to actually take part in politics. But their influence was needed and never more so than at this time.
It was the woman's place to see that their men folk voted
and voted right and this he said (so even we could understand), meant voting Liberal; which brought applause
from the audience.

Mrs. Brown and I had written out two questions and
signed them as we sat at the oilcloth covered table in the
boarding house.

(1) Are you in favor of extending the Franchise to
women? If so when may we expect to have this privilege?

(2) Are you in favor of women having homesteading
rights, and if so, will you ask the Dominion Government
to consider this?

There was a collection taken to defray expenses and
we put our questions on the plate along with our contri-
butions. We saw the chairman read the questions and
show them to Mr. Greenway, who laughed good-naturedly
when he read them and looked down at us with a sort of
fatherly rebuke in his eyes! He was a fine figure of a
man with a full, brown beard, a well-shaped head, and a
merry smile. Then there were more whispers, the other
speaker was consulted and he took the questions, read
them, and shook his head. Then the chairman put the
paper in his pocket, from which it was never recovered
and we were sorry then that we had given our two
quarters.

We stayed and listened, not greatly interested in what
was said. The other party, it seemed, had well nigh
ruined the country. It had been put out just in the nick
of time. Another term would have been fatal. They
must be kept out!

The meeting closed with feeble cheers for the Premier
and I think everyone was glad when it was over.

Mrs. Brown and I were not spoken to, though I saw

men whom I knew, and she, no doubt, knew many. But they charitably ignored us.

We parted at the livery stable, where she too had left her horse. We were indignant at our chilly reception but undismayed and full of plans for further advances. But when I got away from Mrs. Brown my enthusiasm por political life began to wane. It was a sordid, grubby business, judging by this dull meeting with its stale air, and I was uncomfortable all the time I sat in it, knowing we were not wanted.

I rode home through the dark night wondering about what I had heard. The sorrel horse knew his way, without any guidance. . . . Many of the houses were in darkness, for country people go to their beds early even on Saturday night. As I passed Ben Cook's house I heard the mournful notes of a fiddle. Ben and Henry his brother lived at the turn of the road in a little square unpainted house, and did their own cooking. . . . I had skated with them on the lake near their farm the fall before, when we took advantage of the ice before the snow came, and gathered at the lake on the moonlight nights, making fires of driftwood on the shore. I could hear the violin notes long after I passed—they followed me down the dark trail. Ben had been one of the converts at the Judd revival and he played and sang one of the revival hymns now:

> "Jesus Saviour, pilot me
> Over life's tempestuous sea."

The sweet words, drifting out into the night, gave me a sense of security.

I thought of the Judd sisters then, and their work, and how they had changed the color of people's thoughts across southern Manitoba. Marrying and raising children was not the only thing a woman could do; even in that how unfair life and society were to women; laying all responsibility on them and giveng them no training for their work, and then if they made mistakes punishing them beyond all reason. . . . I thought of Louie Smith, poor Louie, who by some mischance had fallen a victim to the wiles of Tom Preston, the bad man of our neighborhood. She had been loyal to him through all, and refused to talk, bearing all the blame.

And Tom still went at large, driving his pacing horse, with his heavy gold watch chain dangling with charms straight across his vest; while Louie had not been off her father's farm since and ran for cover when any one approached. No one had held out a kindly hand to Louie nor had pity on her innocence. Louie had sinned! She had fallen. Hw cruel the world was! How cruel we all were!

I raged in my mind when I thought of her, a fine happy, healthy girl a few months before, weeding a pansy bed, clean and as sweet as a pansy herself in her print dress and sunbonnet, now a prisoner on her father's farm, a fugitive from society. Just a pale, fleeting face seen at an upstairs window . . . doomed to a life of unending and unrelieved labor, for one moment's yielding, and even the church had not spoken out against this injustice. I had take my knee off the pommel and sat straight on the saddle to rest myself and when I thought of Louie I dug my heels into the sorrel horse in my intense indignation, and he, taken by surprise, plunged and bolted for home clattering noisily down the trail with the stirrups lashing him, leaving me on the side of the road.

I was not hurt for I fell on the grassy roadside and I was not far from my destination. I hoped my friends had gone to bed, and so would not know that the sorrel had come home without me. If I had been riding the right and natural way astride the horse this could not have happened. A side-saddle is surely the last word in discomfort for both the rider and the horse; another example of life's injustice to women I thought as I hastened along through the dark.

Everyone was safely in bed and the horse had gone

to the gate, which led to the farmyard and stood there with his head down. I unsaddled him and put him into his stall. Then let myself into the unlocked kitchen, smelling pleasantly of spicy cooking and dimly lighted by the lantern which Mrs. Hornsberg had left burning for me. Mrs. Hornsberg always baked on Saturday afternoon for Sunday. She had left on the kitchen table sliced headcheese, cranberry catsup and fresh buns, and butter and I forgot the sorrows of my sex for the next few minutes, for I was healthily hungry.

When I had eaten my good humor came back. It was good to be back in this cheerful warm kitchen with its reassuring orderliness.

I went into the room where Esther was sleeping and brought out the "Giant" Scribbler where I kept my diary and made an entry detailing the events of the day. Then I went on: "I do not want to be a reformer," I wrote, "I will do my share of the work of the world some other way. I want a big friendly house, white and glistening, under great spreading trees with a huge fireplace in the hall which will send out a welcome to the world. Inside there will be a long table set with gleaming silver and china with rosebuds and when my friends gather there they will look through wide windows at the pageant of the sunset, saffron, rose and flame, and when the night comes down fading the sky to ashy grey the fireflies will stipple the purple dusk of the garden with their dots and dashes and there will be good talk and a great fellowship. No, I do not want to be a reformer and sit in a dull meeting where the air is dead and stale and everyone wondering what I came for. . . . Agnes Wakefield, Florence Doombey, Ruth Pinch did not attend political meetings. Still I must remember that they lived a long time ago and this is a new country. I wonder what C. D. would have thought of Mrs. Brown. Well, I admire her anyway. She has stood up to life."

I decided to sell my horse when I found I could not break him of the habit of bolting for the livery stable every time I rode to town. He had wintered the year before at Curiston's livery barn, and when he came to the foot of that street he began to act like a cat that sees a bed of catnip. I had hoped he would give up the struggle, but he held to the hope he would one day be able to throw me and get back.

Then, of course, I thought of George, who could always use another horse, and who never failed to help any of his friends. I wrote to George and he came down to see me and the horse. I had paid seventy-five dollars for the sorrel; so George gave me ninety and took him off my hands.

I wish all my financial adventures had ended so happily.

CHAPTER XXXVII

MANITOU

A VACANCY occurred in the Manitou School at the end of that year and I sent in an application, hardly hoping, but Inspector E. E. Best had given me two good reports and had said I was one of the best disciplinarians in his Inspectorate, and no doubt I received the appointment on his recommendation. There were four teachers in Manitou School, and my room was next the Principal's.

The school was a grim frame building at the east of the little town, with two rooms up and two down, a hard, worn school-yard, unfenced and unrelieved by tree or flower. The countryside rolled away to the east and south, dotted with farm buildings and clumps of trees, leafless now in January, and swept by wintry winds and brightened only by the new yellow strawstacks and the red and white cattle that foraged through them.

But Manitou was a centre of learning, for we had the Normal School there, one of the three Normal Schools in the province, and the second week I was there, Normal students were sent to each room to watch us teach. It was all very flattering, but embarrassing too. I wished I could be more like Miss Nimmons of the Carleton School in Winnipeg and be really able to show them the art of teaching. My pupils ranged in age from twelve to eighteen.

I was boarding at the parsonage and that was really the highlight of my coming to town. The parsonage was a small frame house facing south, quite near the school. The front door opened into the parlor and beyond the parlor was the dining-room, with a kitchen and woodshed to the right. An open stairs in the dining-room led to three bedrooms upstairs.

The McClung family had come from Port Arthur and the junior members were still bewailing the change. Mr. and Mrs. McClung were ready at any time to accept the ruling of the Stationing Committee of the Methodist Church, even if it took them to the North Pole; though I know they found our little prairie town bleak and barren after the scenic beauty of the head of the Lakes.

Wes and Nellie, Herb and Ed let no sentimental attachment to the church of their fathers put a curb on their tongues, and they mourned for the companions and beauties they had been forced to leave. Besides they found the prairie winter very cold. Having known nothing but prairie winters, I did not know any better, and wondered why they made such a fuss when a pail of water froze to the bottom or frost gathered on the walls an inch thick. That winter of 1892 was a particularly cold one, but I was so glad to have only a hundred yards to go to school that the weather mattered but little to me.

Mr. McClung made a good minister for a scattered flock, for he had all the conquering fire of the circuit rider. He had three services each Sunday; morning and evening, in his own church, and Kingsley and Kaleida on alternate Sundays in the afternoon. These appointments were ten or twelve miles out, and no weather, however, disagreable, kept him at home. Wes, the boy in the drug store, went with him to drive the horse when the weather was stormy.

I will admit (though it would have been considered an unmaidenly confession at that time) that I was much influenced in my desire to teach in Manitou by the presence of the minister's eldest son. I felt sure Mrs. McClung's son must be the sort of man I would like. She had all the sweetness, charm and beauty of the old-fashioned woman, and in addition to this had a fearless, and even radical, mind. I had been to the parsonage quite a few times before I came to board there; and I saw the methods of training her children. Her one girl, Nellie, who was my age, did no more than one share of the work;

being a girl, did not sentence her to all the dishwashing and bedmaking. The two younger boys took their turn and there were no complaints from them. Wes, of course, worked long hours in the drug store, and so he was immune from chores. On the other hand, Nellie had no special favors because she was a girl. And there was no talk of having to be accompanied by a brother every time she went out.

All this I liked, and while I was still profoundly serious in my determination to travel the highway of life alone, giving myself to the world of letters, I liked this tall slim young man of twenty very well indeed, and was glad of a chance to see him at close range.

He told me one day that I was the brightest find of their life, since leaving Port Arthur, but knowing what they thought of the prairie, I did not feel greatly elated. He would have to do better than that.

I loved the life in this little town, and have always resented the condescension with which many people view the small country town. There were many advantages. I began to take music lessons from Miss Clarke, and painting lessons from Miss Victoria Mortson, who had a class in the upstairs parlor at the hotel, where the proprietor's relatives (deceased, I think) looked stonily down on us from their heavy oak frames. We had a teachers' meeting every Friday evening after four, conducted by the principal.

Then there were forty Normalites in circulation, and we had to do what we could to guide their young feet into the pleasant paths of learning.

Besides all this, we often had parties on Friday nights, especially I remember the surprise parties to houses in the country. We did not go unless we were invited, of course, but the night was left open, and the arrangements were made quickly. The young men found sleighs and horses, and the girls provided the refreshments; salmon saidwiches, cakes, a can of coffee, and we were off. All the seats were taken out of the sleigh and plenty of hay put in, covered with robes, with more robes above, and we were young enough to sit comfortably on our heels if necessary.

I remember the moonlight nights, frosty and cold, when the stars seemed twice their natural size in the deep, bright blue of the sky, and the lights in the houses we passed, shone warm and yellow on the snow, blurred by the frost ferns on the windows. We found the Dipper and the North Star and the Bear while the sleigh bells rang out their silvery music, and we were uproariously, unreasonably happy just to be alive and part of life.

When we arrived, what fun we had playing the guessing game, where one person thinks of something and the others ask questions that can only be answered by "yes" or "no". I remember how Jessie McEwen, one of the teachers, held us at bay for a long time at the surprise party at Susie Laidlaw's, when she thought of Mr. Harrison's nose. We found by our questioning that it couldn't be bought or carried away; had been given to the owner; was not as big as a cow; could not be eaten; moved about freely, and did not belong to anyone present but was well known by all and admired by some.

There was no pairing off at our parties—that was understood, but sometimes, coming home, when the moon was low in the sky, looking a bit weary from shining so hard all evening; and when the cold had deepened as the night wore on, there might be a little holding of hands when we sang "Genevieve, Sweet Genevieve" or "Sweet Marie". Nellie Wallen often had cold hands, but not for long.

We had no telephones, picture-shows, radios, phonographs, daily papers or lending libraries. We made our own fun—and we had plenty—the sort of fun you can remember for forty years and find it still warms your heart.

I have lived in several small towns, but I have not known any other place that had such a decided flavor. Manitou was engaging, unexpected, and altogether adventurous. It was half-way between Winnipeg and

L

Deloraine on the southwestern branch of the C.P.R., had been settled since 1882, and had held its early settlers, who, unlike the people in many prairie towns, had come to stay.

The first winter I was there the W.C.T.U. opened a reading room and amusement room, and it became a gathering place for the intelligentsia after four and on Saturday afternoons. I do not know how we managed to be heard above the clatter from the outside room, where there were three croquinole boards always in use, but we were young and lusty and could raise our voices. We had hastily arranged unofficial debates, and could have coffee sent up to us in honest, thick, white cups from the restaurant below, at two cups for five cents, just to give the conversation a continental flavor, and as we argued on annexation with the United States or the relative value of science or literature in the schools, or whether or not it is possible to live without sin, we felt that we were living in the best tradition of the coffee houses of London.

Manitou's weekly paper, *The Mercury*, edited by R. H. Spedding, was an event each week. Even the advertisements tingled with excitement. When one store, wishing to show its popularity, stated in a big headline, "Three men killed in the jam at our Saturday bargains!", the other store came out with the assurance "There are no dead men in our jam." The swift action of changing their ads each week wore away at last, and there came a time later when one ad ran from early August to January. This was Billy M——'s confectionary news, and what was a timely ad in August read queerly when the bitter north wind scoured the frozen streets, and the chief problem of life was to keep the furnaces roaring: "Preserving season is now open," and "Keep Kool at all Kosts, with a Kwart of Ice Kream."

Even our undertakers had personalities of their own. One of them has what he called a "Skidoodle" of prices. The other one always invited the friends at funerals to "Come now, and look your last on the 'diseased'."

The country around Manitou with its rolling prairie and beautiful unfenced lands, was an ideal spot for the training of game-dogs, and four of our citizens had large kennels of Llewellyn setters of great beauty and value. When the dogs were taken out to the fields, many people went to see their performance. The dogs ranged back and forth at right angles to the wind, racing at high speed, and with a graceful flowing motion, to get the scent, then with shorter runs, weaving up the wind to make the point. When a dog reached the place of close scent he suddenly stopped as rigid as if turned to stone, one front paw in mid-air, and his head and tail in line with the bird which, though hidden in the grass, he had located accurately by the scent. He would stand there, a picture of grace and concentration, until released by a word from his master.

Dogs came from as far away as Kentucky to be trained on the Manitou fields, but the Field Trials were held at Morris and Letellier where the wide and level grass lands along the Red River allowed the judges to watch the work of the dogs as they ranged for a mile or more. At the contests the dogs were set down from the crates in pairs, and the test was made between the two. The better dog was the one which made the wide range acting independently of his master, in his zeal to find a bird, though to pass a scent which was picked up by his competitor gave a dog a very bad mark. When the point was made, it must be held until his master arrived. Then at a word the dog, still rigid and pointing, advanced toward the bird, flushing it for the shoot. In the Field Trials which were held just before the shooting season, there was no shooting of birds, and the dogs must have wondered why all their good work came to nothing.

The Manitou dogs were sometimes taken to Kentucky and other southern states to compete, and one of Mr. Wootton's dogs, "Dick Blondell", made a great win one year and had his picture in the *Manitou Mercury* and, no doubt, in many other papers.

I remember one Kentucky dog-owner, a perfect colonial with pointed beard and leather leggings and delightfully soft voice, who came for severel seasons, bringing his wife with him. The colonel had a great fascination for the young crowd, for there was a rumor, unconfirmed but none the less believed, that he had killed a man! But if he had, there was no trace of remorse in his placid countenance.

One of the Manitou dog-owners, whose kennels were behind his office on the main street, played a violin, not well, but persistently, and often far into the night. And sometimes when he had teased the strings into a state of cataphonics, the dogs lifted up their voices too, and the other kennels responded until the little town rang dismally. For a long time no one protested. The game-dogs were part of our village life. But when one of the early settlers went back to his home in the East and married his old sweetheart who had been waiting for twenty years for him to make up his mind, she, accustomed to the sterile silence of that respectable little hamlet on the Ottawa River, made loud protests against the dogs and even wrote a letter to the paper about them. We thought it very strange of her to object. How did she think dogs could always be kept quiet? Of course we had to remember that she probably had never, in her under-privileged life, seen a bird dog turn to stone! We who knew the dogs and appreciated them were divided into two classes—those who said they never heard the dogs, and those who said they liked to hear them.

There was a young Englishman, who lived in the Pembina Valley, twelve miles south of Manitou, who had been sent to Canada to cure him of his drinking habits, but with two hard-working bars twelve miles away, the usual number of thirsty ones ready to drink with him— and no restrictions on the sale of liquor—he went on from bad to worse. But one day, in a furniture store in Manitou, he got into an altercation with the proprietor, who was an old man, and, in his drunken fury, struck Mr. Rossman and knocked him down. When he became sober and knew what he had done, he declared he would never drink again. We knew him for twenty years after that and he kept his word.

There was another young Englishman in the Valley who had been sent away from home because he was not very bright, and "father" did not like to look at him. So he was exiled. His people had plenty of money and supplied him with blankets, guns, knives, saddles—everything but the one thing he craved—permission to go home. He had been out three years before he dared to ask permission that he might go home, even for one day. We all waited for the answer—and hoped. The answer came at last. No, he could not come back; but his mother sent him a book, "Twenty-three ways of playing Solitaire."

There was the young Miss C——— who had mothered the family since her mother died years ago, but who had always cherished the hope that she would some day get her chance. It came at last, and she came to school, a tall, slight, handsome girl of twenty-five. She had the crystalline beauty of Ann Harding. And how eagerly she studied and learned! She was in the principal's room, across from my room, but she often came to me after four, and I was glad to help her with her arithmetic. Her starved mind drew knowledge in with the fervor of its own desire; she would be ready to write for her certificate at the July examinations. One day she came to my door with her books in her arms.

"It's all over," she said, "My brother and his wife have come to visit and they are both sick with typhoid. I must nurse them. So good-bye and I thank you for helping me. Maybe I can come back—I will not say die yet—I'm only twenty-five."

There was a steely glint in her dark blue eyes, and she held her head high as she walked down the stairs.

She tried again, but something always happened. Someone broke an arm, or had a baby, or nerves, or both.

But years after there came a time when she could be spared, and through the influence of a great Canadian doctor, she got a chance to train in the Chicago General Hospital. She was beyond the age, but the doctor knew her worth and got her in. She made a record there among all those younger women, and went into private nursing and was doing well. But the home ties were strong. She loved her own, naturally, having done so much for them. And she came back and did more.

The years have been kind to her. She is still tall, straight and handsome, and still the burder-bearer. She is caring now for an elder sister in Winnipeg, who is under the delusion that her friends have just phoned for her to meet them at the Royal Alexander Hotel, so dressed for the street she waits in the hall, and cannot understand why the front door is kept locked. Over and over, still patient and sweet, the gallant sister explains, reasons, cajoles, improvises and watches—a twenty-four hour shift.

Then there was a gloomy Mrs. Brant who lived a few miles west of the little town, who attended every funeral and saw sin, sickness and death in the brightest day of sunshine. She came to see me when my first baby was three days old, and looking at this marvel of infant beauty, wiped away a tear and said, "Don't set your heart on raising this little boy, he is marked for death—see the blue vein across his nose—he'll never live to wear his wedding clothes."

I wanted to throw her downstairs. Blue vein, indeed! But I thought of it that snowy morning eighteen years later in Edmonton, at the station, when the little boy, grown a tall lad now, went out with the Princess Pats. . .

And I thought of it, with another emotion, twelve years later still, when we stood among the flowers one happy summer evening in Edmonton and heard the throbbing words of the marriage ceremony, beginning, "We are gathered in the sight of God and man to unite this man and this woman. . . ."

I would have written to her to tell her she was wrong, but I did not need to tell her then. She knew.

CHAPTER XXXVIII

SUMMER HOLIDAYS

IN the summer of '92, having saved part of my salary, I went to see Aunt Ellen in Alpena, Michigan. I went by train to Sault Ste. Marie, then by boat to Mackinac where I spent a day and a night, and by another boat to Alpena.

I had promised myself a trip when I had money, for I wanted to see places, the Great Lakes, the locks, big ships; and I wanted to see my Aunt Ellen, who had always been my ideal of women. Mother had good help at this time. Martha Guest, sister of Edwin Guest, had come from Birmingham, a little cheerful English girl. Hannah was teaching at Northfield School and would be at home for the holidays, so I was free to spend mine away from home. More than all, I wanted, I think, a long train trip.

Trains have always fascinated me, and still do. No doubt this love of trains is partly due to the fact that we waited so long for a railway. I love to hear the long whistle of a train trumpeting through the night, and if it wakens me I am glad, but generally it works itself pleasantly into my dreams like sweet music. When I am old, I want to live near the tracks where I can hear the trains at night, pounding the rails and screaming out their signals and ringing their bells. By day I'll see them, hauling their heavy loads, with their smoke plumes darkening and thinning, coming back over their shoulders as they sweep across the plain. With their force and strength, and their minds set upon the far country, they will vitalize me again, and fill me with the joy of living. I hope I will be so near to them that they will shake my house as they pass, and I will sit up and listen and feel their vibrations, and be part of them. And in my mind

I will go with them as far as I can. Then one night, when I am very old and tired, I shall not come back, and the friends will say, "Wasn't it a nice way to go? The old lady died in her sleep. . . ."

But I was speaking of my trip to Alpena. Jessie McEwen went to Merrickville, her old home in Ontario, and Jack and Bell Poole, whom we met in Winnipeg, went to the same part of the country. So we travelled together to Sault Ste. Marie, and there we had a wonderful half-day watching the ships go through the locks. I knew then that geography should be taught by pictures and by exchange teachers, and that a thousand miles of travel is better than many books.

When my friends left me, I had to go alone. It was not so pleasant, but I knew it was good for me; and I wrote copious notes in a large, black-backed note book, and tried to look mysterious and important, as a young lady would who was sent upon a secret mission for her country's good.

I had a wonderful day at Mackinac, and bought an Indian belt at a curio store. I saw the natural bridge in the distance, and remember most vividly of all, that I bought a dozen bananas for fifteen cents.

Alpena, on Lake Michigan, was then a lumber town, all pink and new, with raw lumber houses and with piles of it on vacant lots, ready for building. My cousin, Charley, was the foreman of a lumber company. He came home for a few days and took me to the theatre and to a band concert. My aunt, Ellen, had run a boarding-house for men when she went to Alpena first, and Mary and Maggie, her daughters, had helped her. But when the girls got married and the boys were in good positions, she built a little house for herself on 7th Street. It was at this house I visited her. Her youngest son, Duncan, was still at school, and on Sundays sang in the boys' choir in the Episcopalian Church.

My aunt had changed but little. She still had a laugh in her eyes and a brooky mellowness in her voice.

Charley seemed older than his mother, and in speaking of this, she made the only reference I ever heard her make to the vicissitudes of her life.

"Charley took responsibility too early," she said, "and it has left its mark on him. That's the worst of family troubles. You can't keep it all from the children, and a wound in a child's heart is like a wound in a young tree. It grows with the tree, not out, but in."

Aunt Ellen had many friends and they drove us around, across the sandy country, baked and bleached with the heat and sun, but prosperous too, and I saw saw-mills, shingle-mille and factories. My month went by very quickly. When I came back I had a gold-headed cane for my father, a gift from Charley which I kept under my pillow at night and dreamed of losing, and a quilt which Aunt Ellen had made for my Mother—blue, white and pink, in the pattern which is called, "The Sidewalks of New York."

I had a week at home before school started in September, arriving when the harvest was in full swing.

Mother was rather worried about my attitude toward money. I had been teaching two full years and had saved nothing. I had earned over a thousand dollars and had nothing to show for it but a few clothes and books. Fred Vigfuson, one of our hired men, gave me his support by saying that I had used my money wisely—money was made for spending. Fred had saved all he earned the first five years he worked and then "backed" a friend's note and lost it all. Now he said he had just one rule: "Spend your money so fast no one can steal it from you." The whole question of spending versus saving was discussed when we sat at the long table in the kitchen at mealtime, and though Fred and I were convinced our idea of spending had great merit, we were voted down.

Nap, the old dog, getting a little bit stiff now with advancing years, lived at my brother Will's house all the time—beloved playmate of the children—but when I came home he returned without urging and stayed the week.

Even Leonora, the Queen of the Cats, gave me a greeting, howbeit constrained and haughty. Leonora, under the weight of years, had lost her enthusiasm. She was a real personality who was known all over the neighborhood because of her many descendants. She was our first cat after the tragedy of Sylvia, and was presented to us by Mr. William Ingram, our neighbor, when she was a little ball of fur about the size of a teacup.

Leonora's many kittens were welcomed by the neighbors to keep down the tawny striped gophers which had arrived in large numbers and dug holes in the gardens and ate the young plants. It required no planned sales talk to place kittens at that time. They were a favor, spoken for in advance. Eighteen for the season seemed a very good return. When the next summer Leonora had a mere trifling six, twice, we were a little disappointed. But we did not need to be, for Leonora made up for the shortage by having an extra six in September.

She was a long, slender cat, swift on her feet, and a deadly enemy of gophers. She hunted for sport, not necessity, and piled up the day's catch in windrows for all to see. She lived on praise and demanded it from every member of the family. When she was five years old she left us mysteriously and for no apparent reason. She walked out on us. We feared a wolf or a fox had killed her—she was in no condition to fight when she left —and our grief was all the more acute because of this.

Nap hunted up and down the banks of the creek and all over the neighborhood. Inquiries were made in vain. We had enough cats to go on with, of course, but we sorrowed greatly for Leonora. We were sorry we ever criticized her fertility. She had embarrassed us with this fatal gift for reproduction. Eighteen kittens per season is a heavy stock to handle, even though the prairies were wide and new settlers were coming. There were times when we wished Leonora were not so ambitious. Indeed, there had been some loose talk of drownings. However, she had her revenge on us now. If we loved her in life too little, we loved her in death too well.

I labored hard on a poem during this sad time, in which mournful mention was made of her many excellent qualities, and deep remorse for our criticism.

I think there were ten verses in all—I remember the last two:

"What caused you thus to leave us, Leonora?
Was it a green-field-far-away attraction?
Or did our comments on your swift addition
Drive you to subtraction?

A row of asterisks here indicated the passing of time, and then another verse appeared:

"And while we sorrowed sore for lost Leonora
One day she hurriedly came in the door,
And following her came little cats galora,
Running and leaping on the kitchen floor."

So the story ended happily and Leonora lived out her days, her bright coat fading as the years rolled on and her sunny disposition growing sour and crabbed with the infirmities of age. But her good works and labors of love were not forgotten. She reigned undisputed Queen of the Cats, and was one of the few animals I have known to die of old age. While I was at home I kept a record of her descendants on the smooth side of the granary door, but after I left, this good practice was not followed, and so a complete record can not be given. The score stood at sixty-eight when I left, and the end was not yet!

CHAPTER XXXIX

In Which the First Part of My Life Ends

BECAUSE of heavy storms, and snow-filled cut-banks, I went home at Christmas by Winnipeg. The C.P.R. had a way of keeping their trains moving, which the Northern Pacific had not. Our service on the Morris-Brandon branch was called a tri-weekly service; and some thought the spelling should be changed. But we were not disposed to be critical of it. It had come to us in our sore need and broken the winter of our discontent. It was our own railway, and we regarded it with great tolerance.

I arrived in Winnipeg at 4 o'clock in the afternoon of a blinding snow storm, but a bit of rough weather, did not prevent Helen Hislop from being at the station to meet me, for I was going to spend the night with her. The Hislop home was always open. When I attended Normal two years before I was often there, and enjoyed its high hospitality. Another place could always be set at the long table, and the conversation was easy to enter. The father was an alderman of the city. Jack was in Medical College. Helen had been teaching at Plympton near Winnipeg, and the others were at school.

That night Helen had arranged a party and I remember meeting Edgar Burgess, who afterwards was principal of the Manitou School. I do not remember that we danced, and I know there were no cards. I think we only talked. Mr. Hislop rarely spoke (I know now—there were no open spaces in the conversation), but often shook his head, as he looked at us with his kindly smile.

Mrs. Hislop was a leader in the good works of the city, a woman of fine ability, and a heart as big as humanity's needs. She was president of the Women's Foreign Missionary Society in Saint Andrew's Church and was referred to as the "Foreign Woman" by her children. Her laugh had in it a contagious merriment that made every one join her. She had a driving ambition which inspired her children and her friends, and I have always been grateful to her for the high value she set on learning. She was always busy; doing for other people as well as for her own, but she found time to read many books and could summarize a book with great deftness and skill. She wrote a little book, later, called *Streets of Winnipeg*, which can be found in the Western Libraries.

At ten o'clock Mr. Hislop, true to his Scottish tradition, took the "Book", and read a psalm, and we all went on our knees while he commended his family and friends, his country and her destiny to the mercy of "Him that sitteth above the clouds," and having done this, went to bed, leaving us to go on with our talk. But Mrs. Hislop, who was as young as any of us, stayed on until the last guest had departed.

That night Helen and I talked, until the dawn was showing blue, behind the window blind. We did not know when we would see each other again, and there were many things to be said.

The next morning I left on the Souris branch of the C.P.R. for Treesbank. This line has been extended from Glenboro to Souris and by coming to Treesbank I was within four miles of home.

The pale cold light of a stormy wintry morning lay on the countryside, cattle were huddled close together in the shade of the straw stacks, and the smoke from the houses twisted by the scouring wind soon lost itself in the colorless confusion of the snowy air. I could see muffled figures moving about the barnyards attending to the stock. I knew the hens would be kept in until noon, when the sun would have more power, and even then it would be only the strong-minded hens that would come out, and they would be quite offensive about it and scornful of the timid ones with their tongues. If you wish to hear the

swift jagged tearing of reputations, listen to a flock of
hens, and yet they are always quite impersonal, and dis-
interested.—"It's nothing to me, but facts are facts."

I loved the winter scene, even when the wind whipped
the loose snow into billows, which rising and falling ob-
scured the landscape. Plenty of snow meant moisture for
the soil, and the deadly frost killed noisome insects and
made possible No. 1 Hard wheat, which was our fortune.
There was a kindness in the cold. It made food taste
better, fires burn more brightly, and brought people into
closer family circles. I knew what the psalmist meant
when he spoke of the virtuous woman "who was not
afraid of the snow for her household." She knew it drove
her family into the circle of lamplight and made it easier
to get the children to do their homework, and strength-
ened the bonds of affection.

This was my first time to travel over the long bridge
flung from bank to bank of the Souris, high above where
once the little village of Millford stood. I looked down
at the deserted village below us, as we moved carefully
over the long bridge, where once many people had lived.
The buildings had long since been moved to Glenboro,
and only cellars, old walls and piles of tin cans were left.
Major Roger's dream had come to this!

Treesbank, a mile or so from the north bank of the
Souris, was the new station, and there I found not Jack
waiting for me, as I expected, but Fred Vigfuson, the
man who believed in spending his money as he made it.

Fred was of Icelandic origin, and was somewhat of a
rover. I asked Fred about his trip this year, and found
he was going to California. Fred had seen more of the
world than any of us, for each winter he went somewhere,
returning in the spring, quite willing to work another
summer.

Even when Fred told me my father had a bad cold, I
was not alarmed, though it was seldom that he was ailing.
Jack had gone with Hannah to Northfield school, for it
was her closing concert, and there "were great doings,"

with a Christmas tree as high as the ceiling and a flag drill. I gathered from Fred's conversation that he would have been there himself, but for my untimely arrival. I might as well have stayed a day in Winnipeg.

When we reached home, the house seemed empty, and silent. There was no one in the kitchen or living-room. Mother came out of the bedroom and motioned to me to be quiet.

"He's asleep," she said in a whisper. "He tried to stay awake to see you, but he dropped off. It's just a cold I hope." She looked anxious.

We went down to the kitchen and sat beside the cook stove. Fear had us in its grip.

"You don't think it's serious, do you?" I asked her. My mother knew as much as any doctor.

"Anything is serious, at his age," she said sadly. "He was eighty on the 12th of December. Borrowed time, Nellie. Three score years and ten."

I had intended to write to him, for his eightieth birthday. But I had forgotten, and I knew how pleased he would have been. If I had only remembered!

"We had a roast turkey," she was saying, "and Addie and Fred came. Addie was eight the next day. So we had eight candles on the cake for her. He told her he was ten times her age, but would never be that again; and he was in a great good humour. . . . But there's a change in him now, Nellie! And he does not even ask about the weather! You remember his first question was always, 'What is the day like?' But not now. Not since he took the chill a week ago. He came in from the barn with his teeth chattering, though it was a fine day. I got him into bed and put the hot water bottle at his feet, and hot stove lids. . . ."

The day after Christmas, our local doctor suggested a consultation and Jack drove to Brandon for a well-known doctor, who came, warmed his hands, went in, took a look at his patient, and said in his blunt Scotch way.

"You're a pretty old man, Mr. Mooney, and have lived your life. You can't expect to live much longer.

Father roused himself at that, and sat up.

"I'll live out my time, Doctor," he said. "I am not going to die until I have to; even if you think I should."

The doctor, shaking his head, proceeded to examine him. "A general break-up of the system," he said brutally. . . . "It's a case of the one-horse shay. . . . I don't know why Anderson wanted a consultation. . . ."

Not a kind word, not a friendly observation. The old doctor could not soften his manner, even though his patient was dying.

It was Jack who spoke his mind when he knew what had happened. "You were brought here to do something," Jack said to him, "and you have only discouraged him."

"My dear boy," the doctor said petulantly, "I can't work miracles, I can't save your Father. . . ."

"We do not expect you to work a miracle," Jack said, "but we do expect you to speak civilly, even kindly to him."

"I don't believe is soft soaping," the old doctor said. "Your father probably want to know the truth. He will want to put his house in order in the few days that are left."

"His house has been in order for many years," Mother replied. "He made his peace with God many years ago, and he has not an enemy in the world. . . . We knew he was a very sick man. Our own doctor told us that. But we thought you might be able to do something to prolong his days."

After the doctor had had his dinner, Fred drove him back to Brandon.

Father made light of the doctor's verdict. "That ould trap," he said, lapsing into his richest Irish brogue, "would rather tell a man he was dying than anything else. . . . I'd like to make a liar out of him, and I believe if I could get past March, I'd go another year. . . . Anyway don't let it trouble you. He's right in saying, I've had a long life, and a pleasant one. I've lived near the soil and feel friendly to it. It will lie lightly on my bones."

The next day, Mr. Howarth, the Methodist minister from Stockton, came through a heavy snow-storm and stayed all afternoon. He was a cheerful little man with a hearty laugh and it was glorious to hear Father joining him. We were almost hopeful that day.

Before the minister left Father asked Mother and all of us to come in, and Mr. Howarth read the 4th chapter of John, "Let not your hearts be troubled," and we drank the wine and ate the bread of the Sacrament, and after that a great peace seemed to fall on the house. The last words I heard my Father utter were the words of a hymn:

"The gospel bears my spirit up,
A faithful and unchanging God
Lays the foundation of my hope
In oaths, and promises and blood."

Jack was the most hopeful of all of us; he could not believe the end was near.

At noon on Tuesday mother sent for Lizzie and Will and we all stood beside his bed. As we waited in silence we could see his breath was growing shorter and more labored. Outside the window Nap began to howl. Mother nodded to me and I went out and brought him into the room where he stood as silent and motionless as a dog of stone.

When the great silence fell, and Will had closed his eyes and Mother had gone out of the room to stop the clock, Nap walked over to the bedside with his fur bristled and looked long and wistfully at the still face on the pillow. None of us spoke of it then but we all felt that it was right that one dumb beast should stand among the mourners.

On January the fifth, we laid him away on the hillside in the Millford cemetery, and came back to an empty house.

And so closed the first chapter of my life.

CHAPTER XXXX

LIFE GOES ON, NO MATTER WHO DIES

I DID not go back to Manitou, until the first of February. Hannah had to go for she was going to the Collegiate in Winnipeg for her First Class Certificate, and she had only six months to do the year's work. So the four of us tried to be company for each other; Mother, Jack, Martha Guest and myself. Fred Vigfuson had gone on his annual trip.

Mother and I were getting black dresses made by the Misses Rae in Wawanesa, two Paisley women, who had a little shop above a harness shop. I don't think I ever saw the elder Miss Rae without a few pins in her mouth, but she was a genius at designing dresses. My best dress was of cashmere, and had a pintucked front, with a flaring collar. A rough serge dress, also black of course, had a double breasted basque with large lapels, and smoked pearl buttons. I had a dozen black-edged handkerchiefs, and black-edged notepaper. Mother wore a long crepe veil, draped over her bonnet, and seemed very old to me, though she was only sixty.

Women may not live any longer than they did then, but their expectancy of life has changed. As long as I can remember my mother she was looking forward to her death; and had her shroud made according to the custom of her country. Many a Christmas day my young heart was saddened by her proclamation that she might not be with us next year. By her own attitude she made us feel she was on the brink of the grave all her life. After my father left us, she said she was sure she would not be long behind him.

I believe Jack missed him more than any of us. Father had been his companion all these years, the partner in all his farming operations. Whatever happened outside had to be told to him; how were the pigs thriving? Was the oat straw holding out? Better not let the milking cows drink the ice-cold water, it was not good for them.

Now, when the work was over, Jack seemed lost and restless. Having no man, left him all the chores to do and that helped to fill his time. We must not go out anywhere, for three months at least, except to church. Certainly not to the rink, or to a party . . . . or anywhere that might give us pleasure . . . . and I believe I am honest in saying we did not want to go. We had plenty to do, and that month we read Scott's *Talisman* in the evenings.

I liked to go out to the stables and do the milking in the evening. It was a peaceful scene; the cows looked contented and warm in their stalls; and it was nice to see the cats sitting on their backs, when we made the last trip before going to bed to see that everything was all right. The light of the lantern caught their green eyes that shone like pairs of emeralds down the length of the barn. The cats had their own milk pan and were fed twice a day, and when we gave them their portion, the pan was quickly ringed about with mounds of gray and black fur. These were the barn cats and did not come into the house at all, but having regular food, were law-abiding and gentle, and never molested the chickens. We considered they were a real asset in keeping away rats, weasels and mink.

I left for Manitou at the end of January, sorry to leave, but I wanted to go to the Collegiate the next year, and I must earn the money; and I really loved my work in the Manitou School. Every day was a delight, and the Principal, who was preparing a class for the July examinations, allowed me to come in at four and take the mathematics, and so I got a grounding in algebra, trigonometry and geometry then, which made it possible for me the next year at Winnipeg to win one of the Isbister Scholarships.

The Principal was a born teacher, with a genius for

making difficult lessons plain. And he led us through the intricacies of progressions and permutations, making it appear as simple as long division. One of his sayings was that there was no step in mathematics more difficult than Square Root. I shall always remember him with gratitude and deep affection dyed with heavy regret that, in his dark hours, though he had helped many, none of us were able to help him.

He had acquired early in life a taste for liquor. But had gone through University and had made a brilliant record. He became Principal of the High School in his home town, where every one knew of his failing and tried to help him. But at last, even his friends had to admit failure. He lost two other positions before he came west. For one year after he came to Manitou he had not tasted liquor, and was confident of success. Then he became engaged to a young teacher out in the country. She rode into town on Friday nights, a gallant little figure on her black horse, with a red quill in her hat.

One day he told us he was going to be married at Thanksgiving. He was very happy over the prospect of having a home and had rented and furnished a little house not far from the school. Before the time set for the wedding the crash came. Monday morning he came to school quite befuddled, and with a black eye. Our great concern then was to get him out of sight before the Trustees saw him.

The bigger boys and girls knew, of course, but they were loyal, and that outbreak passed. I never saw anyone struggle harder against an appetite, and, when it became generally known that he was putting up a fight, everyone in that little town tried to help him, including the hotel proprietor and the bartender, Allie Bird. The little girl was loyal, and they were married against the advice of her friends. Her action was a vital theme of discussion. Some thought she might succeed; they were the younger and more romantic ones. The older ones said no woman could reform a man by marrying him.

At midsummer they left, and went to the Coast to make another start. Again we watched the train toiling up the grade with the two of them waving to us from the rear platform. I often thought of her and wondered what I would have done.

I wish I could give the story a happy ending. But it ended in tragedy. After some years of uncertainty, hopes, fears and disappointments, the end came. And so in the loss of this brilliant man, who was everybody's friend but his own, with all his gifts of mind and heart, remembering what he might have been, I have another unsettled account with the liquor traffic.

It is strange to look on these days when men were divided into two classes; they either drank, or they didn't drink. No woman drank, needless to say.

No doubt our severe climate and the pioneer conditions helped to draw this clear line. Man was pitted against the forces of nature every day, and could not afford to be off his guard for one moment. We had no bridges to give safe passage over streams; no road signs, no protecting railings. In summer the work had to be done, and done on time; every day was precious; there was no place for loiterers! And in winter with storms and low temperatures, long journeys and dark nights every faculty was needed; clear eye, strong arm, good judgment, courage, which is quite different from fool-hardiness. . . .

As cold and hard a country as ours has one unalterable law—the survival of the fittest. The incompetent were like little candles in the wind.

When we knew that a man drank to excess, we regarded him with a curious, melancholy interest, knowing that, like the men seen in the Vision of Merza, sooner or later he would drop from sight.

So our attitude had to be one of unyielding opposition, the only alternative being the easy-going, shallow tolerance of the unconcerned.

Mr. Betts, one of the partners of Huston and Betts, announced one Sunday morning in church that if all the young people would come to the vestry of the church the next evening at seven he would organize an Epworth League. He said that there had been some objections to a young people's society in older places, but he believed the objections were trivial and unworthy.

When we got home, we asked Mr. McClung what the objections were, and found that some of the older people believed there was no spiritual value in any meeting of the young people alone, the lambs should be kept with the sheep—because a young people's meeting would naturally be a place where matches were made; in the vulgar speech of that day—"sparking schools." He dismissed the objections by saying it was a very good place for young people to meet and learn to know each other; and so, with his approval, we were launched as an Epworth League. The Presbyterians had a Christian Endeavor, which met the same night, and we honored John Wesley in the name of ours; and incidentally we learned much of the history of the Founder of Methodism.

The time came for me to lead the meeting, and the subject was spring, with the psalm about the voice of the singing bird being heard in the land for the scripture reading. I made adequate preparation, and I was determined to speak without notes. I had had experience in public speaking; yes, indeed, two debates at Normal, and success in both!

I was going to be funny, too; I would give the members a treat. I had no intention of reading from a trembling paper, as some of the others had done. I wrote a paraphrase on the psalm. A little humor was what was needed in the Epworth League.

But something happened when I began to speak. The faces in front of me blurred, melted and rolled away, leaving me alone in a trackless sea. My throat went dry, and my tongue thickened, and the loud silence thundered in my ears. . . .

I don't know how long I stood. When I came out of it and found I could speak once more, I told them I had prepared a speech on the Coming of Spring, but somehow it seemed to have gotten away from me, and Spring would have to come on just as it had always done, unaided and uusung, so far as I was concerned.

No one had ever done so poorly, and I was cast down and dismayed. Mr. Betts was very encouraging and told me about Disraeli and others who had failed in their first efforts. But I knew I was through, I could never try again, indeed, I did not see how I could ever come to a meeting again.

But after I went to bed that night, I tried to decide what had happened to me. I think I asked the Lord quite pointedly why he had let me down. If I had not prepared I would have known what had caused my downfall. But I had worked on my speech. . . . I remembered mother saying it would be a good thing for me to fail in my examination . . . . it would take some of the conceit out of me. I had had things too easy, she said, and it was good for everyone to feel the winds of the world in his face.

I found no peace until I determined to try it again. I knew that when one is thrown from a horse, the only thing to do is to climb on again. The longer you wait the harder it is. I would ask Mr. Bettes to let me try the next Monday night.

I prepared all over again, in a more chastened and humble mood. I began to think of my audience, instead of myself. The Coming of Spring should mean something to them. I thought of the fields ready for the crops, like our minds eager for impressions. I was humbled to the dust, emptied of "self" in the words of the hymn, in true learner's mood, I no longer worried over the sort of appearance I had made. I knew it did not matter.

When Monday night came, I confessed what had happened. Then I told them I had failed because I had nothing to say that was worth saying; I had thought of the subject, superficially, and missed the meaning of it. My talk may have been disjointed and crude, no doubt it was, but it was sincere, and before I was done, my audience began to ask questions. Mr. Betts asked me to go on with the topic the next night. I knew I had kindled a fire, for I felt it in my own heart.

Then I got my first lesson in public speaking, which is to have something to say which you think should be said and never mind how you say it, or what sort of a figure you are making, say it! Get it over to your audience as clearly as you can. If you can use beautiful words, crisp singing words, words that are sweet in your own mouth, because of their association, so much the better, but words are only the paper and string in which the thought is wrapped.

The high peak of social life in Manitou came at the time of the lacrosse games, particularly when our boys played with Morden. Morden was a larger town than Manitou, twenty miles east, and all the rivalry that can be felt between two neighboring towns, swept over our hearts when we even thought of Morden.

The first game of the season was played on the 24th of May, and if the day were warm and fine, the summer dresses and hats came out and made the grand-stand's seats of bare boards blossom like a garden. But unfortunately the Good Queen's birthday was often a sour and sullen day, with lowering clouds of heavy hue, and mean winds that curled up icily through the slatted floor of the grand stand.

The 24th in 1892 was a mean and disappointing day when new dresses had to be left lying on the spare-room beds. Not all either, for the Graham girls had come within the year from Ontario, where the Spring comes earlier and the 24th is considered a real summer day. So Minnie and Mary, blue with cold, but upborne by that fortitude that new and pretty clothes can give, came forth in pink and yellow dotted muslin with parasols to match.

No weather could keep the game from being played, short of a snow storm, and the 24th did not often fall that low. So the game went on; the grandstand, full of Manitou and Morden supporters rocked with emotion, and slander and railings.

Mothers and wives and admirers sat and cheered, encouraged and advised the players. Mrs. Bradley, whose son Tom was one of Manitou's fleetest runners, happened to be sitting directly behind one of Morden's lawyers, an elderly gentleman, who had been a lacrosse player in his youth, in Ontario. When Tom began one of his lightning races down the field carrying his stick and the ball in it, high above his head, twisting, dodging, leaping, foiling all Morden's attempts to trip, waylay or throw him, his mother was naturally excited, and leaned over her seat to direct Tom's progress. Mrs. Bradley, being an English woman, carried her umbrella at all times and never had better use of it than in that tense moment, for she grasped it in both hands and beat with it upon the broad shoulders of Mr. Craik, until her friends on each side forcibly restrained her. For after all, though he was from Morden, he really had not said a word.

The young ladies who came with the team from Morden matched wits with us in describing the shots and failures.

One thing sweetened the performance and kept a measure of good humor in the day. Meals were served usually by the Church Ladies in the Exhibition Building, if the weather permitted, and here mingled victors and vanquished, home and foreign contestants and supporters in the common fellowship of a good meal.

"It's a fine pie, anyway," said big Dave Duncan, with a section of pie neatly balanced on his fork. "Boy, if the Manitou lads could play lacrosse as well as the Manitou women can cook, we'd never get a look in."

"No one would think to look at you now, that you would hit an innocent lad with your stick, and him doing no more than taking the ball from you," said Mrs. Brennagh, whose son Sam was carrying a black eye from the game. Big Dave was full of remorse.

"Say, I'm sorry, Mrs. Brennagh. That boy of yours

doesn't look where he is going, he just runs into things, not blind exactly, but just doesn't care. But I'm sorry he ran against my stick."

The great day came, when Manitou lacrosse team went to Winnipeg to play the "Capitols" for the Championship of Western Canada, and the C.P.R. put on an excursion train, which left Manitou at eight in the morning and returned that evening, and the little town arose, packed up two meals, took the baby and grandma, and went to see their boys play. And they saw their boys win the game in a fair fight; and the silver cup presented to Charley Gordon, the captain. The local photographer had taken their pcture before they left, knowing that history was being made.

In 1893, I went to the Collegiate Institute, in Winnipeg, where Mr. F. H. Schofield was the principal. Hannah had been successful the year before, and received in the July examinations the highest marks that had been taken in the Province. I knew I could not hope to equal her achievement. I would be well satisfied if I could get through.

I went to Winnipeg about December the first and roomed with Hannah, who had received an appointment on the city staff. She lived at a stately home on Ross Street, where our landlady told us quite often that she kept boarders for company only, and really did not need the money.

"We have a business in the city," she said, in the fine old English tradition, and when I found out quite by accident, that it was a livery business, I wondered why she did not say so.

Her parlor was high-ceilinged and cold, with a marble-topped mantle, above the unused fireplace, and was only used by us, when we had callers, by Hannah rather, for she had a theological admirer now, who came once a week. By special concession the parlor door might be left open after dinner, so that some of the heat from the coal-stove in the hall could penetrate its chilling depths. The young man wore his fur-lined coat and Hannah put on her fur coat when she heard the bell ring. However, the call lasted until ten o'clock, and the cold room was not even commented on. We were a hardy race.

Hannah went home at the end of 1893, and took the Northfield School; and I left the lady on Ross street too, and found a much happier place at 464 Jemima St., the home of Dr. and Mrs. W. A. Dunbar and their daughter Jessie. My friend Jessie McEwen, who had taught with me in Manitou, came with me, she too was going to take her "first", at the Collegiate, and we spent six months together very happily.

Jessie Dunbar sang in St. Andrew's choir, and was the centre of a jolly crowd of young people, who were often entertained by her; and we were welcomed by them. But we had to do a year's work in the six months, so we spent our evenings delving into the prescribed text-books, upstairs in our little room, where Jessie used the washstand, and I the bureau, there being no room for a table. But we were comfortable, well-fed, and contented, and we were getting on.

At the Collegiate it was easy to see who among the students were spending his or her own money, and who were still supported by parents. The latter came late, unprepared, talked of parties and dances, and regarded the daily grind of the High School as a tiresome interruption of their good times. We who had been teaching, and had earned our own money, were in deadly earnest, and did everything we were expected to do, listened to the lectures, and never missed a class. No doubt the young ones resented our industry. I know I envied them, and would have been glad to be going to the parties, and wearing pretty clothes too. But it could not be, so I stifled all such vain imaginings in the pasteurized pages of "Green's Short History of the English People."

Mr. Schofield had perfect control of the Collegiate.

We did what we were told without question. Every inch of that forbidding brick structure on Kate Street, was sacred to him, and because of him, to us. We walked the halls soberly, and we walked in the middle of the halls, no one ran up or down stairs; the desks had their shining surfaces, undefaced.

And how we worked!

When the examinations came, I weighed ninety-five pounds. But when I sat down to write, I had a feeling that I knew the course, and with any sort of fair papers I should be pretty sure of passing.

When I went home after the examinations, I slept the clock around for the first two weeks. On August the first, we got the news. Jessie and I had both passed. Mr. Schofield wrote me, and Mr. E. R. Garrett, the history and chemistry teacher, and the whole world seemed to me to be a joyful place.

I had gone to Wawanesa that morning for the mail, expecting the returns and there they were on the third page of the *Manitoba Free Press*. Miss Shields in the Post Office told me, before I opened the paper.

A few days after I had a letter from the Treherne School Board offering me a position, and I accepted it, without delay. Mr. McClung had been moved to Treherne by the Stationing Committee, so I would still be with the family I liked so well. And though the eldest son was still in Manitou he would come sometimes to see us.

CHAPTER XXXXI

Treherne

TREHERNE was then a village of perhaps six hundred people, and had three teachers, in the dark green wooden building, at the south-western end of the settlement. I had the middle room, grades 6, 7, and 8, and sang in the choir, and joined the W.C.T.U. and helped with the Mission Band each Monday evening at seven o'clock.

The social life of the little town centred around the church, whose doors were open, and windows alight each night except Saturday, when everyone was supposed to repair early to bed, after blackening boots and indulging in the weekly bath, or as the English people said, "strip-wash", with a mind sobered and calmed and ready to receive the message at the morning service.

Mr. McClung was an advocate of the early closing of the stores, and preached about it. Indeed he preached about anything that concerned the welfare of his people. He refused to take refuge behind Amos or Eljah, or any ancient authority. The divisions among the Children of Israel were used by him as a point of departure for his sermons, but me quickly arrived at the vagaries and wanderings of the people of Treherne and Manitoba. He denounced governments, bombarded the liquor traffic, but never failed to preach a wide gospel of redeeming love.

He was a small man, in stature, with a fine head of brown curly hair, bushey brows, fine forehead, and large lustrous eyes of steel blue. He was fortunate in having a musical speaking voice, and was independent of choirs and organists, for he could lead the singing like an orchestra,

The family were often worried over his pulpit utterances, and I was too, and wished he would use the soft pedal, once in a while. But when we tried to advise him he knew our voices for the voice of the Tempter trying to turn his aside from the plain, though thorny path of duty, and kept to his high resolves.

He was a man of untiring energy and had a keen memory for faces and names; and was undaunted by circumstances. He was possessed of a shrewd worldly wisdom which contributed largely to his success as a minister. When one of the leading men in Treherne became deeply offended over his blunt and uncompromising denunciation of the government, he went at once to see him, and came back with some of the man's books, and said they had had a wonderful argument. When he found a farmer beating his horses on a slippery hill, because the poor brutes could not hold their feet, he drew off to one side of the road, got out and denounced the driver for his "devilish" temper. Then unhitched "George," his own horse, and brought him over and hooked him to the tongue of the sleigh and helped the team to get to the top of the hill. But the incident did not end there, for he went to see the man the next day, brought him under conviction of sin, signed him up for the "kingdom", and a few Sundays afterwards received him and his family into the Church.

He was as hungry a reader as I ever have known. Every printed page attracted him, and I know it was only his fervid desire to save souls that drove him away from his reading. He cut columns from newspapers, made annotations on the books he read, and spent every cent he could spare, and more, on books and periodicals.

When we were in Treherne I got a copy of Trilby, Du Maurier's much talked of book, and read it with a distinct sense of adventure. Here was a very daring book surely, fascinating but perilous! Before I had finished Mr. McClung sounded the alarm and spoke very seriously to me. An evil book could poison the mind like nothing else, and he believed I should not finish it. He would have been more disturbed if he had known who sent it to me, but I carefully suppressed that information. He asked me to forego the book as an exercise of will pwer. Character was built by self-denial, and character was the object of all our teaching. Under the influence of his eloquent appeal, I agreed that I woould not read the book for a week.

The more I thought of the story, the more I desired to know the end. I simply could not leave Trilby at loose ends.. . . . I left the book on a little table in the hall and waited. . . .

That day when Mrs. McClung called him to come down for dinner he did not hear her and she had to go up and get him, and then I knew my plan was working. . . . He had to go out for the afternoon and I let him have another bout with the book before he went. I wanted him to be approaching the great scene in the theatre before I took it away.

The next day I went into his study and got the book. Mrs. McClung and Nell were both in the plot, and we enjoyed seeing him hunting for it. He couldn't very well ask any of us, and besides we had all gone very high-minded and detached from earthly joys. We talked of self-sacrifice and self-denial, and the joys of renouncement.

"I think you should read that book yourself," I said to him at last. "So you could see for yourself how subtle it is, and fascinating. Indeed I think it might be well to preach a sermon on it."

He looked at me with darkening suspicion.

"It wouldn't take you long to read it—now," I said.

"Young woman," he said, looking at me with his brows drawn down, "you've got me and you know it. I believe you left it there to tempt me. It's the most diabolically interesting book I ever read, and I'm not so sure that it is an evil book either. Where is it?"

I produced the book, and a great silence settled down on the little study while the Chairman of the Treherne

District of the Methodist Church followed the fortunes of poor Trilby.

The publication of W. T. Stead's book, "Two and Two makes Four," in 1891 dropped a stone into the peaceful waters of religious thought, whose widening waves reached as far as Treherne where we read the book with creepy fascination.

Mr. McClung took a firm stand against it, not that he doubted the sincerity of the great Editor, but he believed that it was not God's will that there should be communication between those who had passed over and those who were left. John Wesley's house had been visited by spirits who rang bells, pounded on doors, rattled dishes, moved furniture, and in many ways annoyed and troubled the occupants; but they were evil spirits sent by the kingdom of darkness to impede the great work of salvation carried on by this man of God.

No good end could be served by trying to raise the powers of evil. But we wanted to see for ourselves, and so when Mr. McClung was safely away at his two other appointments, Nell, Herb, and I, and Zella Motheral, who was the local milliner, and organist in the Church, were not above doing a little table rapping in the interests of scientific discovery.

On Hallowe'en night we got the perfect setting for an evening with the spirits. Mr. and Mrs. McClung had gone to Bethel to a Harvest Home Supper, and would stay the night, because of the wild weather. Rain lashed the windows, and the trees were agitated by the wind, whose sudden gusts rattled every window and door in the house.

Nellie and I and Zella were entertaining the Epworth League at the Parsonage, and as the coast was clear, the activity of the evening was table rapping—and how the table did quiver, and rise. It seemed to come up with every heave of the storm.

A load of wheat had been stolen from a field granary nearby, and we asked the spirits to tell us who had taken it. We named the letters of the alphabet, and as

M

the table rapped we wrote down the letter. To our horror the table rapped out the name of ———————— one of the young men, who belonged to the League, but had recently returned to Ontario. He was a College student who had spent the summer working for a farmer, and had gone back to pursue his studies. We asked the table for the first name, and got it. It was not the name we knew him by, but it corresponded with his second initial.

We were rather frightened over this, and felt we were getting into deep water. We did not believe the charge. The young man was the unlikeliest person in the world to steal. He had been drawing wheat to the elevator for his employer; and he could, of course, have taken a load from the neighbor's granary, and it could not be detected. But he wouldn't do this, we felt sure, and we solemnly promised each other we would never tell what the table had rapped out. It was done in fun, and we must not attach any importance to it.

"We must not mistake ourselves for a court of law," Billy Rogers said.

Then we tried a little mesmerism. Tom Simpson, who was a clerk in a dry goods store, and had some experience, would mesmerize me. Tom and I had agreed that we put on a fine act of this kind, and I knew what I was supposed to do. We had talked it over one day when I was in the store. So this seemed to be the night, with every condition right—the wild night, with groaning trees, weird sounds at the windows, and doors, as the storm circled the house.

Tom tied a silk handkerchief around his head to help him to concentrate, and looked me steadily in the eye to give me my orders. I stared back in silence, and suppressed my desire to laugh; the company sat on all the available chairs, with an overflow meeting on the floor, but I held myself rigid and calm, not moving a muscle. The thought-waves were running, and I must receive them.

When the suspense began to be painful, I turned and

walked to the door, slowly, and impressively, looking
straight ahead of me, like a sleep-walker, and went upstairs, returning with a comb in my hand. (Tom had told
the company that this was what I should do.)

There was a distinct gasp of surprise when I came
back, with the comb.

"Now she is competely under hypnotic influence,"
Tom said grandly, "and knows no mind but mine. Murders have been committed by innocent people when under
this influence. Indeed that is a strong argument against
hypnotism in any form. The strong exploit the weak,
and send them on dastardly errands. It is a power for
righteousness, if properly used. I could impose on Miss
Mooney now, a deep hypnotic sleep which would last until
I released her, a sleep in which all the powers of nature
would gain strength, and build up her physical being.
That is the beneficent side of hypnotism."

Nell began to get frightened. "Take her out, Tom,"
she said anxiously, "I can't bear to look at her.
She looks so vacant. . . . I didn't think you could mesmerize her. I thought she had a stronger mind than yours
. . . . She may never come right. . . ."

"I'll give her two more things to do," Tom said, "then
I'll release her."

I knew what they were and I did them. I went into the
kitchen and brought back a sandwich which I gave to Ed
Roberts, and then took off Zella's beads and fastened
them around my own neck.

"Can you make her sing," Zella asked, trembling with
excitement—she had read "Trilby", too.

"I would rather not try," Tom said. "It would be too
hard on her at first. That sort of control takes practice.
There would be no value in it anyway, she would sing
only in her own voice, but with practice I could lend her
mine."

"Do you mean you could make her sing something she
doesn't know?" Billy Rogers asked.

Tom explained.

"At the moment she knows nothing except what I let her know."

"Gosh! that's tough on her, and her a teacher," Billy laughed. "She'll lose her job if that's all she knows."

I wanted to look about me, but I couldn't do that, so I held to the vacant stare, and the audience were plainly impressed.

"Take her out," they were calling.

"I'm scared."

"So am I . . . . this has gone too far."

"I thought it was all a joke at first . . . . but I see it's the real thing."

Tom came over to me and eyed me solemnly. Then he clapped his hands before my face. I stared on. I decided I'd give Tom a few minutes of anxiety. I kept on staring.

Tom turned pale, and began to shake me. There were cries all around me—someone ran for water—Nell was bathing my face. Some one called "I'm going for the doctor."

That settled it—Dr. Lamont was one of my trustees. I came back in a hurry, with a fine show of wakening up from a long sleep. When we sat eating our sandwiches, and drinking coffee, I heard some interesting things.

"You couldn't look like that if you had been fooling us," Zella said, "so empty, and vacant, just like the people in the asylum. At first, I thought you were just doing it for fun, but I soon saw you were really mesmerized; and it's awful. Tom you must promise never to do it again."

"I'm done," Tom said solemnly. "I never had such a scare in my life."

I think our amateur performance had a good effect after all. It convinced us of how easily people can be deceived.

We turned to something saner, and more satisfying after that, for we began the study of the "Trial Scene in the Merchant of Venice," which we put on at the Christmas concert, and repeated it at Midsummer.

There was a peculiar aftermath of our adventure in the realm of physical research which troubled us greatly. Suspicion began to point to the young man who had gone east, and we had a bad time over it fearing that there had been a leakage from our party. It is so easy to throw suspicion. There was talk of bringing the young man back from Ontario to be tried at the Spring Assizes for theft. But in the midst of our anxiety the case was settled anonymously. So the matter has remained a mystery, which, so far as I know, was never cleared up.

I have a pleasant recollection of the lovely autumn days in Treherne.

The parsonage stood beside the Church, and both, facing east, looked out across the road to the deep ravine whose wooded banks broke the monotony of the prairie. The country around Treherne has more trees than many parts of Manitoba and with its deep black loam, and abundant rainfall, the farmers were prosperous and con- tented. Still, even there, the call of the far country had come to some, and Mr. A. J. Cotton left his farm that year, and went still farther west to Swan River to get free land for his boys.

When he wrote back that he had harvested fifty-five bushels of wheat to the acre on his new farm, we found it hard to believe. But knowing Mr. Cotton we could not very well doubt him, and besides we did not want to be like some of the Ontario people who doubted everything that came out of the west, every good thing, I mean. So this story had to be accepted.

When four o'clock came, and I got my desk tidied and the boards cleaned and the last item of the day's busi- ness closed, I was glad of the period of relaxation before supper time. There was a hammock made of barrel staves, with a rope run through auger holes on each end; and covered with a blanket and plenty of pillows hung between two trees, at the North-east corner of the Par- sonage. And there I often lay, when the weather was fine, looking up at the clouds. I always had a curious sense of detachment in that hammock suspended between heaven and earth. My past seemed to be below me, and my future above me, and my whole mentality was quickened and kindled as I lay there. I remember how ecstatically I repeated:

> "Out of the night that covers me,
>   Dark as the pit from pole to pole,
> I thank whatever gods there be
>   For my unconquerable soul."

Or,

> "Who would dare the choice?
>   Neither or both to know?
> The highest quiver of joy
>   The most exquisite pang of woe."

I was often in that grand mood that my family used to refer to derogatively, as being on my high horse, but they were quite mistaken in their estimate of it. It was really an innocent exaltation that always left me the better for it.

It was the one hour of the day, when I let my mind run free, and over and above the sounds of the little town with the clip-clop of horses feet on the hard roads, the voices of children at play, puffs of a gasoline engine at the elevator, there came in from the country the rhythmic sounds of a threshing machine in a grain field near by. Ours was a world of action and effort, a battle against time. I knew the fear that always drives the farmer, of frost, and covering snow, which deprives the cattle of their easy grass, and the finality of the freeze-up. . . . Indoors, I knew busy women were prodding big black stoves to greater efforts; others were frantically peeling potatoes from a wash tub on the floor, long tables were set through "the room," oilcloth covered, with thick white dishes, and a few of the good ones, grudgingly put out for the threshers.

Often, too, as I enjoyed that hour under the trees my thoughts ran into the future with a tingling sense of danger . I knew there was no security in life . . . . no security for women anyway. They could make such tragic mistakes. . . . I had seen it in my twenty years of life. . . . Had I any reason to think I might escape? I was glad I had found the McClung family. . . .

I loved the table conversations and the activities of a parsonage. I knew I had a place in their affections, too, all of them. . . .

If I could only be like Mrs. McClung—sweet, placid, serene, whose life flowed on in endless song, above earth's lamentation", who had a gift for goodness as others have for music. But I knew that could never be! And I wanted to write, and how could I write unless I lived and felt, and sorrowed—and living was dangerous. Still, I had no desire to stand off in the side lines all my life. And besides there was Wes. I never got far in my thinking without coming to him. He believed in me; he said no one could tell a story as well; no one could be more convincing; and when he became engulfed in doubts and fears, and at enmity with the doctrines of the church, and his father's stern theology, and belief in eternal punishment, he had been helped by my exposition of the plan of salvation. I believed that when we are not asked whether or not we wanted to be born, God would not lightly condemn us to suffer for ever, no matter what we had done. I had welcomed the sane theology of *Robert Elsmere* and *John Ward, Preacher.*

Wes and I had walked for miles in Manitou threshing out our beliefs, and I thought of him often as I lay watchin the pageant of the sky. He had suffered in reputation from being a minister's son; not that he had ever done anything very wrong, but because he loved fun and company, and athletics, and had played cards. He had been in Toronto at College when I was in Winnipeg at the Collegiate, and during that time we had written each other every week high-minded letters of theological and literary import, and I knew that a delayed letter made me very miserable.

I would not need to lay aside my ambition if I married him. He would not want me to devote my whole life to him, he often said so. He said I always called out the very best that was in him, and I knew I was filled with a great sense of well-being when we were together, for he seemed to light all the candles of my mind. We wondered if this could be love; we were disposed to think it was, but we had a sort of gentleman's agreement that, if at any time either of us found out that there was something beyond all this, we would not hesitate to intimate to the other that such was so. And there would be no scenes, no recriminations; and we would go on liking each other always.

On my birthday he sent me an opal ring, which I kept in the pocket of my valise and did not wear—to save explanations. I found it always hard to speak of the things that mattered most, and when I heard girls tell of the proposals of marriage they had received, repeating conversations relating thereto, I was distinctly uncomfortable. There was a certain indecency in it, I thought, and a betrayal of confidence at keyholes. So I said nothing at home of the young man in the drug store. There would be plenty of time for that . . . . and if either of us found out we had made a mistake there would be no explanations to make.

I had moments when my conscience chided me for indulging in this period of rest. Hard-working people such as we were, were ever suspicious of leisure, and even sat down with a feeling that had an element of guilt in it. I often wished I could stifle that nagging voice that seemed to tell me all waking hours should be hours of effort.

One day my peaceful hours in the hammock were interrupted. One of the little girls in my Junior Class came to me after four, and I knew she had something on her mind, when she asked me if she could wait and walk home with me. She was an appealing little thing, very

tractable and sad—far too sad for a young thing. I knew
the family history, or part of it.

When we left the school, she took my hand and said:
"Teacher, I wish you would come and see my mother
—not tonight. but some time when I tell you. She is mad
nearly all the time, because she's so tired. There are too
many of us and she's sick again. And she may get another baby soon. She always gets a baby before the last
one can walk, and it makes her mad. And teacher she can
see you in the hammock, and it makes her worse mad.
She says some people have all the luck. She never can
get a rest, because there are too many of us. Please
teacher, maybe you wouldn't go in the hammock no more,
for a while . . . . my mother says hard things about you,
Teacher, just because she's all tired out. Maybe it would
make you mad, if you knew."

I assured little Evadell that I would not be a bit mad,
and maybe we could think of some way her mother could
get a rest, and I would stay out of the hammock tonight,
anyway.

The next day I took counsel with the other teacher,
who had been longer in the neighborhood than I, and who
was always ready to help a family in need. She knew
Evadell's family quite well. She told me the father
worked on the section, drank when he could get it., (Treherne was under local option, but Holland, eight miles
away, had two bars), and was not any too fond of work.
The mother, she said, was a bitter-tongued Irishwoman,
whom it was hard to help. When the Forester's Lodge
had sent her a turkey for Christmas, she was too proud
to accept it and sent it back, telling them to keep their
charity for them that asked for it. She would let her
children go hungry rather than take anything from any-
bady, and she was never so happy as when she was in
pitched battle with her neighbors.

Miss W. ——— did not think anything could be done
for them.

"I tried it," she said, "when I came. I made a dress

for Evadell, and she wouldn't let her wear it. She has a hard time, but she makes most of it herself. I don't even blame her man for drinking. She'd drive any man to drink with her tongue. Go back to the hammock when your day's work is done, in peace, and forget Mrs. N.——. If she weren't mad at you it would be somebody else."

But I did not feel just right about it. The next day I went to see Mrs. N. ——, and I found her in high spirits. She was not the bedraggled, discontented woman I had expected to find. Her conversation rang along the line of past victories over her neighbors, and the acid replies she made to the people who had tried to help her.

"Of course," she said, "I know I have too many children, and there are times when I get out of temper and wish I had never got married. I've often said that if it were not for just the clear disgrace of it, I would rather be a withered-up old maid school teacher like Miss Harris, or what you'll be yourself some day. . . ."

I came away soon after that, and tried all the time I was in Treherne to smooth the path of poor little Evadell, who had been so unfortunate in her choice of a mother.

How inescapable are our family connections! Though we have no voice, or hand, in saying into what family we shall be born, we find ourselves there, bound forever, blessed or marred, helped or hampered, by a relationship which was forced upon us.

CHAPTER XXXXII

THE ROYAL VISIT

LORD AND LADY ABERDEEN were in Rideau Hall at Ottawa at this time representing the Queen in Canada.

Lady Aberdeen had sponsored a plan the year before for bringing English girls to Canada, and in her thorough way had done the work of choosing the girls herself, and selecting the homes. It happened that the Treherne District had received several of these young visitors, and the Governor and Lady Aberdeen were coming to visit their little wards.

Great were the preparations for the official visit; everyone felt the excitement of having royalty come to our little community. The people who had met Lady Aberdeen and her two secretaries the year before were not so panicky as we who had only our own imagination to draw on.

Mrs. Rollins, at whose home Nellie James, one of the English girls, was living, told me when I was at her place for dinner that Lady Aberdeen was just the plainest, loveliest woman anyone could wish to meet. "You'd think she had been brought up on a farm herself, she is so understanding. She asked me for a quilt pattern I was making, mind you, and I think would have been ever more chatty and friendly if it hadn't been for the two secretaries, who were along with her. They watched her pretty close. And Nellie had told me a lot about her Ladyship. . . . I would like nothing better than to have her come and stay a week. But of course she has many places to visit."

Nellie James, the white skinned, brown eyed seventeen-year-old adventurer, who had come across the sea to make Canada her home, was a good ambassador from the old land to the new; for Nellie had the gifts and graces which made her a popular member of the community. She could sing, play the piano, and recite, and she was always ready to do what she could.

One of her popular numbers was the "Cotter's Saturday Night," and as the scene unfolded, it was easy to see Nellie as the eldest girl who came home, "with love sparkling in her ee', perhaps to show a braw new gown, or bring her sair won penny fee, to help her parents dear, if they in hardship be."

Nellie had other selections too, and on the first of July was ready with:

"Breathes there a man, with soul so dead
Who never to himself hath said
This is my own, my native land."

Lady Aberdeen had chosen a good home for Nellie, when she sent her to Mr. and Mrs. Rollins. The nationality was the right one—Scotch from Inverness; they were the pillars of the Presbyterian Church, and owned the one baby-grand piano in the little town, and their big living room was the scene of many gatherings. The night the teachers and the choir of the church were entertained there, Nellie and Fanny Rollins, the daughter of the house, in white aprons and caps (the caps brought by Nellie) served us from a long table which ran through the archway, between the dining room and living room, and Mrs. Rollins told us proudly that the girls had done all the cooking except the turkey dressing; and after dinner Nellie sang to Fanny's accompaniment, "Drink to Me Only With Thine Eyes", "Ben Bolt", and "Cherry Ripe".

Miss E. ———, one of the other teachers, and an old-country woman, whispered to me that the young Scotch girl would be spoiled by being made so much of, and she wondered at Mrs. Rollins putting her forward like this, when she was really only a servant after all, even if Lady Aberdeen had placed her. But no echo of this criticism dulled the radiance of Nellie's triumphs. She continued in her happy way, a cheerful little emissary.

One of the other girls whom Lady Aberdeen had placed was not so happy. She had a good home too, but her face was full of gloom and discontent; she cried often, and could not be comforted. Nellie was sent to spend a day with her, but the source of her grief remained undiscovered. When Lady Aberdeen came to see her, Jennie admitted her mistress was kind, her room comfortable, her work was easy, everyone was pleasant and friendly, but she could not be happy eating with an iron fork and tin spoon, and a knife with a black handle. "I fancy," she said, "that they always taste of onions."

Lady Aberdeen allayed her grief—she would send her a silver knife, fork and spoon for her birthday.

It was the wish of Lord and Lady Aberdeen that no entertainment be given for them, for their time was so short they wanted to spend it visiting their wards. Their private car, standing at the siding, became an object of interest, but we did manage to keep the school children from gathering around it, by constant appeals to their honor. They must not fail in any act of courtesy to these wonderful people, Queen Victoria's representatives, who were trying to help the people of Canada.

One sharp eyed sleuth from my room brought in a fairly full report on the contents of the car, declaring she got all her information quite honestly from the upstairs windows of the section house where her sister lived. She said the secretaries wore grey flannel nightdresses, and that the cook rubbed the pots with an onion, and everyone of them had their own bed.

We knew the Aberdeens would return from the western part of their trip in about a week, and would pass through Treherne on the evening train, which made a stop of ten minutes while the engine took water from the tank beside the track.

Someone conceived the idea of presenting them with an illuminated address. There would be plenty of time to read it, and it seemed to be a fitting and courteous way of thanking them for coming. The post master, Alan Ross, our local poet, wrote the address.

For a while there was some uncertainty in the matter of the reading of it. A minister was the first choice, and we had four Protestant Ministers and a Roman Catholic priest. At first the Anglican seemed to travel next the pole on account of His Excellency's connection with the Established Church in England. But it was urged by some of the Non-conformists that the Anglican minister would not read without intoning and besides this was a citizen's affair, and should have no ecclesiastical flavor. Some one suggested the auctioneer as a highly suitable reader, accustomed to public speaking, and this would carry the matter away from denominational controversy.

The address set down in Alan Ross' neat writing, and tastefully framed in golden oak, looked rather bleak and bare, and a bit austere, so someone suggested that it be illuminated in gold and colored ink. There was a man who lived back in the hills, who could do beautiful work, and had india ink, and gold and silver paints. It would cost five dollars, but what of it? We had not the privilege of addressing the Queen's representative every day!

The address was illuminated or rather decorated. It came back in a scroll rolled on an oak roller, and from the faint glimpse I caught of it, and from the auctioneer's description afterwards, "illuminate" was the one word which should not be applied to it.

It had birds with tape flowing from their bills, acorns and oak trees, summer cottages and ships at sea, and for a background there were clouds and elevators, threshing machines, and haystacks to give local color, and the script was done in early English, in four colors.

When the train pulled in a messenger went to the private car, and asked their Excellencies if they would come into the station, which they did, umbrellas in hand, for the night was raining with all the black insistence of a November downpour.

The station was full and all the bracket lamps were set in high gear, but unfortunately were placed too high on the walls to be effective, so some of the company carried lanterns. There had been some delay in getting the address back from the illuminator, but it arrived just as the train drew in, and when their Excellencies had lowered their umbrellas, and were placed under the brightest lamp, the address began. The Reeve had briefly stated that it was the unanimous desire of the citizens to present a few words of appreciation; and then the auctioneer started in very well:

"To Your Excellencies,

Lord Aberdeen, Governor General of Canada, and Lady Aberdeen:

We, the citizens of Treherne, desire to express to you our deep appreciation of your Excellencies' visit to our part of your Dominion and also—"

Dan stuck fast here. He said afterwards it looked more like a piece of knotted fringe than a word.

"Where's Alan Ross? He wrote this——"

Alan Ross was in the crowd but had not brought his glasses.

I was wedged in behind a big man and could not see very well, but I saw a lantern was being held up by someone over Dan's head, and after an uncomfortable pause, a new voice, deep and foreign, was reading:

" 'Successful'," I think that is the word, long S's you know—a bit confusing in the old English script." "Successful efforts of Lady Aberdeen in the matter of colonization.——" "I believe that is what it is. . . Very kind, I am sure," the deep voice commented. The Governor General of Canada was reading his own address, and replying to it, and doing all without embarrassment or condescension.

Dan took hold again.

"We beg to assure you, that by your united efforts the bonds of the Empire are being drawn increasingly closer——" but there he stuck.

The Governor took the address and got another sentence from it, which put Dan back on the track. With a mighty effort, and a little improvising Dan got through with the address, and though the sentiments may not have been all that Alan Ross wrote, it conveyed the idea very clearly that we were trying to tell the regal visitors that we liked them very much.

The Governor thanked us for the address, and told us he would always prize it, and Lady Aberdeen thanked us, and the rain poured down in a river from the sloping station roof; and the night was a black as ink, as we stood watching their car at the rear of the train, as it pulled away from us over the long trestle across the big ravine, and we sang:

"For they are jolly good fellows," with right goodwill. And I hope every address they received carried as deep an admiration as ours.

The only other time I saw the Aberdeens was in Fremont Temple in Boston, in 1917, where they were speaking on their Anti-Tuberculosis work in Ireland. I was lecturing for the National Suffrage Association and had a place on the same program. I had tea with them afterwards and reminded them of the address presented to them in Treherne that rainy November night. They remembered it very well, they told me; and said they were "much touched" by it.

CHAPTER XXXXIII

The Farm in 1895

In the summer of 1895 when I went home for the holidays I could see that I was needed at home and so sent in my resignation to the Treherne School Board. My sister Hannah was married and living in New York State and Lizzie and her husband and their little son George had gone to a farm eight miles from Holland, and Mother was rather sad about these changes.

"No matter how many children you have", she would say, "It all comes to the same in the end and when you need them they are gone". We were fortunate in getting a relative of my Mother's to come and keep house for us and she was glad to come with her little five-year-old girl. Mrs. Brown was a very efficient and amiable young woman but even if she had been less efficient or amiable Mother would have made light of her short-comings for was she not of the household of faith, having had one of the Scotch aunts from Holland and formerly from "Enbro' for her grandmother?

I am always glad I had that last year at home for I saw then the western prairie in full bloom, with its bewildering abundance, and I like to think of it as it was then with work enough for everyone and a clear assurance that anyone that would work could be clothed and fed and be able to lay aside something too for their old age.

My brothers, Will and Jack, had a threshing machine then and with all the fall work promised, and with fine clear weather and a heavy crop the whole neighborhood hummed with activity. In the harvest time under deep blue skies the country lay one great golden tapestry shaded from the tawny hues of the ripe grasses through the greens of the late corps into the solid yellow gold of the ripe grain. Machines at that time had not driven out the men and the harvest fields employed, not only all the available men in Manitoba, but every fall the railways brought out men from Ontario and Quebec.

At threshing time, many prayers ascended for good weather in the churches in the accustomed phrases. Equally fervent were the strange voices that "troubled the gold gateways of the stars" with the same request. "God knows I am not one of these pests that bother Him about every little thing," said old Bob Peters, who lived beside the river, "but I certainly do got down on my knees at threshing time and ask for decent weather. It is nothing to Him and it means a lot to us." Threshing time healed up many an old sore too, for everyone was needed and the old feuds had to be forgotten.

"I would not have put up with her sauce," a woman said of her sister-in-law who had been visiting her all summer from the States," only I knew I needed her in threshing time."

It was for the threshing that sauerkraut was put up in barrels (chopped by a new spade) and green tomato pickles were made; red cabbage and white were chopped up with onions, vinegar. cloves and sugar, corn scraped from the cobs, and all kept in stone crocks. Every sort of cake that would keep was baked and hidden. The woman who had nothing ready for the threshers was almost as low in the social scale as "the woman who had not a yard of flannel in the house when the baby came."

What a day it was when the machine pulled into the yard with the great powerful engine drawing the high and cumbrous separator. The old horse-power drawn by three teams of horses though really more picturesque, was never such a sight as the snorting Traction Engine drawing its great red and white trailer, followed by the water-tank. And what a deep mark was left in the earth by the huge engine-wheels with their lugs patterning the black soil. Even though the work in the house was press-

ing everybody came out to witness the arrival of the
Machine as it made its way majestically to the first set
of stacks and drew in between them cautiously, and what
a temptation it was to wait to see the carriers run up
and the canvas spread and the great belt beginning to
turn, and the pitchers climbing up on the stacks from
the highest part of the separator, there to wait for the
signal to start to throw down the sheaves to the platform below where the two band-cutters stood with their
knives to cut the bands. When the word was given
and the great belt began to turn and the white canvas
of the carriers slowly revolved, gathering speed every
second until the rhythmic sounds settled into a roaring
hum the yellow straw was thrown from the top of
the carriers like a cloud of gold smoke that veered and
twisted in the wind! When the pile of straw grew so high
it had to be removed the "straw horses" advanced without anyone telling them, one on each side of the straw
pile, and by means of the straw rake to which they were
hitched one at each end, they drew the pile to one side and
turned around stood at attention until the pile was again
high enough to be taken away. When a team was trained
to do this they became valuable possessions to their
owner and their services were well paid for.

The best paid-for job was that of the engineer and
the next best the "feeder", that is the man who stood
between the band-cutters and fed the sheaves into the
machine. This was not only hard work but it had considerable danger in it both from the knives of the band-
cutters and from the mouth of the machine where a
hand might be caught in the cylinders. Will was the
separator boss and did the feeding himself. Jack was the
engineer and it was a matter of great pride that there
had never been an accident of any kind around the
machine.

Will and Jack paid big wages and expected their men
to work long hours, and not waste a minute, for the
time element was everything in threshing. Always there

was the danger of a break in the weather. Wet weather was everybody's loss. The men received no wages when they were not working and the farmer had to go on feeding the gang. So everyone hurried the work along without a grumble. . . . I have seen the machine running by the light of burning straw to get a stack finished. But if the men had to work hard and long, Jack and Will worked harder than any of them, for when the work was over for the night they often had to stay behind to repair something on the engine or separator. But so far as I can remember everyone remained good humored. One man did say that working on the Mooney outfit was like heaven in one regard—there was no night there!

For three weeks that fall—1895—I helped to cook for the threshers, beginning at Will's place, then our own and then George's, with two days or so at a neighbor's whose wife had no help. It was hard to get help in the house for the farmer's daughters all had plenty of work at home and there were no Employment Bureaus for women in the cities and very few women had come from the Old Country. There were the Crofters from Scotland who lived in a settlement in the Tiger Hills, but they had their own small farms and seem to have work enough for all their women too. I remember hearing one woman who lived in Wawanesa at this time lament the fact that everyone in the country was so well off that no one needed to work for anyone else.

The farmers kept no hours when the crop was being handled and the whistle of the engine tore through the dark dawn every morning when it seemed the room had hardly had time to get dark after we had blown out the lamp. But in a second or two the raucuous voice of the alarm clocks repeated the message both upstairs and down that it was time to get up and in a few minutes lights twinkled from the windows, and before there was light enough to see columns of smoke were rising into the morning air and the business of the day had begun. Even the roosters would begin to crow hearing the bustle

in the farmyard and the hens would scold drowsily knowing well that they had no call to be up before daylight.
But there was no rest after that first blast from the
engine, for the fireman, who had been out since three
o'clock getting up the steam would sound a longer blast, if
the lights did not show in the windows.

The first man up put on the fire in the kitchen stove
and put on the kettle full of water and then went out to
feed the horses. No matter how the fire crackled in the
stove I always came shivering into the dark kitchen and
found it hard to waken up bright and ready for the day's
work, but there was no time to think about personal con-
cerns for the men had to be fed. We prepared all we
could the night before and had sliced bacon and
peeled the boiled potatoes and had pans of them ready to
put in the oven dotted over with pieces of butter and
sprinkled with pepper and salt, and soon two frying pans
of bacon were sending out their cheerful incense and
another pot of eggs was set to cook. Boiled eggs were
easier to get ready than fried ones and to have to stop
to remove the shell slowed the men up a little, and that
was a good thing for them for they were disposed to eat
too quickly. The coffee was made in big blue enamel pots
and there was no question of timing or measuring. There
was just one rule—plenty of coffee and let it boil until the
men came in.

It seems to me that the coffee was always excellent
and it was not dated or even fresh. It came from the
store in big paper bags and was kept in a stone crock with
a lid and no one knew how it had been dried or ground or
when. The table, made as long as the size of the room
allowed, was covered with oilcloth and had sugar-bowls
and cream pitchers at intervals with a cruet-stand in the
middle, a fine big silver affair with at least five compart-
ments for pepper and salt, mustard, oil and vinegar in
glass containers. And then there were glass pickle dishes
set in silver stands with a hook on the side to hold the
fork and the glass was colored, one in green the shade

of an unripe tomato and the other one ruby-red and very beautiful.

We sliced bread, a loaf at a time, and the table had plates of baking powder biscuits and pitchers of syrup and prints of butter. I thought our print was prettier than any of the neighbours' for it had three heads of wheat on it with a Greek key border.

At noon we often had soup as well as the meat and vegetables, though some of the men were disposed to belittle the value of soup for they said it filled you up but you soon got hungry after it. It did not "stick" to your ribs like meat and potatoes," but I noticed we never had any left over. There was a keen satisfaction in cooking for people who enjoyed their meals like these hungry men, and I loved to see the great platters of hot roast beef beginning to show the pattern, knowing that a further supply was being sliced off in the kitchen, and that big pots of mashed and buttered potatoes and turnips were ready, too, to refill the vegetable dishes, and that the oven was full of baked rice pudding well filled with raisins, and that the big white pitchers on the table were full of thick cream, and if the worst came to the worst, that is if they cleaned up everything, we still had the pantry shelves full of pies and a brown crock full of doughnuts.

There was considerable friendly rivalry in the matter of feeding the threshers and there were dark stories told of certain places where they got no raisins in their rice pudding and nothing but skim milk to eat with it, and where the pies were made of dried apples even though at that time we were able to get barrels of gravensteins from Nova Scotia and northern spies from Ontario.

In spite of the presence of fresh apples, raisin pie held its place in popularity. My brother George had a house-keeper that fall, a Mrs. Porteous from Kincardine, who could make a wonderful pie of what she called "pluens," an open pie with whipped cream, and these vanished like the mists of the morning, when the "gentry" as she called them caught sight of them. I objected to whipping the cream saying that plain cream was just as good but the old lady held firm. "Whipped cream is a bit of style" she said, "which I daresay threshers never have had before, and they won't forget it. It is something extra and will surprise them. Did you ever hear of the second mile? Well that is what this whipped cream is and to see those pies sitting there all fluffed out white as snow rests me more than an hour in bed.' '

She was a stout old lady who could not get around very well but she sat at the table and rolled out pies and biscuits. We had a young fellow to peel potatoes and carry water and wood for us, and someway we managed to feed the men. But when the three weeks were over and I could go back home my bones ached with fatigue.

The farmers in these days were rugged individualists. They changed work when necessary but each kept his affairs to himself quite jealously. The first real co-operative effort came when someone suggested a "Beef-Ring", and outlined a plan whereby each farmer might have fresh meat in the summer. Once a week an animal was butchered and divided according to a diagram. The next week when another farmer did the butchering there would be a different distribution of the meat so that as the season went on each farmer would receive the same amount and portions of the meat.

The plan worked very well at first, but with the coming of better crops and prices the farmers began to reason that they were foolish to bother with their own meat when they could buy it at the butcher shops. Wheat was the thing that brought in the most money and to the raising of wheat they set all their energies, despising the slower penny-pinching ways of former generations. It was not long until there were farms which had not a cow or a hen or a hill of potatoes. Particularly was this true when the younger generation were in command. The older people watched this development with alarm and disapproval, and shook their heads. No good could come of it they said.

I am glad I knew the farm in the days of abundance before the evil days had come when machinery had driven out the horses. I am glad I can think of the farmyard with a ring of horses heads gathered around the sunken tub below the pump or in a row across the pasture bars; when the brood mares roamed the pasture hills, later to be followed by frisking colts on their too-long legs. I am glad I knew the farm when there were cows grazing along the creek in deep contentment or lying in some shady place out of the wind in the crisp October mornings when I went to get them and where many a time I was glad to warm by bare feet in the place where they had been lying. Even the pigs, though they were greedy, squealing and ungrateful brutes had their uses too, as we found when we changed their pasture and used the old one for a garden, and never had a growth of cabbages and potatoes and onions and peas, and flowers that grew as high as the fence.

The first encroachment of the machine came after Will and Jack got the threshing outfit. From then on Sunday changed in its spirit and essence. Sunday had always been to us a day set apart; a day when every activity on the farm ceased. Even the hens were late in getting out on Sunday mornings; the cows knew they would not be milked early, and took their time in coming up to the bars. It was the one morning of the week when we saw patches of sunshine on the floor before we left our beds, or could watch the golden radiance on the walls. Everyone got dressed-up on Sunday with blackened shoes and "other clothes"; even on the Sunday that had no church service in the Schoolhouse, for then there would be visitors. Sunday's work, as much as could be, was done on Saturday, the house was made clean and tidy, vases were filled with flowers, and the pantry shelves with cooking. So Sunday was not only a day it was a feeling of rest, contentment, friendliness, a sense of peace and well-being. Even in harvest time, Sunday held its place, horses were turned into the pasture for their day of rest too, and before we had driving horses, we walked to church rather than drive a tired team!

But after the threshing-machine came Jack and Will lost their day of rest. Sunday was the day the machine had to be overhauled or one of them had to drive to Brandon or Glenboro for repairs. There was always something that must be done. The dominance of the machine had begun and none of us were far-seeing enough to know the end.

CHAPTER XXXXIV

COMMENCEMENT

MY last six months' teaching took place at my old home school, Northfield, whose bare surroundings I have described in the *Second Chance*. It stood alone on a wide expanse of prairie, for the land to the north was gravelly and poor and there were no houses within a radius of two miles, but the road from Wawanesa to Stockton and Glenboro ran past the door. The country west, south, and east, was thickly settled.

We had one visit a year from the inspector, Mr. E. E. Best, who lived in Manitou, and although his coming was unheralded, officially, we always had an intimation that he was hovering near. When that news was flashed along the grapevine telegraph, that is, someone had seen him near Glenboro and heading west, there were house-cleanings, window-washings, wood-pilings, and the teacher, regardless of expense, wore her "other" dress and shiny shoes every day. The children were urged to deal lavishly in soap and water.

Blackboards that at other times carried forward the struggles of yesterday, were now cleaned each night, and their upper, unused sections were decorated with a stencil, purple grapes aind green leaves, with an edifying and uplifting motto framed therein, inciting to greater industry.

The pupils entered into all these preparations heartily, for if the Inspector were pleased he would proclaim a half-holiday. We did our own janitor work in the country schools then. The first person who arrived lit the fire and we took turns in sweeping the school. Twice a year it was scrubbed, and had its windows cleaned.

That year Mr. Best tarried long in his coming and we

had to scrub the floor twice before we had our visit. Mr. Best was an ideal inspector and put every child in good humor when he entered the room.

He had inspected Northfield when I was a pupil there and had inspected each school I had taught, so I knew him well. But I had a wholesome regard for his good opinion. There was no sentiment in his inspection, but a fine sense of blindfolded justice.

Mr. Best travelled the prairie trails in all sorts of weather, covering an area of a hundred by sixty miles, and nothing was hidden from his eyes, after he had spent half a day in a school, but any teacher who was sincerely trying to bring the pupils along need have no fears. Unlike most inspectors, Mr. Best was a great teacher, and took full charge of the classes. When he began his work in a school it was no mere march-past that took place. He carried copies of *The Popular Educator* and the *Ontario School Journal* with him, and always had some new books to recommend.

The routine of my life at Northfield was a pleasant one. I got up at seven, in the cold dark of the farmhouse, opened the dampers of the round coal stove in the front room and dressed beside it. Meanwhile Mrs. Brown was preparing breakfast in the kitchen, porridge, bacon and eggs, tea and toast—if she had time to make it.

I set out before sunrise, walking toward the kindling east, the quarter mile to Will's house. Then we drove to the school, with the sleigh box filled with robes, picking up the Kennedy children half way. The big, round heater filled with dry wood soon drove out the cold, and the business of the day began.

No doubt we spent much energy in fighting the cold, but we did not mind, and with furs and woollen clothing managed very well.

January and February were cold months, but spring was on its way, when March came blowing in with a great snow storm, and in April we would hear the meadow larks, and know that our deliverance was at hand. Even the cattle foraging through the straw stacks, hunting vainly for a green blade, lifted their heads when they heard the first liquid note of the little gray messenger.

The winter had its compensation too, in the skating and curling rink at Wawanesa, and though it was three miles away, Jack and I went two nights a week, and skated until the manager began to turn out the lights. When we came home gloriously hungry, we always found a banked fire in the kitchen stove with oatmeal porridge slowly cooking in the double boiler and this with cream and brown sugar made on "After the Game" supper, which has never been surpassed. I had no fears of being overweight then, for I was trying hard to make the even hundred. Mother was quite content to go to bed on these nights and not worry about me, for had I not the protection of a male relative?

The last night of the skating came, when the soft ice, warned us that the spring was upon us, and before the evening was over little poools of water had gathered in the corners of the rink. We had the band that night, and the music, no matter what the tune was, had a fateful and solemn sound, for it was the end of the season— and before another time of ice had come there would be changes and partings, and the old crowd would be broken up—we, who had such pleasant times together.

Beside the skating rink lay the curling rink, where the older men threw the stones each night, and from which the thunder of rolling stones travelling on ice, cracking together and rolling away again, mingled with the band music. It was all part of a scene which I like to remember—and which I knew that night would not come to me again, for life was moving rapidly in my small world.

I was going to be married the next summer. I had begun to think seriously of marriage after Jack had told me he was going to get married soon. I was quite settled in my mind, and I knew I could be happy with Wes. We did not always agree but he was a fair fighter, and I knew I would rather fight with him than agree with anyone else. I would not be afraid of life with him. He would never fail me. He was getting on too. He had the drugstore now in Manitou, and there were four little rooms above it where we could live.

Wes. had come to see me in January, and to my great relief was received by my family with real enthusiasm. I had been a little bit anxious about this meeting from both sides. I wondered what he would think of my people—would they seem to him just plain country people who ate in the kitchen, in their shirt sleeves—I wondered! Or would he see them, as I saw them, clear thinking independent people, more ready to give a favor than ask for one. I thought of my mother especially—would he see what a woman she was? Fearless, self-reliant, undaunted, who never turned away from the sick or needy; for whom no night was too dark or cold, or road too dangerous to go out and help a neighbor in distress, who, for all her bluntness had a gracious spirit, and knew the healing word for souls in distress; who scorned pretence or affectation, and loved the sweet and simple virtues. I wondered would he see all this, or would there be just a trace of condescension in his manner, of which perhaps he migth be unaware—

It troubled me, for I know that was one thing I could not take, and he could not help. But these were my people, and I would stand or fall with them.

I need not have worried. The first night he came, looking so smart and handsome in a rough brown tweed suit, he settled into the family circle like the last piece of a crossword puzzle. He and mother were so enchanted with each other I thought it best to leave them, when eleven o'clock came, and went to bed.

The next morning mother came into my room before I was up and said to me. "Nellie, you have more sense than I ever gave you credit for, and I like your young man—I couldn't have picked out a finer one myself. Now, if you cannot get on, I'll be inclined to think it will be your fault—and you certainly are getting something to look at, as you always said you would."

But the next night, which was his last—for he left on the early train the next day, when I thought we might have had a little time to talk, and Jack had obligingly gone to bed early—mother announced that it was ten o'clock and time for me to go to bed—

And I went—without a word, I went!

We were married on August 25th, at a quarter to eight in the morning. The day before had been the perfect harvest day; with a heavy amber sunshine, lighting up the golden fields, and gladdening the harvesters as they drove the binders around the dwindling rectangles of standing grain. There was not a breath of wind, or a cloud in the sky, and the whole countryside was steeped in the golden glory. Through the still air came the clickety-clack of the binders; the drowsy sounds of contented farm yards, cheerful barking of dogs, and cooing of pigeons on the roofs of barns.

Wes. came on the four o'clock train, and I drove into Wawanesa to meet him, and as we came along the winding road, with its lovely foliage, beginning to mellow into the autumn tints, and up to the level of the plain, with the Horse-Shoe Slough across the river, perfect in its symmetry and grace, we stopped the horse to look at the perfect scene of prairie beauty. We had not heard of William H. Davis, but we knew what he meant when we read, years afterwards, about the rainbow, and the coo-coo song coming together, once, and perhaps never again.

The next morning we were all astir early, for this was the day of days. But what a change had come in the night!

The dark and stormy sky—the raging wind that tore the leaves from the maple trees, and levelled the standing grain in the fields, and rattled every window in the house, were poor omens for a wedding day!

We reached the church at 7:30—the Presbyterian Church on the river bank (which had been kindly offered

to us, because it was larger than the little Methodist
Church), decorated now with sheaves of wheat and
beautiful flowers, and filled with the old friends from far
and near. I remember walking up the aisle with my
brother Will, while Miss Hopkins at the organ played the
wedding march—and I remember the solemn words of
the marriage ceremony. . . . A sea of faces, everyone
friendly—good wishes, and a great confusion of voices—
and a feeling of haste. Again the high wind whistle of
the train, as it came down the grade beyond the river,
heard in a lull in the storm, and a lot of rice, and laughter
—and mother, waving her hand, and the whole scene
moving away from us, as we stood on the back platform.

The trees were bending in the gale which seemed to
grow in fury and the rain which had held up until we
were up again on the plain, lashed the windows and
rattled like hail against the ventilators over our heads.

The pleasant harvest scene of the day before was
blotted out; cattle huddled in the shelter of the barns;
as we passed Ashdown and Hilton, the fields were deserted; the wheat and oats were bending and shelling.

Suddenly the rain stopped and the wind too, grew less.
I think we had reached Baldur where my dear old teacher
lived, when we went out to the back platform holding the railing, just as I had done six years before, leaving home for the first time, fearful, although the sun
was shining. Now I was leaving again, and there was
no sun; nothing but dark and thunderous clouds covering
all the sky, but I was not afraid.

Fear of the future did not cross either of our minds.
We were sitting on the top of the world. Not that we
had any money to give us assurance. We had the four
little rooms above the store to go to and the rent was
paid for one month in advance. We had enough furniture to begin housekeeping, bought on the instalment
plan, and we had agreed to pay interest at the rate of
2% a month. Wes. had an insurance policy for $2,000.
I cannot remember what we talked about, but I know we

were hilariously, unreasonably happy, and confident, rich in the things we did not know.

Even in that gloomy, threatening morning to ride on the back platform of the train gave me a glorious feeling of speed and adventure. We were off, and away!

Suddenly the landscape began to brighten, and the farmhouses, barns, and fences lifted themselves out of the gloom, and a gleam came on the steel ribbons running out beneath our feet. We looked up, and saw the clouds were parting, and a bit of blue sky was showing over the shoulder of a black cloud.

It was clearing in the West! Tomorrow would be fine!